Wholeness in Later Life

MMB MUSIC, INC.

CONTEMPORARY ARTS BUILDING
3526 WASHINGTON AVENUE
SAINT LOUIS, MISSOURI 63103-1019 USA
314 531-9635; 800 543-3771 (USA/Canada); Fax 314 531-8384
http://www.mmbmusic.com

of related interest

Grief and Powerlessness
Helping People Regain Control of their Lives
Ruth Bright
ISBN 1 85302 386 8

Quality of Life
Philip Seed and Greg Lloyd
ISBN 1 85302 413 9

Wholeness in Later Life

Ruth Bright

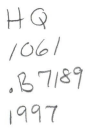

Jessica Kingsley Publishers
London and Bristol, Pennsylvania

The right of Ruth Bright to be identified as author of this work has been asserted by her in accordance with the Copyright, Designs and Patents Act 1988.

First published in the United Kingdom in 1997 by
Jessica Kingsley Publishers Ltd
116 Pentonville Road
London N1 9JB, England
and
1900 Frost Road, Suite 101
Bristol, PA 19007, U S A

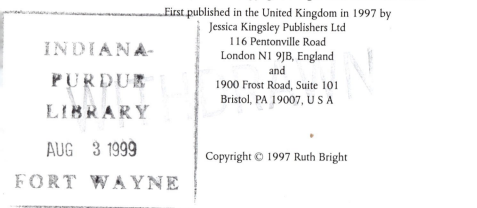

Copyright © 1997 Ruth Bright

Library of Congress Cataloging in Publication Data
A CIP catalogue record for this book is available from the Library of Congress

British Library Cataloguing in Publication Data
A CIP catalogue record for this book is available from the British Library

ISBN 1-85302-447-3

Printed and Bound in Great Britain by
Athenæum Press, Gateshead, Tyne and Wear

Contents

Acknowledgements

This book could not have been written without the help of a number of people, and their support is gratefully acknowledged. In particular I would like to thank by name the various library staff who have helped me by obtaining the books and journal articles that were needed in the research which preceded the actual writing: Chitra Karunanayake and Tina Casey at Rozelle Hospital; Jacqui Ristau at Cumberland Hospital; Ruth Mitchell at Royal Rehabilitation Centre; Kathryn Walker at Hornsby-Ku-ring-gai Hospital.

I have also been encouraged by these people and my other colleagues from all professions, not only in my writing but in clinical work over many years.

Introduction

**A note on the readership for whom this book is intended
and other personal comments**

The book was written for everyone who is concerned with life in later maturity:

- for those who are living it and want to know how they may achieve and retain a sense of fulfilment, and
- for professionals involved in medical and psychosocial care of older people who require support and treatment.

Because of this wide readership, some chapters will be of more interest than others, depending upon the background and expertise of the reader, but in any case the intention is to publish not an authoritative textbook on all aspects of ageing, but an overall view of later maturity with summaries of the various challenges which we face as we get older.

There are lists of 'recommended reading' at the end of some chapters to make it easier to follow up particular areas of interest.

As the book is written by a music therapist, much of the clinical work which is described is related to the practice of music therapy, but the underlying themes are of common interest.

My professional involvement with ageing has extended beyond music therapy, and has included: work as a member of the Board of Directors (for some six years as president) of the Gerontology Foundation of Australia, which funds research into physical and psychosocial aspects of ageing; service on the Committee of the New South Wales branch of the (Australian) National Association for Loss and Grief, and – as a continuing responsibility – service as a professional adviser to the Australian telephone support service, Grief Support.

Because I have now reached the age of 'later maturity', I realise my good fortune in living in a state where retirement from the public service merely on the grounds of age is illegal, but I am keenly aware that this is a privileged position and that many people who still have much to give to society are prevented from doing so in any formal way simply because they have reached an age which has been arbitrarily set as requiring retirement.

My book *Music in Geriatric Care*, published in 1972, was seen as important by geriatricians because it reminded them (or, for some, made them think for the first time) that their patients were whole people, individuals, each with a unique life-story, a unique set of needs, not necessarily connected directly with the disability or illness which brought them into the ambit of a hospital or health professional. Because of this totality of needs, the present book is wide-ranging, looking at the wholeness of older people, as far as anyone can presume to describe either 'wholeness' or 'old-ness', and there are two main sections. The first covers the theoretical background and the second covers practical ideas drawn from my profession of music therapy. Several chapters aim to raise awareness rather than to give answers; for example, there are chapters on how people cope with later life when they have had life-long disabilities or long-term disabilities.

None of us has all the answers but, by being alert to challenges outside our own speciality, we can call upon others to give help as necessary. If we ignore every profession but our own, we risk making mistakes and thereby diminishing the wholeness of the individual.

For similar reasons, many different clinical aspects of old age are discussed throughout the text. We cannot have an empathic understanding of what challenges and disappointments people experience unless we know what life is like when one is frail or has a disability. Although no description can provide more than a shadowy picture of the reality of these experiences, we must use our knowledge as we try to 'walk in another's mocasins' or – more appropriately for some of the matters discussed here – to 'sit in another's wheelchair'.

There were difficulties in deciding how to divide some of the topics into chapters. We are not justified today in discussing psychiatric disorders as if they had no physical components, or vice versa. We are becoming so much better informed about biological aspects of mental illness and the emotional and psychiatric impact of physical disorder that we must think of them as linked. There are similar areas of commonality when we discuss neurological impairments which cause both physical and psychosocial problems. But practicalities of organisation demand that a book is divided into categories; there are, therefore, separate sections on physical difficulties, psychiatric problems and on mental retardation, but with cross-links between them.

Although the chapters in the second section are of special interest to music therapists, because these sections discuss practical suggestions as to how music therapy can contribute to the well-being and life-satisfaction of older people, they will be of interest to many others also.

There is some confusion about nomenclature, that is, which descriptive word should be used by a professional to refer to the person one is trying to help. Should it be 'patient' (too patronising and 'medical model'-ish); 'client' (too uncertain of meaning, it can describe someone visiting a lawyer or a prostitute); or 'consumer' (politically-correct but also uncertain of meaning)? Even 'customer' is sometimes used, and that is even worse! However enthusiastic we are to emphasise the autonomy of the person receiving therapy, both 'consumer' and 'customer' fail to recognise adequately the nature of the therapeutic alliance which develops between the people concerned, based on a shared wish to improve the quality of life for the individual who is seeking help.

In fact it matters little what words we use. If our attitude is right, we shall contribute to older people's sense of wholeness, but if our attitude is wrong, then no correct terminology will make any difference. For this reason, I have generally used the word 'patient' and hope that, as with 'mental retardation', this will be accepted as being in the interests of accuracy and not in any way disparaging.

Because in this book I have in a sense 'changed sides', so that older people are no longer 'them' but 'us', there are several personal comments and I have in any case rejected the convention of the indirect ('the author', 'the present author') and have instead written as myself, using 'I' and 'me'. I make no apology for this, trusting that it is not perceived as being an attempt (as in *The Mikado*) to 'give artistic verisimilitude to an otherwise bald and unconvincing narrative'! (Gilbert and Sullivan 1885).

PART I

CHAPTER 1

Wholeness and Old Age
Realities and Vulnerabilities

Introduction

The reasons for writing this book were:

- to distinguish between 'wholeness' and 'perfection'
- to discuss aspects of life in later maturity
- to discuss the risks to our wholeness of physical and psychiatric disorders
- to increase general awareness of cultural aspects of ageing
- to describe the manner in which music therapy can enhance our sense of wholeness, even when we are affected by frailty or disability
- to heighten awareness among geriatricians and others of the special needs in later life of those whose lives have (since birth or for many years) been affected by disabilities and who are now (because of those disabilities) experiencing an accelerated ageing process, which has both physical and psychosocial impact upon their quality of life.

Even this wide agenda is incomplete, and I hope that others will fill the gaps, and take my preliminary thoughts further.

The context of ageing: when are we considered to be 'old'?

Concepts of oldness have changed over the last 2000 years, and although the maximum possible life span of 100–110 years has been the same for probably 100,000 years, the average life span has changed. In 1993 the average life expectation of a new-born baby girl in Japan was 76 years, whereas for a new-born Neanderthal baby it is estimated that the average life span was only 18 years (Albert and Catell 1993, p.27).

Concepts of oldness (our own or those of observers) may also depend upon our activities and employment. An Olympic gymnast is considered 'too

7

old' by the age of 20 (and perhaps far earlier), whilst a parliamentarian of 50 may still be described as 'one of our younger politicians'. The athlete depends for success upon the youthful agility of the body, whilst the politician's success depends (one assumes and hopes!) on agility of mind and on the wisdom which generally comes only with chronological maturity. This success then tends to influence social position and income.

We see accelerated ageing of people who have had a long-term disability, who (having achieved independence in life outside institutions) lose that independence relatively early in life because of the physical strains of coping with the disability. When this untimely ageing process takes them back into long-term care (often into nursing homes where most of the residents are from a different generation and may suffer from dementing illness), their quality of life is greatly diminished.

There is a two-way process by which sociological concepts and the biological aspects of ageing interact, and the attitudes of individuals and groups are subject to many and varied influences. There is a correlation between the developed state of a country and the life expectation of its inhabitants, arising from standards of medical care (especially in childbirth and childhood years), general nutrition, poverty and wealth (Albert and Catell 1993, p.45). Life expectation is also influenced by wars, or by persecution, which reduce the numbers of people from given groups.

Erikson (1973, pp.239–261) uses psychological developmental criteria to denote stages of maturation and ageing, but Foner (1984), throughout her book on intergenerational conflict, uses chronological physical and social role as the defining criteria.

Even with chronology it may be difficult to know precise age because not all cultures regard birthdates as significant. Under a bureaucratic system, in which a birthdate decides matters of pensions, employment and other issues, people are accustomed to the idea that precise age is significant, but this system is far from universal outside the Western world.

The idea of enjoyment and creativity in the post-menopausal life of women is relatively new, and – even at the end of the twentieth century – it generally remains the privilege of women in highly-developed nations. We may wonder why human beings live past the menopause, why our biological time-clock allows so many of us a long period of time when (for women at least) the possibility of reproduction has ceased. Mature-age students complete post-graduate study and attain higher degrees, or start university studies for the first time; older people are involved in political action, professional groups, hobby associations and individual ventures of all kinds.

What can older people really do?

The Terman Study (named for its first researcher) is an on-going longitudinal study of giftedness which started in the 1920s, when the 1500 subjects were children; despite attrition, there were in 1986 still over 1000 subjects in the study. The research demonstrated some years ago that giftedness does not 'wear off', as the myth of the day insisted ('early ripe, early rot'), but continues throughout life. It also showed the falseness of the other 1920s myth, which held that gifted people were strong only in one direction but weaklings in other areas of intellectual achievement, in leadership, relation-ships and physique.

Older people can take heart from the sixth volume of the series, describing recent findings on achievements in later maturity. Research showed that gifts from earlier in life do not disappear simply because of advancing age, and that giftedness remains an all-round quality of living (Holohan and Sears 1995).

It is interesting to consider the possible associations between:

o the findings of the Terman study

o the (fairly modern) folklore that 'if you don't use it, you lose it', which teaches that we must use our intellectual capacity if we are not to lose it by dementia, and

o the findings about greater head size (and therefore brain capacity) as a protective factor against the worst ravages of dementia (Graves *et al.* 1996).

Can it be that those who are motivated to continue with intellectual or semi-intellectual pursuits never were greatly at risk of severe impairment by dementia? In the folklore about using one's brain as a preventative measure, are we seeing the familiar *post hoc ergo propter hoc* fallacy?

A belief in the capacities of older people is, however, not yet widely accepted. People in later life hear astonished comments: 'Are you *still* working? Isn't it time you sat back and took life easily?' or 'How can he start a new degree when he is 71?' The Biblical phrase 'three-score years and ten', as marking the normal life-span, still has an influence, even though the words were written at a time when it was normal to die at about that age. A man who was otherwise thoroughly up-to-date in attitudes said, 'Having reached my three-score years and ten, I am now living on borrowed time.'

Although in France the expression *mon vieux* is commonly used as a term of endearment and friendship, many English-speakers use the word 'old' as a 'distancing' term: 'Did you hear about old...?' or 'Poor old...' commonly refer to a person of any age who has had a heart attack or a major illness, because there is a strong conceptual link between ill-health and ageing.

When the retirement age was 60 for women and 65 for men, those milestones commonly shaped perceptions of the beginning of old age, but the changes to legislation in some parts of the world, by which it is illegal to force someone to retire on the ground of age alone, have helped to counter some beliefs about ageing. The legislation has, however, caused some resentment amongst younger workers who feel that their rightful paths to promotion are blocked by the presence of older staff. Ageism remains a powerful and a destructive force!

Concepts of ageing have undergone major changes in the last 20 years. Health professionals rarely describe 70-year-olds who are in good health as 'old', but we may hear them spoken of as 'the young old' if they are having to cope with some level of disability or illness. Older persons who continue to enjoy good health and happiness are referred to as 'the well-aged', often with the comment 'They chose their ancestors wisely!' because genetic resources do affect our prospects for health and long life. Those aged 85 or more are thought of as the 'old old', and some may suffer from limitations, but many people of that age are truly involved in life despite limitations.

Wholeness and perfection

If we expect to attain perfection in later life, we shall have unrealistic expectations and face disappointment and, perhaps, depression. Our biological time clocks impose upon us various indications of advancing age (not all of them for all people, but common to most): greying and thinning of hair, decreased acuity of sight and hearing, shrinking height as spinal discs reduce in size, occasional memory lapses, thinner and wrinkled skin, some aching joints, less upright posture.

If we expect perfection as we age, we condemn ourselves to secret strategies, pretences and anxieties. If we expect wholeness, we can accept these changes as natural, and although we may take pride in our appearance and make the most of it, we enjoy life as real people and not as frightened puppets who dance to strings pulled by fear.

In the fourteenth and fifteenth centuries, 'whole' meant 'intact', 'complete' (the word is still used in that way to differentiate between a stallion and a gelding) or 'healed after injury'. It is worth noting that in Jesus' instruction to his followers – 'Be ye perfect' – which has led to feelings of guilt and despair in so many of his followers, the Greek word *teleios* is equally correctly translated as 'fully developed', a far more attainable goal, so that the command could be expressed as 'be ye whole' or 'be ye mature'.

If we are to feel whole, our needs and the priorities of these will differ with the individual, but would probably include:

- physical health and financial resources sufficient to maintain our independence and autonomy
- the ability and the right to make decisions for ourselves, in health and in sickness
- areas of life in which we feel successful
- positive feedback from others, which builds our self-esteem without patronising us, even if we have a disability or if things go wrong
- the opportunity for affectionate two-way relationships
- to be able to give something, however intangible, to others
- to feel part of the community and exercise our democratic rights
- to participate in religious worship if this is important to us
- to be accepted as we are.

Each of us will have special personal needs but the list above is fairly comprehensive.

Vulnerability

A life-long sense of wholeness is built on our own inner certainty but also, depending on our vulnerability, on the opinions of others. Many children grow to adulthood emotionally scarred by misunderstanding and unkindness because of handicaps. They include:

- those with learning disabilities, pilloried as 'stupid'
- those of 'different' build or appearance, labelled as 'weird'
- those who stutter and are teased, so that the speech problem gets worse
- those whose skin colour is different from that of their class-mates, leading to bullying and teasing.

The list is endless of the cruelty of child to child. Is it the result of parental teaching or the child's own fear of the unknown?

Legislation allowing abortion of a malformed foetus can affect adults with disabilities, whose inner wholeness is diminished as they wonder whether their parents wished they had been aborted. The legislation tells us that, in society's eyes, to be disabled is worse than death, and perhaps also that society should not be asked to pay for the additional support disabled people require to lead a normal life. The final tragic domino to fall is that of so-called euthanasia, in which handicapped persons are brain-washed into requesting death (or, worse still, are exterminated, as in Nazi Germany) on the grounds that they would be 'better off dead', or that the state cannot and should not pay for their maintenance (Ralph 1994).

Such a series of steps may seem unthinkable, and yet there are suspicions that in Holland (where euthanasia is countenanced even though it is illegal) a significant proportion of planned deaths are not in fact voluntary but based on the decisions of others. So far there has been comparative silence from older people about their fears of the pressures from individuals and govern-ments, that there is not enough money to support them in old age and ill-health and that they should ask for death. But such fears do exist and, with the increasing proportion of older people, who are supported by a smaller taxable population, the situation may worsen. I heard an after-dinner speaker from the legal profession say (in what was only marginally a jocular manner) that, because of the changes in population, there would in future be suicide centres to which elderly people would go, make their wills and commit suicide.

At any stage of life, whether disabled or not, we are vulnerable to feelings of uselessness and inadequacy, not necessarily because of what people say but because the subtleties of their behaviour make us believe that we are not good enough, do not measure up to the expectations of others. This can happen simply because we have grown old.

Society today often asks 'What do you do?' with the implied query 'and how much money do you have?' Those who are handicapped may feel guilty at being unable to answer this question in any triumphant way, and some older people look back regretfully at their modest lives.

Can attitudes towards ageing be influenced by social class, and by the availability or scarcity of money which may be linked with social class? Writers on social class and identity describe feelings and fears which are linked with social position. Men who fear that loss of hair is seen as a sign of their being too old to work in a senior position or of being accepted in fashionable society may spend lavishly on hair 'restorations'. The less affluent (those who are lower in social position) cannot do so and yet their social position may be less affected by fears of baldness. Women, under pressure from advertisers to see wrinkles or loss of hair colour as indicating lost social position or sexual desirability, may spend lavishly for cosmetic treatments which attempt to hide the ageing process.

Wealthy nations have resources which are not available to poorer nations to pay for medical and surgical treatment which prevents premature death or the ageing effects of at least some conditions. They also can provide prostheses of all kinds, amenities and services which reduce the impact which disability has upon the lives of those who are disabled.

We are vulnerable in old age (especially if we are alone) to the advances of our biological clock, and to the effects of events and circumstances which are of great importance to us but which may appear to be quite minor:

- ○ The death of the spouse or partner after many years of happily shared companionship impairs our wholeness to the extent that people say 'I shall never get over it', and although some adaptation occurs, life is indeed for them never the same. Resolving grief of all kinds and at all ages consists not only in expressing sadness but also in adapting to change.

- ○ The neighbouring house changes hands or an adult child moves away on business. The person who used to put out the garbage bins, change light bulbs or mend electric fuses has gone, and similar relationships with new neighbours take time to develop or fail to flourish. The older person is vulnerable because there is no longer a listening ear in times of loneliness, nobody to notice if health is diminished or actual illness occurs, rubbish is not cleared (with consequent risks to health), the house is darker because light bulbs are not replaced so that falls are more likely, and so on. Even when helpful family and neighbours are available, the list of risks caused by the possible frailty of old age is endless.

- ○ We develop hearing losses, so that using the telephone is more difficult and we are lonelier; visual losses, so that reading instructions on medication is harder and reading the telephone directory impossible; difficulties with hand function, so that opening some packets or bottles of medication is impossible; mobility impairment, so that walking to the shops is difficult and using public transport impossible. Memory losses may cause us to leave pans on the stove to catch fire, or gas jets to remain unlit; failure of judgement leads to danger with electric heaters placed close to bedding, food left out of the refrigerator so that it becomes inedible, rubbish left uncleared with risk of infection and infestations, and so on.

Personal emotional vulnerability to negative images of ageing or to personal events is particularly important when health is poor and there is a risk of depression. Because it may present as physical illness, depression frequently remains undiagnosed in elderly people (Kane, Ouslander and Abrass 1994).

Community support

Some communities accept responsibility for such matters: buses are fitted with hydraulic steps which can be lowered to allow people with disabilities to get on, bus routes are changed so that retirement village residents can go shopping, ticket offices are fitted with 'induction loops' so that those with hearing aids can use the T-switch to converse easily with the booking clerk as they purchase tickets for travel or entertainment. Churches and theatres commonly have audio-loops, and one middle-aged ex-serviceman – deaf as the result of exposure to gunfire and explosions – experienced renewal of his spiritual life after his place of worship installed a loop.

In the UK, at least one big chain of supermarkets employs a deaf person to train all staff in communication with customers who have hearing problems, and, in the same chain, staff are employed specifically to assist disabled people who have difficulty in reaching down into freezer cabinets or up to high shelves for articles which are out of reach.

All such provisions help to maintain wholeness as we age or cope with disabilities throughout life, and speak to us of a society which accepts us despite age or disabilities. But not all societies are financially able to make these provisions and, even amongst those which are affluent, the willingness to do so may be absent.

Stereotypes

Ageism and destructive stereotypes influence our lives. 'Ageism' is the attitude based upon stereotypes which relegate older people into the 'no longer any use' category. Today's practice of marking foodstuffs with a 'use-by' date has added a new 'joke' (?) to the conversation of many older people, as we wonder whether we have passed *our* use-by date!

Common stereotypical beliefs are:

- Old people do not understand present-day life; they are out-of-date and should keep out of present-day affairs
- Old people all lose their memories
- Old people cannot learn new ideas; they are stuck in the ways of the past
- Old people automatically disapprove of what young people do
- Old people all have strong religious faith
- Because their ideas are too old-fashioned to have any value, older people should get out of the work-force and allow younger people to move into their positions

- Once you are at retirement age, you should relax and enjoy only hobbies and recreation

- Old people are a-sexual beings; they have forgotten what it is like to be in love

- Old people should all be nice, kind, good listeners

- Old people should accept gratefully whatever is done for them without asking questions and without ever grumbling.

Many of these have some basis in reality for some older individuals, but the dangers of stereotypes are that they are believed to be universally applicable. We must challenge them, refusing to bow to a belief that all older people are incompetent nincompoops!

Other stereotypes contribute to ill-health in old age: these are the (dangerous and unfounded) beliefs people hold about themselves that there is no point in trying to change. We now know that even modest increases in physical activity bring benefits to elderly people, improving cardiac capacity, lessening mortality and improving the quality of life (Wenger 1996). We now know that it is well worth giving up smoking even late in life, in order to lessen the many risks associated with coronary heart disease – ventricular fibrillation, myocardial ischaemia, platelet adhesiveness and so on (Tresch and Aronow 1996). The stereotype which says 'It is too late to change' is dangerous indeed, if we are sufficiently naive or gullible to believe it.

Asian cultures have traditionally given respect to the wisdom of older people, and, even in technological Western society, the person who reaches the age of 100 will find that his or her opinions on life will be quoted in newspaper interviews and accepted as having value – but only for the day of the birthday!

But are cultures changing today? Is the ready familiarity of younger people with terminology and attitudes of the computer age leading to the discarding of the wisdom of the aged? The strangeness of some of today's vocabulary, and the neologisms which label aspects of electronic communication (e.g. 'surfing the internet', 'virtual reality' and 'cyberspace'), can leave older people feeling bewildered and useless.

'What on earth is a modem?' asked one 75-year-old. But when it had been explained to her she was able to understand what an acquaintance had meant when he said that his normal phone line was tied up by a modem so he needed to use his mobile phone instead. She was perhaps exceptional in having the courage to ask what the words meant rather than pretending she knew or withdrawing from the conversation because she felt out of it and stupid. In such a situation, the risk is that one feels too embarrassed to ask, for fear of seeming out-of-date, and this confirms the negative views of the onlooker about old age. The apparent out-of-date-ness of elderly people may be a consequence of their fear of acknowledging their ignorance of jargon, and the stereotypes of ageing become self-fulfilling prophecies.

Needs of those who become unwell or disabled in old age

Those who have become frail, disabled or physically or mentally impaired need help, but their needs are not always met. There is a (false) belief that a high percentage of older people need full-time care in a nursing home. This is damaging to society's concept of old age. It causes resentment about rising taxes to help pay for this care, and it also damages the feelings people have about their own old age, present or future.

Figures provided by the Council on the Ageing in New South Wales, Australia (Mathur 1996) show that only 3.3 per cent of the total number of people over the age of 65 are in full-time care. Of those who are over 70 years of age, 4.68 per cent are in nursing homes and of those who are over the age of 80, 11 per cent are in nursing homes. This is far from the pervasive sterotype of unavoidable and universal decrepitude!

Statistics cannot give a complete picture of the factors which cause admission to a nursing home; they cannot describe the relative importance of physical factors and social factors in making it necessary for someone to live in a nursing home. Total assessment by the geriatric team of all factors, both physical and psychosocial, is an important precursor to placement, so that people do not lose their independence unless it is absolutely essential for their care and protection.

But for those who are in need of full-time care, why has this happened? Some conditions may have been present for many years or may have been life-long, but the limitations and impairments which they impose can worsen as age advances. Can we be sure that each individual is assessed adequately, or will the attitude be 'Oh well, what can you expect at that age, of course he is getting worse!' Some conditions are more common in old age, but it is dangerous to assume that they are unavoidable.

Culturally-based stereotypes can cause conflict between generations. A professional young woman in Spain described how it was taken for granted by her frail mother-in-law that she would give up her work in order to provide care. But the younger woman believed that she should continue her career and pay for professional care for the older woman.

A similar stereotype is that married women will leave work to care for a sick husband. Will older women with careers do this or pay for professional help? Will men give up their professions to provide full-time care? The matter is contentious both generally and professionally.

The expectations and self-image of an older person may bewilder younger people because they do not fit the stereotypes. A 90-year-old referred to a hemicolectomy for bowel malignancy as: 'This bloody cancer, it has wrecked all my plans for the future!', when most people had assumed that he had no plans for the future. It was encouraging to hear his surgeon say that the man probably would achieve his plans, of travelling from Sydney to London to see his sister, because his anger would fuel his recovery.

The flow-on effects of our vulnerabilities are enormous. Those who become frail or ill as they grow older may well find themselves in nursing homes, and their future happiness will depend largely upon the morale of the home and the skills and attitudes of the staff. In some places (but not all) people find decisions being made for them on every imaginable topic, from choice of what (if anything) is shown on television, to the time and content of meals or times of waking and sleeping, with no understanding that individual preference and habits should be encouraged.

Ellen Newton, in a book which did much to change public attitudes on decision-making and freedom for older people in nursing homes, described the interview in which she was told that she would not be going home from hospital but would be going to a nursing home (Newton 1979, pp.4–5). Little empathy was shown to her own needs, and there was certainly no choice for her in the matter. Consequently, she was left feeling like an object and not a person.

Empathy and appropriate planning are essential when older people are ill. An elderly person cannot, for example, be discharged from an acute hospital to a nursing home at an hour's notice because the hospital bed is needed for someone else. For successful transition, there must be investigation by a trained professional of such things as:

- the atmosphere and ethos of the nursing home, whether or not residents are seen as individuals with unique needs, physically, emotionally, cognitively and spiritually

- languages spoken by staff and residents

- ease of mobility within the buildings and garden

- the capacity of the individual or family to pay the fees if these are required

- nearness of the home to family so that visiting is easy

- ○ the possibility of continuing treatment in physiotherapy, speech pathology and so on.

These investigations must then be followed by adequate psychological and emotional preparation of the individual for the transfer, and so the process goes on. It is a highly professional challenge and not a task for a few phone calls in the odd half-hour. The following 1996 vignette described by a social worker shows that a hasty, unthinking approach can still happen.

An inexperienced doctor, working at a weekend, decided, despite instructions to the contrary, to discharge a frail elderly woman from an acute hospital because he saw the bed as being 'blocked'. Without discussion with the family, he made a few phone calls, did some paper-work and ordered an ambulance to take her to a (very expensive) nursing home some distance away.

On Monday morning, the family telephoned the hospital to ask why this move had been made, saying that the nursing home was too far away from their home to make it easy to visit their mother and that in any case they could not afford the fees required, which were far beyond the pension. The patient then had to be returned to the acute hospital to await the availability of a bed in a nursing home which the family could afford and which was near enough for them to be able to give the patient emotional support at this difficult time of sadness and loss, when disability had robbed her of the capacity for independent living and led to the sale of her home.

Because of the emotional trauma caused by two (ill-advised!) trips by ambulance and the emotional stress of being moved around from hospital to nursing home and back again over a short period of time, the patient actually stayed far longer in the acute bed than would otherwise have been necessary.

If assessment and preparation are not done properly, the person may suffer from additional illness (justifiably described as iatrogenic), and, far from saving money for the acute medical service, become still more of a liability for funding! The vignette also demonstrates the continuing need for newer members of health-related professions to be helped to understand the vulnerability and range of needs of frail elderly people, and to develop an empathy towards the needs and wholeness of the people concerned, rather than seeing these as unimportant and irrelevant.

Despite the emphasis on community care, there can still be times of crisis. One hopes that, with better funding for community health teams, there will be a diminishing number of tragedies, in which an elderly person is found dead after several days because neighbours have not been able to make contact or have not known of the person's need. But this can still occur.

Whilst we all wish to preserve our autonomy and privacy, some older people can have a fall or a major health crisis without warning, or do not recognise in themselves the urgent need for help. If they have locked the house securely against intruders and have not given a key to someone else, nobody can get into the house to find out what is wrong, and so the person may die in misery and loneliness.

Music therapy

Music therapy in the home gives pleasant stimulation and enjoyment, and a non-threatening contact with someone outside the neighbourhood. For those who are not receiving delivered meals or visits from domiciliary services, there is an extra benefit, in providing regular contact with someone who is trained to notice changes in health and behaviour. Such changes include risk-taking behaviour, abuse of alcohol or other substances, poor lighting of steps which can lead to a fractured femur, smells within the house which suggest forgetfulness and dementia or depression, loss of weight which needs investigation, and so on.

I have been involved in such work, and although on one occasion, when arriving at the house with musical instruments, I was told 'Not today, thank you, I don't buy at the door!' this was only a temporary set-back and the person soon remembered who I was and why I was there!

On another home visit, I found the neighbours in a state of anxiety, wondering what to do because their elderly friend had not taken his milk bottles off the doorstep but – because the house was locked up like a fortress – they were unable to find out what had happened. Gaining instant authority as 'the lady from the hospital', I rang the police and the ambulance and went with them as they forced entry into the house. We found the man on the bedroom floor, unconscious from a stroke, the phone dangling off the hook. I saw him a week later for music therapy in hospital, and was able to comfort him both by music and by our conversation. He was reassured that I had been there and had come in with the police and ambulance officers, so that he was not entirely with strangers in his crisis.

Summary

Older age can bring sadness in the bitter fruits of events long-past but not forgotten, as well as gladness in memories of past happiness. Often the two feelings co-exist: we remember happy events but grieve that they are only memories.

Ageing can also bring its own fulfilments, when greater maturity permits us to put behind us the hurts and disappointments as well as the responsibilities of the past. We can then move joyfully into 'The Third Age', whether we use our leisure to follow up new-found interests and hobbies, study at a professional level a subject which has been 'on hold' for many years because of lack of time, or take on the responsibility and the fun of caring for a grandchild once a week!

It seems that the truism 'You are as old as you feel' is not as trite and unreal as it sounds. If we feel well then we probably are well, or are at least able to live life on the basis of well-ness, and not ill-ness. But we are also vulnerable to events over which we have no control, to unavoidable illness, to the opinions of others, to losses and to grief over loss.

For health professionals of any discipline the challenge is to try to match our aims for any individual with the reality of his or her whole state of health, the state of 'being whole'. We need to facilitate the contributions of the individual and the family in the planning process so that, if possible, all individual needs are met, with minimum distress or disappointment and maximum satisfaction.

For those of us who have achieved older age, we need the courage to be ourselves, to continue to enjoy our sexuality and our friendships, our practicalities and our spirituality, to be willing to stand up for what we believe in and to demand what we need, even if those demands sometimes seem to fulfil the stereotype of older people as being 'difficult'.

Politically we must strive to inculcate appropriate attitudes in politicians, public servants and taxpayers so that older people get their fair share of the health dollar or pound, that there is enough money available through taxation or better government housekeeping to fund adequate community care. Resources must be coupled with the right attitudes so that each person is seen as a person with unique needs of mind and spirit and not of body alone, a recognition that 'one size does *not* fit all.'

If, despite society's stereotypes, we can achieve all this – or even set it in motion! – then we have indeed attained wholeness, no matter what our chronological age.

CHAPTER 2

Cultural Aspects of Growing Older

Introduction

The word 'culture' means different things in different contexts:

- Ethnic origins and the influences of these on our language, relationships, customs and behaviour; these may cross national boundaries and may include matters of law as well as of tradition

- National patterns of thought, custom, language, a few of which will have expression in legal requirements or absence of these

- Religious beliefs and customs, which are not necessarily but may be linked to ethnic or national boundaries

- The way of life associated with a particular tribe or clan, sometimes equivalent to a national grouping

- Patterns of behaviour born of social class or family customs, which may or may not differ strongly from ethnic or national boundaries

- Patterns of behaviour and taste in other professional, social or interest groups, matters pertaining to education and to artistic taste and endeavour.

These may be separated into macro- and micro-cultures, the first growing from cultural identity on the large scale and based upon ethnic origin, nationality and religion, and the second from matters of social class, family traditions, education and individual interests or preferences. They all influence attitudes towards ageing and wholeness, ill health or frailty, personal feelings about our own old age, and the capacity of older people to participate in society, to be maintained and supported by society, to be held in respect or rejected as non-persons.

Macro-cultural influences

How far is 'race' equated with 'culture'? We cannot do controlled studies on the similarities and differences between race and culture. We cannot move children from one race or culture to another, remove all possible sources of statistical ambiguity and measure the outcome. All we can do is observe what has happened by chance and speculate as to the possible significance of various factors. There are some genetic aspects of race which will influence culture, so that the colour of one's skin, the shape of one's eyes, the shape of one's skull may influence us and those with whom we come into contact. The precise outcome of these influences is varied and can include antipathy or solidarity, and both of these will affect our lives in ways which can be classified as cultural.

But in my view, culture is chiefly learned. Children who are adopted at birth and who live in a family of different race generally take on the cultural patterns of that family, in early childhood and perhaps permanently: their speech, style of dress, food habits, attitudes on class and religion.

In some places children whose racial appearance differs from the local population may be teased at school because of that appearance, but in places with high migration it may be the locally-born who are different. This was seen recently in one Sydney school where there were 35 different languages, symbolising 35 different cultural groups, and it was the 'local' population which was in the minority.

The beginning of adult life may, for some inter-racially adopted children, mark a stronger recognition of differences in colour and other racial characteristics and, for some, this leads to a yearning for the culture of the natural parents, and a wish to make contact with them. This wish for contact is, as we know, found in a high proportion of adopted children, even those adopted within the same race. For those whose adoption involved a migration across the world, contacting the family usually remains a dream, but contact is more easily achieved if the adopted child and the natural parents live in the same general area.

In young people whose adolescence is marked by rebellion and protest against the family way of life, the yearning for their cultural roots can become part of that protest. One such young woman bitterly resented having been taken from a remote African village to live in an Australian professional family in a large city, and felt that she was deprived of membership of any culture. Although she acknowledged that her adoptive parents had seen their action as humanitarian, she also felt 'owned' by them and her actions were often motivated, she said, by her need to be different.

Her rebellion led to difficult behaviour. Was this young woman unique or is a sense of racial and cultural confusion common in migrants (and particularly in those who are adopted outside their race) as they become adult?

Race and culture are not synonymous but inter-connected. Ethnic and national boundaries are not necessarily synonymous; this is seen in countries divided up by treaties which bring war to an end. Those of similar ethnic origins may find themselves with different nationalities, or a single country may have has as citizens people of widely different ethnic backgrounds.

Differences in law may cause difficulties in cultural matters; for example, funerary practices (such as exposure of a body for destruction by vultures) which, whilst normal in the country of origin, are illegal in the new country of residence (Bright 1996, p.82). Other cultural–legal problems affect medical practice (Bright 1996, pp.81–84), for example with female genital mutilation ('circumcision') which, for some people, has been practised in the country of origin but is illegal in the new homeland.

We see blurring of national and religious boundaries during war, as in the 1939–1945 conflict, when the groups on opposing sides share similar religious beliefs. During the 1939–45 war, several German prisoners of war worked in the gardens of my school and they attended Chapel services on Sunday evenings. It was customary for at least one hymn of Lutheran origin to be included in that service so that, whilst we sang it in English, they could sing it in German and feel that they were joining in the worship and were welcome. Even as a schoolgirl, I was well aware of the irony of the situation, that nations could be at war but individuals or small institutions could still act in a kindly manner to individuals. This awareness has remained with me as a life-long formative influence!

Migration

Migration and the arrival of refugees cause cultural diversity, which may or may not be a happy experience for the newcomers, despite their having sought the move, and is sometimes an unhappy experience for the host country. There can be resentment in the original inhabitants of the areas which have thus been summarily re-allocated if their original culture is changed by the new arrivals, and, when a country has been thus re-divided politically, the new citizens may regret or resent losing their previous cultural identity.

When, as in Australia, migration programmes reunite families, elderly people (not the usual target for encouragement to migrate) are helped to join their now-established families. The older people frequently have difficulty in feeling part of the new wider community because of language and custom, and tend therefore to remain within the boundaries of their immediate family and ethnic group.

Members of the health professions experience bewilderment and frustration when cultural factors prevent adequate examination and treatment, as when a male doctor is not permitted to examine a Muslim woman. Her health is jeopardised if a woman doctor is not readily available. Accepting the authority of women (doctors, nurses, therapists, police, members of the legal profession) is also culturally difficult for some.

Racial differences

Race may also be perceived as one aspect of culture, whether we consider skin colour and shape of the eye or the myriad other genetic influences which shape our lives. We see today general changes of attitude about race, so that there is, in many countries, a general 'official' climate of acceptance, even though individuals may still hold on privately to their prejudices about race and skin colour.

Such changes may be of very recent origin; it is relatively recently that racial segregation has ended in the USA and apartheid has ended in South Africa. But we are still far from universal racial tolerance, and there may be some ambiguity about cultural differences and racial differences, whether the two are or are not synonymous. People may be confused as to whether, for example, achievements in education outweigh racial differences so that a professional person of another skin colour may be an acceptable marriage partner whereas a blue-collar worker of the same racial origin is unacceptable.

We have known for some time that there are diseases or disorders which are more common in one race than another, without there being any identifiable reason for this, except that it happens! Homozygous ß thalassaemia is one such disease, common to people of Mediterranean racial origin, and causing severe illness and, frequently, death in childhood (Beeson and McDermott 1975, pp.1456–1457). It may be considered medically advisable to refrain from having children, especially if both partners carry the gene, and yet because many affected families have religious views which forbid contraception, a dilemma occurs and the spiritual, psychological and emotional difficulties can be profound. In Australia, the Thalassaemia Society provides support for affected families in their multiple and complex griefs arising from these problems.

Janicki reported results for a study of the distribution of cerebral palsied (CP) persons with mental retardation, in which he looked at the total CP population over the age of 45 years, examining statistics for the total and for three cohorts of persons aged 45–59, 60–74 and 75 or over. He found that there were racial differences in distribution, with the elderly group showing a significantly lower percentage of persons of black and Hispanic origin (Janicki 1989). No explanation was given, but it is worthy of note as indicating that racial factors can have an influence in a wide variety of matters.

These may or may not be classed as 'cultural' differences, but any racial group which is prone to a particular disease will have particular cultural attitudes towards the disease or disability. Thus racial differences lead to cultural differences.

Sexuality and culture

Great differences exist in attitudes towards sexuality, whether we look at heterosexual or homosexual relationships. Much is written about the former but, it seems, little about the latter. It has been noted that in many cultural or ethnic groups, homosexuality is either rejected or barely accepted, and in some bisexuality is either accepted or quietly condoned (Klinger and Cabaj 1996, p.117). Therapists need to be aware of cultural norms on sexual relationships and attitudes in any given group, particularly regarding homosexuality since, usually, this is not openly discussed.

It is important to differentiate between behaviour or beliefs which are bizarre from those which are normal in a given culture, and also to be aware of the possibility of culture-bound disorders (American Psychiatric Association, 1994, p.xxiv and pp.843–849).

Revaluing traditional cultures

A feature of the latter half of the twentieth century has been the re-assessment and resurgence of traditional indigenous cultures. the way of life of 'First Peoples'. In some places this has included a change of name to denote a change in value and attitude. For example, the erstwhile Eskimos are now correctly referred to as Inuit people, and (although the term 'Aboriginal' is still used) some Australian native peoples think of themselves as Kooris and others use the name of their tribe; the existence of many different languages supports the use of separate names for the various Australian tribes or peoples.

Responses to this resurgence have varied, but on the whole older people are more valued amongst First Peoples than in the past because of their role as 'rememberers', those who can recall the old ways, who can teach younger people the stories of the heroes and the spiritual background to the culture (in Australia, the stories of the Dreamtime). One may hope that some of this sense of the past as a living influence may be communicated to others. First Peoples have strong associations between spirituality and culture. A Sioux grandmother, for example, grieved about her grandchildren's loss of awareness of the spiritual aspects of the traditional Sioux ways of life (Weibel-Orlando 1990, pp.119–125).

Indigenous peoples experience varying degrees of anger about the long periods of being devalued and dispossessed, their traditional culture damaged by people who saw themselves as developers but who were seen by the indigenous peoples as invaders and conquerors. In Australia, for instance, this anger continues to have an influence on politics and provision of funding. It is a source of controversy for some, who wonder how long the anger can, or should, continue to evoke guilt in the descendants of those early settlers, how long before the process of forgiveness and reconciliation is achieved, and what can be done to speed the process.

Australian native peoples are rediscovering the value of their own heritage and although there is a risk, as elsewhere in the world, of this becoming a mere tourist attraction without the underlying essentials, many of those who visit traditional cultural areas do so from genuine concern and not simply to produce startling holiday photographs and videos.

Micro-cultural influences

Social class has strong influence on culture, and in the twentieth century there has been far greater social mobility between classes than in the past. Regional accents are heard on BBC radio today whereas in the past only 'southern received speech' was acceptable. But today's social class distinctions may be on different bases from those of the past.

In some cultures academia has created a new upper class. Educational achievements help the individual attain an upward social acceptance which would not have been possible in the past, when family origins had a profound social separating effect. Money can also help people to achieve upward social mobility, although in some places the degree of genuine acceptance may be more apparent than real.

Family culture often reflects the cultural mores of the surrounding community, but may differ from it quite strongly. In the one society one finds some families who maintain life-long relationships in marriage, but others for whom marriage is either transient or is an unwanted formality. Some families are emotionally open in happiness and sadness, while others proclaim their strength of mind by asserting proudly that they do not show their feelings – both in the one so-called homogenous society.

Such areas of study are of special concern to anthropologists and sociologists, but because of migration and the arrival of refugees, all those involved in health and social welfare also need to acquire knowledge and understanding of these cultural influences.

'Culture' is also used when referring to special interest groups:

- 'Pop' culture, those who are devotees of the current fashion in popular music

- 'Internet culture', those who use the worldwide computer network for communication and information

- 'drug culture', referring to illicit substances, their sale and use and the social network of relationships and behaviour which is linked to drug use

- the 'Old School Tie' culture and network based on attendance at specific schools.

The supportive nature of specialist sub-cultures, such as those associated with the law, the military, medicine, the arts, the priesthood and so on, which are enclaves within secular society, promote 'gerontophillic conceptions' by presenting older people as setting ethical standards for society (Guttmann 1980, pp.429–447). Whether this is true in the late 1990s is questionable: some people resent what are perceived as authoritarian attitudes of the legal profession, the medical profession and the clergy, and The Old Boy Network or The Old School Tie (unique perhaps to English-speaking countries) is derided. There is also resentment of the wealth, imagined or real, of these professions – although the clergy are, justifiably, not generally resented on those grounds!

Guttmann believes that, in upholding traditional mores, these professional enclaves are the modern equivalent of the folk traditions of the past, and that it is the increasing urbanisation of the world which has led to an erosion of gerontocracy. He also comments, however, that to return to the ways of the past would not be useful because it would lead to the disenfranchisement of women.

Culture and old age

All these cultural matters have effects upon people of all ages, and are not specific to old age. What cultural influences affect our capacity to be whole people in old age? How far are we personally affected by cultural influences from the past and the present? How does culture influence our capacity, when we are elderly, to develop and expand our skills, find new areas of interest, be perceived as creative people who have things to offer the community as a whole? Does culture affect possible avenues for medical treatment if we do become ill? Does it affect opportunities for rehabilitation and re-establishing ourselves in the 'well community'?

The 1939–1945 war was a major agent of social change for society. Women went into the armed services, worked on the land, took over civilian tasks which had previously been strictly male areas of employment. An Australian newsreel of the period showed women working on public transport, delivering the mail, working on the assembly line in munitions and other jobs (Cinesound 1942). The commentator's remarks are of interest:

> If the cautious see major post-war problems growing from the wholesale transfer of women to male jobs, there is only one answer to them. War stands on no ceremony and this is a war we must win, *no matter how much our social structures may suffer in the winning.* [emphasis added]

At the time, the idea of social structures *suffering* because of the emancipation of women probably aroused none of the public anger which would explode now, fifty or so years later, if such thoughts were aired. (We may, however, speculate on the private thoughts of women who saw that newsreel!) Today's women have cause to bless one aspect of the war, that of having started the recognition of women's competence and abilities.

There always have been women who achieved great things; names which come to mind are Florence Nightingale, Hildegarde of Bingham, the Abbess Hilda of Whitby, and others. But these were exceptions, and it must not surprise us if some of our elderly people now feel that the world is moving too fast for them to keep up. Betty Friedan (1993) writes powerfully of our need not to be pushed out of active life because we are old. She describes her own anger with the newer feminists who put her on a pedestal but in so doing denied her any present influence.

The results of the Terman Study, which has followed the same group of gifted people from childhood to old age, cannot all be extrapolated to another generation, since these people went through World War II and the depression, both of which affected study and employment opportunities. Nor can we generalise from the gifted group to the population as a whole. The present-day achievements of these gifted people do, however, refute the common belief that all elderly people lose creativity and drive (Holohan and Sears 1995).

War and civil conflict

Early interest in Post-Traumatic Stress Disorder focused upon experiences in war, but we now know that its long-lasting deleterious effects upon the lives of those affected also occur in the civilian population. The experience of organised violence, which led to Vietnamese people becoming refugees, was still having seriously harmful effects upon them some three years after their re-settlement (Haugg and Vaglum 1995).

In Cambodian culture the family is extremely important, and one of the after-effects of relocation as refugees is the guilt experienced at having left family members behind in Cambodia. It was found that two generations suffered from these guilty feelings, a measure of the cultural significance of family loyalties (Sack et al. 1995).

Somasundarem and colleagues have examined the after-effects in a civilian population of civil strife in Sri Lanka, and commented upon the chronic effect of such trauma. It seems probable that it will still be apparent when the people concerned have entered old age (Somasundarem and Sivayokan 1994). We can safely assume that civil war is especially productive of cultural shock and a lasting grief.

Reviewing the impact of trauma, Bromet (1996) emphasises the long-lasting nature of emotional responses to trauma. We must therefore expect that elderly people who have suffered from persecution, violence, torture, cruel imprisonment, forced re-location as refugees and other fear-filled circumstances, will continue to show adverse effects all their lives (Bright 1996, p.90).

In 1996 our attention was drawn to this problem in an article (Joffe, Joffe and Brodaty 1996) about the fears of elderly Jews, victims and survivors of the Holocaust, of whom there are at least 35,000 in Australia alone. Ageing is found to be doubly difficult for them when they need to consult a doctor or go to hospital because of remembered experiences.

Doctors were often actively involved in Nazi extermination (so that white coats or other features which say 'doctor' have terrifying associations) and hospital smells such as ammonia and chlorine (unobjectionable to most people) bring back terrible memories of camps and grave pits. The authors also remind us of the associations for concentration camp victims of having had to leave their homes and familiar surroundings, so that a move from home to a nursing home may be additionally disturbing.

All these instances should be regarded as having cultural implications in that particular cultural groups have been the victims, and the responses to the trauma may well have a cultural basis. We need to be alert for signs of Post-Traumatic Stress Disorder in our older patients or friends, aware of the frightening nightmares and the flash-backs which interrupt ordinary activities, the time-slip which afflicts some people (perhaps in the early stage of a dementing illness) who re-live the past as if it were the present, either with unavoidable associations from the past or actually misinterpreting chance events as threatening.

When we ourselves have not shared in such tragic experiences, we can have no idea of the long-lasting nature of the trauma nor of the way in which emotional arousal occurs with unrelated events, even if one's brain says 'This is not persecution or a death threat, this is different'. It is easy to diagnose such people as psychotic because this misinterpretation is perceived by the observer as 'ideas of reference' (and thus diagnostic of a major illness) and not rightfully recognised as the long-lasting emotional trauma of stressful life events, coupled sometimes with an incipient or actual dementia.

Attitudes towards ageing and death-hastening behaviour

Anthropologists have studied the attitude of non-industrialised people towards clan or tribal members who become old and frail, and whose support is burdensome to the group. Sokalovsky comments that older people were shown in a 1968 study in Denmark, in England and in the USA, to have rejected the 'arms length' status of being seen as 'old', imposed upon them by bureaucratic structures. He also discusses the cultural significance of the feminization of the aged population in industrial society as contrasted with societies which have not become industrialised, where the genders are more evenly balanced. Safer childbirth is one cause for the difference, and one may also speculate that attitudes towards the birth of female children (whether or not baby girls are allowed to survive) may be another (Sokalovsky 1990, pp.1–11).

What, one wonders, will the future balance of genders be in China? There is medical technology to permit the fairly accurate identification of gender of the foetus and to abort the unwanted child in order to fulfil legal requirements on family size. Given the known Chinese preference for a son, one wonders how many women there will be to grow old?

Rosenberg writes of the rapid rate of change that can take place in social custom, describing the !Kung people (the '!' represents a sound, one of many glottal stops and mouth clicks which are unique to this group). She tells us that in the early 1960s the !Kung people were hunter-gatherers with traditional social structure, and living in extended-family clans in camps of fifteen to thirty people, moving two or three times each year.

Between 1968 and 1978, however, the picture changed completely. A shop, school, airstrip and medical clinic were established, nutrition and leisure activities changed, portable cassette players became commonplace and young men were pressed into South African Police service as trackers in pursuit of the South West African Peoples Organisation.

It is significant that part of the charm to city dwellers of the film *The Gods Must be Crazy* (produced in South Africa in 1980 and later shown world-wide) was its portrayal of !Kung traditional culture as still extant, but Rosenberg tells us that this was not so – traditional ways were already threatened and altered. The elders attempted to maintain their traditional cultural practices and attitudes, but how long will it be, Rosenberg asks, before these are all lost, the elders themselves de-valued (Rosenberg 1990, pp.19–41)?

Writing under the heading 'By any other name, it is still killing', Glascock compares the treatment of the elderly in America and in other societies. He draws a convincing parallel between the causing of death in the USA by withholding or withdrawing treatment or by actively killing in so-called euthanasia with the death-hastening behaviour of primitive peoples (Glascock 1990, pp.43–56). He reminds us that, despite our modern technical skills in preserving and saving life, we are not the first people to face the dilemma of whether to support the life or (by failure to provide adequate care or by actively killing) to hasten the death of those who have become a burden on the group.

Other writers on cultural aspects of ageing have commented that the capacity of a group to maintain and support a decrepit member (someone who is affected by chronic disease and not simply old) will probably depend upon 'the prosthetic environment' (Albert and Catell 1993, pp.227–233). The poorer the economy, the less any given society will be able to afford the equipment which permits maintenance and support for its decrepit members.

Although this applies to non-industrialised society, it may also apply to any group where there are financial restrictions on the amount of money available for health and welfare. Any society where there is a shortage of money may find it easy to develop convincing arguments in favour of euthanasia. Are there cultural parallels between legalising euthanasia and existing legal decisions to allow the abortion of an imperfect foetus and the practice of some primitive peoples of abandoning the imperfect elderly or newborn because it is impossible to cope with the burden of care?

Those who are elderly today have lived through great social changes, and it is not surprising if they feel bewildered by today's social practices, even yearn for the past 'when one knew where one was', as one older person expressed it. There is a popular myth that the old days were best, that older people were properly valued and nurtured in earlier or in primitive societies, that it is only in industrialised society that we devalue and get rid of our frail elderly citizens because we cannot afford to look after them.

But Nydegger prevents us from ever again believing that everything would be fine if only we could get back to the past, 'the Golden Age', or to some idyllic primitive state, 'the Golden Isles' (Nydegger 1983). She provides telling evidence to prove her point, that there has been no 'before' and 'after' in our style of dealing with elderly people. We cannot ascribe our apparent cold-heartedness simply to industrial development. The dilemma is as old as humanity itself.

Elder abuse

Glascock's extension of death-hastening cultural behaviour as including elder abuse, and seeing this as part of cultural devaluation of older people, is logical. Both death-hastening behaviour and elder abuse arise from a capacity to stand back from the elderly man or woman, to see him or her as a non-person.

Described in 1975 under the name 'Granny bashing' (Burston 1975), abuse of an elderly person was often perceived as being a consequence of family stress in response to sharing a residence with an elderly relative. When violence occurred, it was because the carer's patience was over-stressed by that relative's repetition of questions, incontinence, getting in the way, interfering with children's activities and so on.

It is now recognised, however, that elder abuse is more than an under-standable impatience followed by a 'shove' out of the way. We know today that it is alarmingly common and that it can consist of sexual abuse, physical violence, financial exploitation, psychological abuse, and that there may be single or repeated acts. Medical officers who work in accident and emergency units should develop a high degree of suspicion and scepticism about how the injuries of elderly people were sustained when they are brought in for treatment (Kurrle, Sadler and Cameron 1992).

Elder abuse also includes failure to provide appropriate care or withdrawal of that care; a lack of appropriate action in a relationship in which there is an expectation of trust, which action or lack of action causes harm or distress to an older person (Vernon 1996). It therefore includes actions and omissions in professional as well as in personal relationships.

Even if the abuse takes the form of 'only' verbal denigration and bullying or unkindness, these too can be life-threatening for the helpless elderly person, either because it may lead to suicide or because the resulting unhappiness and distress causes depression and loss of heart so that death results.

Too often one observes impatient, short-tempered behaviour and sometimes punitive behaviour to older people: unnecessary delays to bringing a bedpan for a nursing home or hospital patient, talking over the top of someone as the bed is made as if the person in bed were not really present, the patronising tone of voice which says 'You are a non-person and I do not need to address you as an equal', rough handling so that fragile skin is damaged, and so on. All this is abuse and is clear proof of the existence of a culture in which older people, especially the sick and frail, are devalued.

One of the strengths of music therapy is the sense of individuality and choice which it brings to people, the dignity which is possible in making decisions, even if that decision is to stay away from music!

Iatrogenic disease

Because abuse includes not only harmful acts but lack of appropriate action within a relationship in which there is an expectation of trust, we must extend it to include iatrogenic disease. This includes not only mistakes in active treatment but also failure to treat, omissions of professional responsibility. Elder abuse includes many aspects of neglect by health workers (Gorbien, Bishop and Beers 1992).

- the development of decubitus ulcers caused by poor skin care and failure to move regularly an unconscious or paralysed patient

- the too-common (and potentially lethal) failure in hospitals and nursing homes to provide proper diagnosis and treatment for a condition which poses risks to health and well-being

- the spread of infections (e.g. arising from multi-resistant staphylococcus) which arises from negligence in infection control – a negligence which seems to be more prevalent with older patients than with acutely ill younger surgical or medical patients

- falls, occurring because an incapable person has been left unattended on a commode or because a seat belt has been left unfastened on a wheel chair

- tying elderly people into chairs for long periods. This is elder abuse on two counts: (a) because it is illegal in most countries and (b) because it is a cause of falls; the muscles become so wasted that the person is more liable to fall when he or she is occasionally asked to stand or walk (Evans and Strumpf 1989)

○ poor nutrition, the outcome of ignorance of nutritional needs and
   cost-cutting (with the excuse 'Oldies have such small appetites, a
   quarter of a banana is quite enough fruit for each person!').

A horrifying instance of abuse was described in 'A case of death by physical
restraint' in which the strangulation of a dementing patient was described
and illustrated, showing how a restrictive device (labelled by the manufac-
turer, we are told, as 'A Reminder to Stay in Bed') killed the woman as she
tried to escape from its straps. The writer comments that this type of disaster,
or a near-disaster from the same cause, is appallingly common (Miles 1996).
It can arise only in a culture which denies dignity to the elderly.

Reciprocity

A less immediately alarming topic but one which has far-reaching consequences for some older people is that of reciprocity, the giving of something
in return when one receives a gift or service.

In Japan it has been noted that the giving of love and affection is sufficient
return for a gift, so that older people who do not have the resources to return
in kind nor the health to return in reciprocal service are not humiliated by
receiving help from younger members of the family. There may, however, be
difficulties because the wife of the oldest son has preference in relationships
with the mother-in-law, so that, if the mother-in-law is widowed or otherwise in need of support and care, the blood-daughter may hold back from
offering help for fear of trespassing against this cultural tenet.

But this capacity to accept without giving in return is not universal across
all cultures. In Western countries there is a yearning for reciprocity which,
in some people, far exceeds any logical principle. In palliative care I have
noticed that one of the most difficult features of terminal illness (for some)
is constantly 'being on the receiving end'. For this reason we try to give
patients an opportunity of doing something for someone else: teaching the
music therapist an old song which the therapist does not know and which
may be enjoyed by someone else; asking a patient to ring the bell for an even
more frail patient when that person needs help, and so on – reciprocity on
a small scale but not without meaning.

Because their frailty prevents them from doing anything in return for
kindness and help received, people in nursing homes are deprived of
reciprocity with the result that they feel no longer whole people. They suffer
what has been called 'the awful burden of having to be grateful' (Shield
1990, pp.331–352). An elderly woman, disabled by arthritis, said 'I've

always helped other people and now look at me! I can't do anything for anybody. I wish I were dead!'

Some places do, however, support reciprocity:

○ Grandchildren are dropped off for care at a nursing home in Samoa as their mothers go to work (Foner 1984, p.150).

○ In a country town in Australia, the physiotherapy department of the hospital–nursing home was designed also as the meeting place for the Country Women's Association so that residents maintained membership of that group, continuing to assist the community and be involved in making decisions

○ Patients in a suburban Sydney nursing home sell their craftwork to support an orphan in the Third World.

But such opportunities are rare.

Those who are only frail (not disabled or dying) can feel humiliated by accepting help because they cannot repay in gifts and cannot return the help. Families remind the parent (and it usually is a parent) of his or her own tireless work and generosity in parenting. But usually it makes no difference, the parent still feels a need to do something in return. For the affluent, this need is often assuaged by paying school fees for grandchildren, giving lavish birthday gifts or sums of money to help pay off a debt on a house purchase, and so on. For elderly people without money, there is a greater challenge but the wise 'child', whose parent is unhappy about dependency, finds something about which to express gratitude.

Summary

Culture is more than race, national or ethnic background, spirituality, skin colour, the shape of eyes or family and local tradition. It is the intangible feelings and attitudes within ourselves which colour our relationships and our behaviour and which can either bring us together or separate us from each other.

Can we achieve a more empathic and loving cultural approach? This can be achieved only by hard work by society as a whole. The task is many-faceted and includes a sense of history and anthropology with a willingness to understand the cultural mores of our indigenous peoples, our migrants and refugees, especially as these relate to frailty, illness, medical or surgical treatment, dying, death and the hereafter.

Understanding ourselves is important, and an honest appraisal of our own prejudices and needs, coupled with a willingness to change, can lead to a warmer cultural approach, whether to people designated as 'patients', 'clients' or 'neighbours'.

CHAPTER 3

Sexuality and Relationships

The word 'sexuality' is sometimes used exclusively to refer to the capacity or wish for intercourse. Here it is used more widely, to indicate awareness of oneself as male or female, awareness of similarities and differences in the ways men and women may think, feel or behave, the risks of stereotypes about gender and sexuality, and – above all! – how sexuality affects our view of ourselves and our wholeness as we age.

Sexual stereotypes

Do women behave and think differently from men? The matter is increasingly controversial, with conflicting reports. The old assumptions ('Girls don't need education when all they will do is marry and have children', 'Women wouldn't be able to cope with the competition of business life') are largely discarded. Some cultures, however, forbid the emancipation of women, as in religious groups such as Muslim fundamentalists. There are also pockets of resistance within cultures which are, officially at least, committed to the idea of women sharing in employment at all levels.

The topic is too broad to be dealt with here, but we must be aware of the enormous and widespread changes which, in their own lifetime, older people have seen in the lives of men and women; some older people find these changes bewildering and even objectionable, for a variety of reasons.

But the business and professional achievements of women are not restricted to the latter half of the twentieth century. The Old Testament section of the Bible described the good wife as buying land and planting a vineyard with her profits, organising her weaving and selling her cloth; her husband is told that he is fortunate to have her and that he is respected in the community for having such a wife (King James Bible, Proverbs 31, vv. 10–31).

Elizabeth Garrett Anderson (1836–1917) was the pioneer of women's place in the medical profession, starting her work in early adult life, when (after a struggle) she achieved membership of the (London) Society of Apothecaries, but it was not until 1870 that the University of Paris awarded her the degree of Doctor of Medicine. It is fitting that there is a memorial to her in Tavistock Square in London, a place associated with medical organisation and study.

It is, however, only relatively recently that women have had a choice between motherhood and a profession, with the chance to combine the two. Even now, some older women are angered by the decision of some younger women to reject the responsibility of a family and choose instead a business or professional career.

The reason for the anger is not always obvious, and it may be a defence mechanism, a 'reaction formation', which has its origin in the wish that they had been free to make the same decisions. Reaction formation has been defined as:

> ...the unconscious adoption of behaviour opposite to behaviour which would reflect true feelings and intentions. For example, excessively prudish attitudes to sex are sometimes (but not always) a reaction to the person's own sexual urges that he cannot accept. (Gelder *et al.* 1996, p.136)

We may perhaps see a risk in the new stereotypes which seem to say 'A woman must have a career, any woman who finds full satisfaction in home life is a traitor to her sex.' Although not usually expressed so forthrightly, this is not far from the view which some women express, and has led to some disenchantment with the extremes of the women's movement.

Betty Friedan, whose writing contributed so much to the earlier initiatives for freedom of women to develop their gifts and talents, has expressed irritation with some of the later developments of feminism, and has written especially strongly on their failure to support older women. Friedan's view is that today's feminists see older women as 'they' rather than 'us', that they act on the assumption that only young women are in touch with reality (Friedan 1993, p.xxi).

The Terman Study on giftedness draws attention to some cultural differences in outlook between men and women. It was found that men usually measured their success in terms of educational and occupational life, with emphasis upon status and achievement, whereas women were more likely to mention family events as important and as being turning points in their lives. It was also found that women were also more likely than men to see spirituality as important (Holohan and Sears 1995, pp.200, 213).

I have heard many older women describe a kind of shame that they were 'only housewives'. This can be seen as a natural response to the feminist position summarised above. It is a comment to which I respond strongly, reminding the speakers of the struggles they had compared with the life of today's housewife. They had no freezers and refrigerators but had to do their shopping every day or two, no car to travel to the shops so that they had to carry their purchases home (except for the more affluent who had things delivered). During the 1930s depression, when many of today's older women were bringing up their families, they had little money; in Australia many men were away from home trapping rabbits. The social services of the day were organised in such a way that recipients of food tickets felt at best patronised and at worst humiliated, and were suspected of trickery if they were not obviously poverty-stricken. Such situations were common, not only in Australia.

A woman suffering from dementia, but whose memory was jogged by music of the depression time ('It's only a shanty in old shanty town...'), described being widowed and left with seven children, and how the teacher at the local school said that her children had the cleanest feet of any of the children at the school – 'feet' because there was no money for shoes!

Older women who battled with such challenges need have no shame at their accomplishments, even though these would today be seen as highly gender-specific. There were many instances in which women were exploited, marriages in which there was bullying and denigration, either because women were genuinely perceived as less intelligent, less competent than men or because these beliefs were convenient to society. In prostitution the blame was assigned only to the women and not their customers; until the 1939– 1945 war changed social patterns, women who had to work were badly treated and exploited, and so on.

Elderly men too may feel bewildered by the changes they see today in gender roles, in the employment of women in jobs they used to see as exclusively male, even in engineering and other work which would have at one time seemed too dirty, difficult or dangerous for women. At the University of Melbourne, the Engineering School figures for 1996 show that 16 per cent of students are female and that, in chemical engineering, 40 per cent are female.

Some older men find it strange to see the greater acceptability of emotional behaviour in men, who are now not only permitted but also encouraged to show their feelings. There have always been some men who were able to do this, but it did not fit the stereotype of the 'real man'. The description 'the sensitive new-age guy' is not simply a cartoon character, but (without the label) does symbolise a change in attitude which allows men to enjoy what had previously been seen as mothering roles, to acknowledge grief and anxiety instead of merely drinking to dull the pain, and so on.

This is not yet universal, and there are even today many men who find it difficult to accept a nurturing role with their children and men who have suffered brain damage because of the stereotype which says 'If you are a real man you must not let anyone see you are upset, just get drunk.' Some may see here a social or educational class difference, but our responses are strongly influenced by personal and family attitudes, less so by educational or social status.

We should not then be surprised that older men feel astonished and perhaps irritated or even frightened by the changes they see in men's attitudes and behaviour. We may speculate that the irritation arises from the thought 'What was wrong with the way we did things that they are changing it all?' and from wondering whether perhaps their way of doing things was wrong.

Family relationships

Other sources of confusion and distress to older people are the changes they see in marriage and family relationships. Since these frequently affect their grandchildren, their distress is not merely theoretical but born of life experiences.

The decision of so many people to live together 'as partners in a relationship' is hard for older people to understand. It causes anger and distress when it leads eventually to their grandchildren having several sets of parents, step-parents, different surnames from their half-siblings and step-siblings, conflict as to which person to invite to a school prize-giving or concert. The grief and anxiety of the older generation is comprehensible.

Such changes are frequently perceived as being the consequence of sexual licence and promiscuity, and of the failure of loyalty and stability. Older people look back to the apparent stability of their own family relationships, forgetting that some of them were loveless relationships, lacking in compan-ionship and friendship, marriages which held together because finances forced them to do so, or because convention and religious scruples made separation impossible. They also fail to recognise that much of the emotional disturbance of children of divorced parents is due to the stress of having lived in an atmosphere of conflict before the divorce rather than to the divorce itself.

Homosexuality

Homosexuality is another matter which can cause feelings of confusion and anger or distress for older people, damaging their sense of wholeness because of their bewilderment in becoming aware of this preference in those around them or in members of their families. The obvious exceptions to this are those who have themselves had a long-term homosexual preference.

Whether one perceives homosexuality as an abnormality, as a disorder, or as a normal expression of human sexuality will depend upon several factors: one's place in history (in classical Greece homosexual relationships were highly valued), one's social environment (homosexuality is frowned upon in some parts of society today and fostered or at least accepted in others) and one's profession or employment (homosexual relationships are more common in some fields of work than in others).

Klinger and Cabaj believe that homosexual individuals cope better with old age if they are satisfied with their sexual orientation, have been open about it and have a supportive network. But they remind us that few retirement communities are supportive of homosexual people as couples, and the enforced separation causes grief, isolation and loneliness (Klinger and Cabaj 1996, pp.117–8). The grief after bereavement by death is as intense for a homosexual individual as for anyone else, but may be disenfranchised by society's attitudes (Bright 1996, p.100).

Homosexuality is no longer generally categorised as a psychiatric disorder unless it involves acts with children, or involves acts with adults which include sadism or masochism or both. The legal position varies in different parts of the world and even in different parts of the same country there may be separate legal systems.

Despite this wider acceptance, and many efforts to establish biological features which make homosexual preference inevitable rather than a matter of choice, the evidence on an organic basis for homosexuality is uncertain. In a review editorial published in the *British Journal of Psychiatry*, Bancroft (1994) examined the available evidence and concluded that, although there may perhaps be some indication that some lesbian women may be hormonally different, none of the studies published in the past claiming a biological basis for homosexuality are now accepted because the results were not replicable.

For example, a theory that there is a difference between men and women in the dimensions of the *corpus callosum* is now known to be untenable. Bancroft also comments that, although homosexual behaviour is found in other species, it is only in the human population that one finds individuals with an exclusive preference for homosexual behaviour.

His conclusion is that homosexuality is a developmental process in which biological factors play a part but in which psychosocial factors remain crucially important. He also comments that the moral and political issues (which have clouded the issue in many controversies) must be resolved on other grounds than these.

Repugnance is not restricted to the elderly; some younger people share these feelings. Sometimes the responses may be explained by their being a reaction formation. It is possible therefore that those who have been unable to deal with such tendencies in themselves are strongly repulsed by homosexuality because of this unconscious defence mechanism.

Oppenheimer has discussed the attitudes of staff to sexual partnerships in long-stay facilities. She comments that a romance in a nursing home between people of the opposite sex is commonly approved, unless it complicates an existing marriage, and a wedding between such people is a matter for rejoicing. But the same approval does not extend to the growth of a homosexual relationship.

Nursing homes will also encounter problems when an elderly transvestite or transsexual person is admitted to long-term care. It may be difficult for all staff to accept without comment the gender preference of the individual and the practical arrangements which therefore need to be made for the person's care (Oppenheimer 1991, pp.889–890).

Homosexual relationships are not necessarily long-term (nor, today, are heterosexual relationships), and we do not yet know what the outcome is for older people who have had a life-long homosexual preference. If partners have stayed in the same relationship for many years, growing old together, how does one partner cope with the death or the long-term disability of the other? Although their grief is the same, they appear to receive less community support than is given to those who are bereaved after a heterosexual relationship, and may suffer from the same disenfranchised grief as is experienced by young homosexual people (Bright 1996, p.100).

Disenfranchised grief has been described and discussed as being the grief which is (for one reason or another) forbidden, illicit, unrecognised; an experience by which the grieving person is denied recognition of feelings about a loss and excluded from formal expressions of grief (Doka 1989). This is seen, for example, in the grief of an unofficial lover of any age whose grief over the death of the loved person is disenfranchised because there was no public acknowledgement of their relationship, because the relationship was unacceptable to the person's family or because there was no legal bond between them. This is particularly painful for the lovers of those with AIDS, who may find themselves, because of family shame, forbidden to visit the dying partner or, later, attend the funeral.

What isolation and loneliness is suffered by people whose homosexual relationships have always been short-lived and who, as they age, find it harder to establish new relationships? Has the focus upon HIV and AIDS, which mainly affects younger people, denied older gay and lesbian people emotional support in times of loneliness? Because many older people find the idea of intense, romantic love between persons of the same sex incomprehensible, especially when it includes physical intimacy, they may see the AIDS epidemic as associated with sexual licence and promiscuity of a type which is outside their understanding. There is therefore a deep shame for some older people in acknowledging that an adult child is HIV positive or has AIDS.

One such woman was blocked in her grief over her son's death because, so it seemed to staff, she feared that, if she let her feelings have expression, she might inadvertently reveal that he had died from AIDS and not, as she insisted, from cancer (Bright 1996, pp.95–104). We have much to learn about problems and challenges facing persons who have a preference for others of their own gender.

Personal sexuality

Damaging stereotypes about sexuality in later life include opinions that older people are asexual, have lost all interest in the opposite sex, that anyone who shows sexual awareness of another person is 'a dirty old man'. Usually it is a male who is thus described, although in the same circumstances a woman may be described as 'abnormally sexy'.

A research project on stress in nurses who care for persons with dementing illness (Bright 1987, pp.129–144) revealed some interesting contrasts in attitudes to sexuality. A questionnaire included questions about perceived stress in response to a variety of behaviours, including incontinence, aggression towards staff and towards fellow-patients, and various other behaviours which may be regarded as difficult. Respondents to the questionnaire included people at various levels of seniority and expertise, ranging from people at the peak of their profession as directors of nursing in large establishments, to nursing aides who had only basic training.

One of the questions was concerned with responses to overt sexual behaviour. Results showed that there was no correlation between the stress reported in response to sexual behaviour and the experience, training or seniority of the respondents. In fact there was greater difference between reported stress levels in response to this behaviour than to any other. No questions were asked which might have revealed the reasons for this discrepancy.

The conclusion was that attitudes of nurses towards sexuality in older people are highly variable and highly personal, and it is probable that a survey of the general community about attitudes to sexual behaviour in older people would elicit a similar result. Informal discussion suggests that it may be the place in which sexual behaviours take place rather than the behaviours themselves which elicit staff stress, so that masturbation or heterosexual petting in public is stress-inducing for carers but does not induce stress if the behaviours take place in the privacy of the bedroom.

Many middle-aged or young adults find the thought of their own parents' sexual life difficult to accept, a matter which psychoanalysts and others have discussed. This may well be extrapolated to the older generation as a whole, and may help to explain some of the responses in the research described above. Such feelings may also explain why some nursing homes do not provide shared accommodation for married couples, and may even place the two partners at opposite ends of the building with few opportunities to meet.

Some geriatric rehabilitation units do admit happily married couples into double rooms, because they have the wisdom to recognise that anxiety of one partner over the other's well-being is detrimental to progress and can lead to the request for early discharge from treatment when the person in hospital is anxious over what is happening to the spouse at home or vice versa. The style and quality of the marriage must be understood before a decision on sharing a room is made, so that estranged couples, or those who have not shared a room for many years, are not forced into an unwanted and potentially destructive propinquity.

Is it true that we lose interest in sexual activities with our partners as we grow old? We must distinguish between intercourse and affection. Some-times, in the 1990s, we seem to focus so strongly on 'relationships' – whether 'good', 'destructive', 'working', 'neighbourly' or any other – that we forget about 'liking' and 'loving' and sharing affection!

There can be practical difficulties in achieving intercourse. Our partner may have died and we may not be inclined to look for another, either on a temporary or a permanent basis. Illness and the surgery or medication used to treat it may have led to male impotence or to loss of full sexual function. Physical weakness and fatigue may make coitus almost or completely impossible.

Post-menopausal women experience hormonal loss leading to vaginal problems which can make intercourse uncomfortable and they may not seek the help which is available to deal with this. One imagines that this discomfort may well have been the cause historically of the myth of sexlessness in older women.

Arthritis, hemiplegia, amputations and other problems can lead to sexual intercourse being so difficult that the partners can only enjoy closeness without coitus. If the quality of love has in the past been shown only through coitus, without it there is loss of emotional intimacy.

Despite these challenges to wholeness, marriages can continue to be a source of companionship, love, fun and mutual support in times of difficulty. It is not unknown for people (often those who have been previously married) to marry for a second time late in life, enjoying several years of shared companionship and happiness with the new partner.

Kellett (1989), writing on 'Sex and the elderly', discussed the need for continuing sexual behaviour in old age, emphasising that it is important to understand the causes of changes when these do occur, such as delay in arousal, diminished (or changed quality of) orgasm, and so on. He commented that older people may need permission to enjoy behaviour which is different from the behaviour in early married life. He also recommended a handbook (produced in 1985 by the UK organisation Age Concern) entitled 'Living, Loving and Ageing' as being a helpful source of guidance and reassurance to elderly people.

Comments about Kellett's article drew attention to the particular problems of women who have had gynaecological surgery, especially when this was for cancer and when there was also a need for radiation. Such women (and, one assumes, their partners) need information about the effects of treatment, with strongly supportive counselling. The authors quoted statistics as to the high percentage of women surgical patients who were sexually active. Of women over the age of 65 who had cancer of the vulva, 25 per cent were sexually active; for ovarian or endometrial cancer 33 per cent, and for cervical cancer 50 per cent. Such figures disprove beliefs about sexual inactivity in old age (Lawton and Hacker 1989).

But sexuality is more than the genitalia, more than our sets of reproductive organs. One person who suffered greatly, who may or may not have been typical of a particular group, was a nun, vowed to life-long celibacy in a religious order. I spent time in music therapy and counselling with her during her rehabilitation after excision of the vulva because of cancer, and it was difficult even to mention her loss or help her to speak of her feelings of repugnance in enduring intimate examinations, surgery and subsequent nursing care because, it seemed, she had never come to terms with her own sexuality.

For this woman, religious vows were associated with the problem. But similar difficulties are likely to be seen in any elderly unmarried woman, who grew up at a time when sexuality was never discussed with unmarried women, and when sex was, to many, solely a means to procreation and not to pleasure. The elderly unmarried women whom we meet today grew to maturity at a time when, for most women, to be unmarried meant to lack all sexual knowledge and experience.

Oppenheimer has useful reminders about sexuality in older people, that we must not have stereotypes at either extreme. We must not believe that all older people live their lives without sexual intercourse and those who do enjoy sexual relationships are seen as atypical, perhaps as abnormal. But it is equally important that we do not behave towards people on the assumption that all elderly people must enjoy a full sexual life, and that failure to do so is atypical or abnormal (Oppenheimer 1991, pp.872–900).

The Department of Health in New South Wales (Australia) produced in 1988 a video called *The Heart Has No Wrinkles* which emphasised the joy of continuing or new intimacy in old age. It demonstrated the damaging nature and the incorrectness of the stereotypical belief that it is abnormal for older people to see themselves as sexual beings. The video was also helpful in emphasising that we must not equate love with intercourse, that affection can bring joy even when there is male impotence.

Some research on sexual adjustment and the quality of relationships in persons suffering from spinal cord injury in paraplegia is helpful to our general thinking on sexuality in old age (Kreuler, Sullivan and Siösteen 1996). The researchers concluded from their investigations that psychosocial rather than physical factors are important for a satisfying sexual life and relationship.

The factors they found to be important included shared activities of various kinds, feelings of being sexually attractive, willingness to use a variety of approaches in gaining sexual pleasure. They found that age, gender, education, duration of the relationship, employment, previous sexual experience and orgasm were not correlated with the emotional quality of the relationship.

The implications of this study for older people are clear. If one feels oneself to be still sexually attractive, and when the relationship includes shared activities and interests, the relationship retains a sexual quality even if intercourse is difficult or impossible.

Probably the most important factor in both individual and shared contentment later in life is that we see ourselves as sexual beings. Whether or not we have the opportunity and capacity for intercourse, we are still men and women who can enjoy our differences as well as our similarities – *vive la difference*, and let no one convince us otherwise!

Sexuality and disabled people

It is known that the partners of people with Alzheimer's disease are often unhappy about sexual relationships for a variety of reasons:

- because the dementing partner forgets what to do to achieve intercourse

- because the dementing partner makes inordinate demands for intercourse, having forgotten an incident earlier in the evening

- because the spouse feels uncomfortable at the idea of having such intimacy with someone who cannot remember his or her name or remember that they have been married for many years.

In such situations, professionals need training to provide appropriate guidance and emotional support for the non-demented partner (Litz, Zeiss and Davies 1989).

Although the main concerns of older people are focused on their own needs or those of family members, the matter of sexuality in younger people may sometimes need discussion because of a disability in a child or a grandchild.

Whether we are concerned with mental retardation or a pervasive developmental disability such as autism, or a physical disability such as cerebral palsy or spinal cord injuries, it seems to be easier to think of people with disabilities as asexual beings, perpetual children. The other common view is that people with retardation are over-sexed and uninhibited, and so are a risk to the community (Szollos and McCabe 1995). Szollos and McCabe comment that little is known with any certainty of the attitudes of the intellectually disabled people themselves but it seems that they are generally lacking in understanding of and knowledge about their own sexuality, and the World Health Organisation's classification reminds us of the vulnerability of mentally retarded persons to sexual exploitation (World Health Organisation 1992, p.226).

By thinking of disabled persons as asexual or as perpetual children, we avoid having to consider ethical issues such as exploitation of a lower functioning person by a higher functioning person. We do not have to work out ways of satisfying the needs of physically disabled people for sexual intimacy when the usual ways are unavailable to them. We do not have to plan appropriate accommodation so that intimacy can be achieved and long-term partnerships established. We do not have to provide appropriate education on matters of sexual hygiene and contraception.

In the past, and perhaps also today, disabled people encountered opposition from families who saw it as improper, even indecent that someone with, for example, spinal cord injury should contemplate marriage, particularly to a non-disabled partner.

For those who suffer from a severe level of mental retardation, to have the responsibility of bringing up children is challenging and perhaps not wise. It is, however, possible to arrange contraceptive measures which do not depend upon remembering to take a nightly pill, although the ethics of long-term hormonal anovulants or of permanent sterilisation are highly controversial, and the focus of legal disputation.

Marriage with parental support, perhaps in a separate flat attached to the parents' house, has proved happy and successful for people with moderate levels of intellectual impairment. But not all families are able to support such a relationship, for reasons of their own attitudes towards sex and disability or because of finance.

It is vital for a long-term relationship between people with disabilities, especially if one partner is not disabled, that they have made sure that the relationship is not based upon pity or 'rescuing' but upon a realistic understanding of the challenges which are involved.

Many counsellors advise people with major disabilities who are contemplating permanent relationship with either another disabled person or a non-disabled person to have a trial period in which there can be a realistic assessment of whether or not they can be happy together within the unavoidable limitations. Although this is not a decision which older people will often need to make for themselves, they may be concerned at decisions being made by younger relatives with a disability who are contemplating a serious partnership.

But they themselves may also decide in later life to marry, and may encounter opposition similar to that described above from relatives who see it as indecent for elderly people to enter marriage. Financial implications can also be the cause of such opposition, when it is feared that money may be willed to members of the new partner's family.

In 1990 an article was published about the assessment of persons with Alzheimer's disease who were living in nursing homes or other institutions to determine their competence in decision-making, specifically on a decision to enter into a sexual relationship with a fellow-resident. In those for whom the possibility seemed reasonable, it was important to discuss the matter with the family, and although staff had expected to meet opposition, this was not so. Their statistics showed that it is not a decision which will often need to be made. Of 130 people whose competence in making decisions was assessed for this reason, only two were adjudged competent and encouraged to make this change in their lives (Lichtenberg and Strzepek 1990).

Sexual behaviour in institutions

In the past there has been clear disapproval of sexual relationships in institutions, whether we are thinking of the old charity 'workhouses', in which families were split up to live in dormitory-type accommodation, or of large long-stay hospitals, which had similar segregation. Sexuality between residents of institutions remains today a matter of contention and embarrassment.

Those who have lived for many years in institutions have perhaps come to believe of themselves that sex is inappropriate, or even that sexual needs are wrong. In such circumstances it is difficult to set up ways in which older people can begin for the first time to recognise their own sexuality.

But, even in institutions, flirtations can flourish and, without any significant relationship being established, these experiences add extra colour and fun to people's lives. It is sexuality on a minor scale, but worthwhile despite this. To have a boyfriend or a girlfriend is good for the morale of those with mental retardation as well as for others, even if the relationship can flourish only on the basis of occasional meetings at functions or in a sheltered workshop.

With the increasing practice of de-institutionalisation, we are seeing people, including some in later life, who have been for many years in institutions but who are now being moved into smaller group homes. Decisions may need to be made for some of them about what house rules are to hold for sexual relationships. Normalisation, as concerned with sexuality, does have some hazards. For example, a person with a moderate or high level of functioning is distressed and bewildered as to why sexually-coloured overtures to a staff member are rejected (Bright 1996, p.73).

I was a director for many years of a small group home where, with the support of a house manager, four people live together who are of very widely differing levels of functioning; the attitude adopted was that a family atmosphere pervaded the home and that it was best for residents to feel brotherly and sisterly affection towards each other rather than have the life of the house complicated by sexual intercourse and sexually-based rivalries. Such an attitude also avoids the risk of exploitation which arises when residents are widely different in their competence and understanding.

Sexuality was not frowned upon as such (parties were arranged for visiting men and women, friends from sheltered workshops) but sexual activity was discouraged between residents of this particular house. There would be those who would see such a decision as infringing the rights of the individual, despite the risk of exploitation which the organisers foresaw if this decision had not been made.

Further comments on harmful stereotypes

Just as we must reject the idea that marriages and personal lives cease to have a sexual component in old age, so we must not accept the stereotype that, for older people, marriages were always perfect.

Many of those older people who have been referred to me for grief therapy following the death of the spouse have in fact been trying, often unsuccessfully, to cope with their hidden feelings of relief that a difficult relationship was over. When marriages have been extremely unhappy and full of conflict, and both partners have become frail, we need empathic understanding of their needs (with additional information from adult children, however difficult this may be for them) to ensure that we do not perpetuate the unhappiness by an enforced propinquity.

It is vital to admit happily married people to a place where they can be together. It is desirable, if people have had long-term unhappiness in a relationship, to help them achieve reconciliation and a new relationship if this can be done. But it is equally important to accept that the renewed intimacy may not be possible.

When they are in good health and living in their own homes with friends nearby, unhappily married people can live their own lives with different interests but in a nursing home this is more difficult. Enforced propinquity, based upon an assumption that all married couples must want to spend their time exclusively with each other, damages those whose wish is the exact opposite. It may even be necessary to arrange their accommodation in different places or in different units of the same establishment. A middle-aged woman described how her father's mood deteriorated when his very difficult and demanding alcoholic wife was admitted to the same facility where (following a stroke) he had been living for several years, and how his depression and isolation eased only when his wife was moved elsewhere.

Divorce has been available for many years, although in earlier times it was extremely difficult, particularly so for a woman to divorce her husband. Convention, religious beliefs or rules and financial problems have resulted in people staying together when there was neither love nor alliance but only fears of disapproval or the bonds of finances or children to hold them together.

Cultural attitudes to sexually-based relationships

Even today there are religious and cultural differences in whether it is easy, difficult or impossible to dissolve a marriage and whether or not it is exclusively the prerogative of the male partner to bring the marriage to an end. Migration can bring cultural problems and amongst these is the question of the dissolubility or the permanence of marriage. Because this book is concerned mainly with older people, the matter is not discussed here except to remind ourselves that older migrants may find it hard to accept the practices of their new homeland, since (even if their own marriages are not at risk) marital conflict can affect their adult children and their grandchildren.

We can speculate that it may be hard for older migrants from some cultures to accept that the failure of the wife to give birth to a son is not, in their new homeland, *a priori* grounds for divorce. They might find it hard to cope with what is perceived as a threat to the continuity of the family name and heritage when their daughter-in-law does not provide them with a grandson. Although failure to bear a son is not in itself a cause for divorce, it may lead to such a breakdown of the marriage that divorce eventually occurs. There is a strong association between cultural factors and sexual attitudes.

Friendship

Friendships are to most people a source of affection, happiness and strength, and it is a sad experience for many older people to find that it becomes more difficult to maintain friendships as one becomes more frail and disabilities reduce our ability to visit and to communicate with friends.

One of the disappointing and perhaps unexpected effects of today's focus on homosexuality is that some people are embarrassed about having a close friendship with a person of the same sex lest it be perceived as having a sexual basis. One hopes that this hypersensitivity of both the individual and society will disappear because friendship and the affectionate support of friends, whether of the same or of the opposite sex, is part of society's fabric!

Sexuality of older people may well be the least understood aspect of life in later maturity, but it is far from the least important!

CHAPTER 4

Spiritual Aspects of Old Age

Religious beliefs and practices are highly personal and, to some, highly controversial, and so this chapter discusses spirituality as it affects older people whatever their beliefs or absence of belief. Most of us perceive ourselves as being something more than a mere combination of body and mind, and feel that we have some other essential component, that of 'spirit'. In some contexts there are similarities between what we mean by 'spirit' and what we mean by 'personality' and it may be that the two are closer than the words would suggest.

Personality

Wherein lies the personality? What a debate there would be if we could gather together, in some celestial debating chamber, those philosophers across the centuries: René Descartes and John Locke from the seventeenth, David Hume and Immanuel Kant from the eighteenth, Sigmund Freud and Jean Paul Sartre from the twentieth. But whether there would in the end be consensus of their views on thought, feeling, experience and personality we shall never know!

To me, 'personality', sometimes expressed as 'personhood', means that essential core of the individual which remains intact despite changes in communication from whatever cause, despite apparent changes in behaviour wrought by a dementing illness or a psychiatric disorder, and sometimes despite unconsciousness or coma. It is this essential person whom we meet when we play music to an unconscious person and see tears on the cheek, when we sing familiar songs to a person with advanced dementing illness, a catastrophic stroke or a major depressive illness and see the face light up, see a toe tapping in time, perhaps hear music emerge as the person sings the tune.

It was that inner being of the woman, angry, miserable, lost and dysphasic because of dementia, who responded to quiet reassurance that 'despite the "fog" and confusion you feel, you are still the same person deep inside and people still care about you!' She smiled and touched my arm, saying 'Nice you say, nice you say.'

This is the personality, the personhood; how far does it differ from the 'spirit' of that person, even perhaps the soul? One can play with words, argue about semantics and etymology, and thereby lose the heart of the matter, which is that we are not merely our intellect and our behaviours, we are something more, and that 'something', call it what we will, may be eternal.

A strictly behaviourist view, that we are nothing more than the product of our environment, nothing more than learned behaviour, loses some of its authority when we ask ourselves 'If this is so, what was the learned behaviour which led the behaviourist to this belief, and how valid are theories based upon it?' I remember with gratitude my late headmistress, Joan Elliott, who made a group of 16-year-olds think about this question.

Spiritual attitudes

Our beliefs and feelings about the spirit and the soul are influenced by many factors. Although most people are capable of change in adult life, important formative influences include our social and cultural background, our childhood upbringing and the attitudes about spirituality which were instilled into us in that process. We may decide as adults to reject those influences, to take on the philosophical and spiritual attitudes of a different group with whom we choose to live, or to take strong personal steps in a different direction. These are not necessarily a once-only matter. We may in the course of a lifetime change direction philosophically and spiritually more than once, sometimes returning to the family attitudes of early life, sometimes moving to something entirely new.

In her book *Fountain of Age*, Betty Friedan describes people's need 'to nurture a sense of the sacred' (1993, p.595), quoting a long-term antagonist of religion as having astonished his readers by such comments. She also describes (1993, pp.552–3) the long-time editor of the *New York Times*, who, at the age of 70, arranged to celebrate his Bar Mitzvah, which he had not had as a boy because of his father's antagonism to Jewish faith and ceremonies. Change in spiritual matters is possible even in what many would call 'old age'!

Although spiritual attitudes are not immune to change, there is a strong link between them and culture. A family's spiritual attitudes have not necessarily grown *de novo* or from long traditions. They too may have been affected by external factors such as ethnic and national culture, migration (whether by choice or as refugees), marriage, or other circumstance.

We can argue that the concept of spirituality has its origins in the powerlessness of primitive man and his need to feel that there was a way of bringing control to the uncertainty of living, a way of escaping the fear of that uncertainty.

We can argue that the mind itself is only a product of the body, since damage to some areas of the brain result in changes of thinking and apparent change of personality. Since, however, we may in this be seeing only changes in brain connection causing changes in behaviour rather than a fundamental change in personality, this matter will be left for another arena!

Observations in psychiatry show that behaviour, and what therefore may seem to be the personality, can change because of a disorder such as mania, schizophrenia or psychotic depression. Nevertheless, appropriate treatment restores the 'real' person. This is further demonstration of the separateness of behaviour and personality.

Those who do have a sense of that third dimension of being human, of having a spiritual component to life, can argue that the behaviour had to start somewhere. Who taught primitive mankind that we are not simply body and mind? Plato's doctrine of ideas, which he set out in his *Republic*, attempted to solve this dilemma by postulating that there are absolute values, 'ideas', and that these provide us with a way of recognising goodness, truth and so on in our everyday world. These principles seem to be close to theistic views of life and morality, and to the origins of spirituality.

Even in the early artistic works done by Australian Aborigines there were carvings and paintings in ochre not only of the animals sought by the hunter, but also of spirit figures. These clearly demonstrate a feeling for the numinous, and one cannot but be moved by these as one looks at the art-works on rock platforms and cave walls in the bush areas around modern Sydney or in Central Australia. They also force us to think about the boundaries and the links between spiritual and artistic creation, links which today have been clouded by the conventions of the industrialised world, in which there is a general separation between religious and secular works.

Australian Aborigines are today strongly aware of their spiritual heritage of the Dreamtime, and we must recognise that the practice of 'going walkabout' (still happening in some places outside urban environments) is not associated with food-gathering but with the need to visit sacred sites and teach growing children about these. Evidence of spirituality in 'primitive', pre-development man is not, of course, confined to Australia, but is found in many archaeological sites as well as in the contemporary spiritual life of First Peoples.

Whether an awareness of the spiritual dimension of life necessarily implies also an awareness of the individual soul is open to discussion. It is fairly common for people to have a nebulous feeling that there is something more to life than body and mind, even that there must have been a creator of the universe, yet some people feel this without any personal involvement with the spiritual, and without any belief that the individual soul will continue as a separate entity after the death of the body.

In a video comprising two interviews with women who were facing the immediate prospect of death, they spoke about their spiritual values. In their comments one sensed profound differences in attitude towards death and the survival of the spirit because of their upbringing and culture, one came from a fairly conventional Christian background and the other from a North American Indian culture (Mount 1990).

We must not confuse spirituality with formal religious observance and it was interesting to find, in a book of interviews with elderly Australians (Deveson 1994), how few of them spoke of formal spiritual creeds or a belief in life after death, yet how many spoke of belief in a creator spirit of the universe. One wonders whether this was because their early teaching on religion had alienated them from a God whose only focus, as so many children were taught, seemed to be on punishment and quasi-parental autocratic control (Phillips 1986, pp.3–21), or whether personal experience of tragedy made God seem remote from human suffering.

For some people, however, there is a strong and abiding sense of having a soul, a personal bonding with the creator, of having a personal spiritual existence which is in some way separate from the life of body and mind. At the same time the soul interacts with body and mind so that the soul can be harmed by evil actions. Some people have an added trust that human suffering is not planned by the creator but is mainly the fruit of man's misuse of the world and his environment.

It is to me profoundly tragic – and wrong! – that so many older people see illness or disability as punishments for some wrong-doing. 'I must have done something to deserve this illness even though I can't think what it could be.' Such beliefs are not restricted to elderly people but are seen in some faith-healing groups which give the message that if you have not been healed from your illness it is because you haven't prayed hard enough, haven't repented of your sins deeply enough, or some equally destructive implication, stated or unstated. But it does seem to be particularly common in older people and is sometimes described as Christian (or Catholic) guilt.

Bereavement too is seen by some as retribution to the survivor for having loved the person too much, been dependent upon the person instead of on God. In some people, especially in those with depressive illness, there is a feeling of guilt at having in some way caused the death. Because depression is so common in elderly people, they may be specially at risk of such feelings.

The spiritual needs of elderly people must he acknowledged, whether they are people who are facing imminent death, those who are coming to terms with a life of continuing frailty or disability, or those who are starting to have difficulty in maintaining their previous levels of involvement in corporate religious observance.

Although not all wish to do so, continued participation in organised worship is still possible for those in good health, and two research projects have looked at associations between participation and mental health.

A group working on a three-generational study in Mexico found that religious attendance was associated with life satisfaction. Although attendance at church was less common in the youngest generation in the study, such observance had salutary effects upon the depressed affect in that generation (Levin, Markides and Ray 1996).

In discussing the distinction between suicidal ideation and actual attempts, Schmid and colleagues found that religion is the best single predictor, with attempting suicide usually linked with Protestantism, and suicidal ideation linked with Catholicisim or Judaism (Schmid, Manjee and Shah 1994). We would be wise, however, not to use this finding as justification for ignoring risks in particular groups.

Fear of death

Fear of suffering and death is common. If we work with those who are dying or who are facing a life of disability and dependence, it is important that we think through our own attitudes towards suffering and the treatment of those who suffer, towards life and death, life after death, and the other aspects of human existence which form an uncertain and undefined area (fraught with ethical dilemma) that lies between treatment and philosophy.

Only by deep thought on these matters can we equip ourselves to work sensitively with clients or patients and their families. Even if in the end we come to no personal conviction or decision, the effort to reach understanding will have been helpful in achieving empathy with those in need.

Not all elderly people are able to continue with their accustomed ways of worship. Most hospitals and nursing facilities include visits by clergy of different religious groups in their regular programmes, and some employ full- or part-time chaplains. The therapist who finds that a patient is distressed over a spiritual matter, but who feels personally unable to give any counsel, can seek assistance from the appropriate spiritual adviser attached to the facility.

How does this link with our theme of 'wholeness'? Is it necessary to have a feeling for the numinous in order to feel whole, integrated? There are those who have lived happily without any belief in a spiritual life except in a humanistic sense of seeking the common good as being something worthwhile and as more important than personal satisfaction. As they face death, they are content in their belief that to die is to come to an end, and that they will live on only in the memories of the people who knew them, perhaps in the work they did, and, if they leave descendants, in the gene pool of the family.

In one of the first books to be published which dealt with death and dying (Hinton 1967, p.84), findings were reported of those with a weak religious faith who seemed to have more fears of death than were experienced by those without faith, who therefore had no expectation of eternity.

We must have deep respect for the beliefs of others whether these are theistic, atheistic or agnostic, Buddhist, Hindu, Muslim, primitive animism or any other. Our professional responsibility, however strong our own thoughts on spiritual matters, is not to convert to our own creed or absence of creed, but to support those who are emotionally and spiritually vulnerable because of illness, disability, impending death or other difficulty.

When speaking at chaplains' meetings and conferences, I have found in discussion that their attitudes on this are very open, with a notable absence of proselytising zeal but instead a positive attitude of loving acceptance of the individual, no matter what his faith or lack of it. There is no desperate struggle to achieve a death-bed conversion, although some lay people find it impossible to match such unconditional acceptance.

The words come to mind 'There's wideness in God's mercy like the wideness of the sea', and 'We magnify his strictness with a zeal he will not own' (Faber, 1862). Obviously, today's chaplains who support the spiritual needs of those in distress need no such reminders!

The health departments of various states in Australia have for many years given formal recognition to the importance of spiritual aspects of life by funding the salaries of chaplains in public hospitals. There is a public acknowledgement of the diversity of human need in times of illness and crisis, and the wholeness of the individual which encompasses not merely the body or the mind but the spirit as well.

How do older people express their spirituality and, in this context, how do we feel that we are 'whole people'?

Most religious groups find strength in their older members who in turn benefit from loving support of the congregation. For some, however, changes in the structure and wording of services can be difficult to accept. For them the words, rather than the meaning of the words, have been something of a transitional object, a security blanket giving comfort in times of stress.

For others the use of 'songs' instead of traditional 'hymns' is tiresome. These feelings are not necessarily associated with chronological age – some younger people also feel that the songs are ephemeral, the music banal, and are thus an inadequate means of expression of their spirituality. But few spiritual groups concentrate solely on songs of short-lived popularity, so that older people are able to express their spirituality through familiar music and forms of worship, in services which provide a mixture of styles.

A discussion had taken place with a group of elderly hospital patients about their preferences in spiritual music at times of unhappiness or anxiety, and I had noted (not for the first time) the comments that 'at times like this', they remembered 'Sunday School songs' or music associated with early participation in religious observance.

A few days later, I asked a young guitar-player, a key member of a religious 'rock' music group, what music he would turn to for solace in the future if he were in distress. His reply surprised me at the time but has since been confirmed by others of the same age. He said, 'Well, it wouldn't be rubbish like this, it would be something that had lasted – something like…', and he went on to name some music by Bach. The precise choice depended upon the musical experience of the individual, but there was a general agreement that, in times of stress or unhappiness, one needs music which has persisted, not the fashionable and ephemeral.

What conclusions, then, can we draw about wholeness and spirituality as we age?

- that there is a widespread belief in a creator spirit who planned the universe, and advances in scientific knowledge appear to have strengthened a disbelief that it could possibly have happened by chance

- that such a belief in a creator is not necessarily linked with belief that the creator has any personal investment in the individual, and, because of the tragedies and conflicts in the world, some people have deliberately rejected such a concept

- that there is a deep sense of personhood, personality, which may or may not be equated with belief about the possession of an immortal soul

- that there is a wide diversity in the nature and strength of spiritual beliefs, and that many people gain strength, joy and inspiration from their faith, especially when this includes belief in a personal and loving God.

- that this strength is often but not invariably linked to a Christian belief; for example, we have seen how Jews were able to withstand Nazi oppression because of their tenacious faith.

We also know that, for some people, there is a growth in spirituality as they 'attempt to resolve some of life's paradoxes and contradictions' (Wilkes 1993, pp.305–312), and this may occur as part of acceptance of disability or impending death.

How can we help those who fear death because their faith gives them a belief in eternal life but no certainty that they themselves will reach 'heaven'? The official chaplain of the appropriate faith may be able to give reassurance on this, because his role gives him an authority which other staff members lack, and it is encouraging to see the changes in mood which occur after empathic and supportive counselling.

There is a feeling of wholeness which pervades happy or contented people of any age, and this usually includes some awareness of a dimension to life beyond mind and body, even if it includes spirituality only in a belief in human goodness as being stronger than human evil. This dimension I describe as 'the spiritual essence of being', no matter what the formal beliefs or lack of belief, and no matter what the age of the person.

However strong our own beliefs or denial of belief, we must support the wholeness (and do nothing to destroy it) of those who face the end of life, whether in imminent death or in the last phase of living through disability and frailness.

Recommended reading

Philip Yancey's writings are recommended for those who wish to consider problems of human suffering in the context of religious belief:

Yancey, P. (1977) *Where is God When it Hurts?* Grand Rapids, MI: Zondervan.

Yancey, P. (1988) *Disappointment with God. Three Questions No One Asks Aloud.* New York: Harper-Collins.

CHAPTER 5

Physical Challenges to our Integrity

Introduction

As we age, many of us develop physical difficulties which challenge our integrity and our wholeness, and the physical cannot be separated entirely from the emotional. How do we cope with these? Can we retain our sense of wholeness despite these difficulties?

There can be no single answer to a question which has such global implications and much will depend upon the severity of the condition, the response to medical or surgical intervention, and on people's attitudes – our own and those of people with whom we come into contact.

What is certain is that to hear people say 'Oh well, what can you expect at your age!' (or comments of similar meaning) is damaging to one's self-esteem, and likely to engender feelings of powerlessness and hopelessness. We may well feel angry at such comments, and try with great determination to prove the comments wrong. Although such anger and determination can be useful in fuelling our rehabilitation or recovery, they can also lead to the 'as if' behaviour, with all its potential for harm.

Some conditions are more common in old age, and some of them are discussed in the following sections.

Strokes

It is perhaps surprising that we still use the word 'stroke' (dating from 1599 to describe a sudden catastrophic illness, often 'apoplexy'), surprising that it gives the name to a major journal and that the word is used every day by professionals to describe the circumstance in which an area of brain tissue dies. Yet the suddenness which is implied by 'stroke' is true to life for both sufferer and relative.

There is a wide interest in the occurrence of strokes, and a seven-country study has been in progress for some time (Menotti *et al.* 1996). It seems that the incidence of strokes is decreasing in industrialised society (Beaglehole

1993; Bonita *et al.* 1994) but, because of increasing numbers of people surviving into old age, the actual number of people having strokes is not diminishing, with a suggested figure of 200,000 per year in the USA (Sin, Beers and Morgenstern 1993).

We must not, therefore, be complacent about the number of people with major needs, and suffering impairment of their feelings of wholeness from the results of a stroke, whether these involve gait and mobility, perception, communication, independence or relationships, or all of these.

Strokes are caused by loss of circulation in part of the brain, either because a blood vessel is blocked or because a haemorrhage deprives more distant tissues of their normal blood supply and damages the area where the bleeding occurred.

The results of a stroke in someone's life will vary according to the severity of the event. A transient ischaemic attack (TIA) in which temporary reduction of blood supply to the brain causes short-lived signs and symptoms such as muscular weakness, confusion of speech, clouding of consciousness, will resolve in a matter of hours and yet is usually a forerunner of a serious stroke in the future.

A minute embolus (a blood clot or piece of tissue, for example from the fatty lining of a blood vessel) will block only a small blood vessel so that only a small part of the brain is deprived of blood circulation, but a larger embolus will cut off the blood supply of a correspondingly large area of brain tissue and cause wider and more serious deficits, even possibly to the extent that life is no longer possible.

An intra-cortical haemorrhage will deprive the area of brain normally supplied by that vessel of its blood supply, and therefore deprive the area of oxygen, and the area invaded by the bleeding will also suffer. Unless the blood is promptly removed, even bleeding outside the brain itself (as in a sub-dural haematoma caused by a blow to the head) has serious after-effects similar to that of a stroke because of the pressure exerted upon the brain contents.

Effects of a stroke are highly diverse, and, as mentioned above, some strokes are so severe that continued life is impossible. Even in those who survive, however, results differ in their severity and the time in which any recovery occurs. Effects may include immediate loss of consciousness or a confusional state and loss of general intellectual capacity; there is likely to be a loss of power in, and perhaps total paralysis of, a limb (on the opposite side from the brain lesion), loss of speech (usually following a stroke to the dominant, right-hand hemisphere) and loss of various higher cortical functions such as awareness of part of the body.

Other effects are often only recognised later, when the immediate threat to life is over. These may include a hemianopia, in which part of the visual fields is lost (potentially bewildering to sufferer and family alike); apraxia, in which the person cannot perform planned movements; agnosia, in which the understanding of the identity or use of objects is lost; a condition called somatolateral agnosia, in which the person ceases to know that the affected half of the body belongs to him or her, and so on (Heilman, Valenstein and Watson 1985, pp.153–84).

When it is certain that life will continue, neurological and other assessment takes place to assist in planning for the future. Precise forecasts cannot always be made but it is usually possible to make a decision as to whether rehabilitation is feasible or whether only long-term care in a nursing home facility can be provided.

Stroke rehabilitation

Rehabilitation focuses upon regaining use of impaired body parts and impaired functions so that, depending upon what has been impaired, professionals in occupational therapy, physiotherapy, speech pathology and other therapeutic approaches will plan rehabilitation programmes to suit the needs of each person. The social worker will also be involved, for family conferences and especially at the time when discharge is planned.

The prediction of length of stay in rehabilitation of stroke patients is of interest to health professionals and planners, and has been examined by a number of researchers. Galski and colleagues concluded that higher-order cognitive function may be a deciding factor governing the time spent in rehabilitation, so that assessment of comprehension, memory, judgement and abstract thinking are essential in early management (Galski *et al.* 1993). One may ask why they did not include more detailed discussion of social and psychological factors in their study, since there have been several studies of post-stroke depression (Robinson *et al.* 1985).

We must therefore consider the extent to which the effects of depression will influence the outcome of rehabilitation, either because the person is denied access to rehabilitation (as lacking motivation and energy), or by being discharged from the programme (due to failure to respond).

Penington (1992) described a rehabilitation programme for elderly people (not exclusively stroke patients) who had been rejected by other services and found that there are both economic benefits to the community and psychosocial benefits to the individual in such work.

Morris and colleagues have shown that the perceived adequacy of emotional support influences the occurrence of depression in stroke patients

(Morris *et al.* 1991). They also found that men are more likely then women to suffer post-stroke depression, perhaps, they comment, because men are less able to adjust to their dependency, or because the loss of physical capacity has greater salience for men than for women.

Cultural factors may also influence outcome in rehabilitation, as described in a cross-sectional study of the correlates of disability in elderly Taiwanese people. One of their findings was that elderly men are adversely influenced by expectations of what a man does or does not do for himself, so that, for cultural reasons, elderly men are more functionally disabled than women, who are more willing to do things for themselves (Hsieh *et al.* 1995).

Stroke sufferers and their families are usually able to make use of the support and information given by stroke recovery clubs, which are common throughout the world, and community information offices or hospital social work departments will have details of such groups. Usually such participation in groups starts when rehabilitation has been completed.

Some degenerative neurological disorders

Parkinson's disease causes several distressing symptoms: rigidity (called 'lead-pipe' rigidity because of its characteristic plastic stiffness), the tremor which gave the disease its original name of 'the shaking palsy' (this is described as a pill-rolling movement and is referred to as a resting tremor because, in the early stages of the disease at least, it is present only during inactivity and can disappear as one makes a purposeful movement). In fact 'resting tremor' is a misnomer because total rest obliterates the movements, but it is so named to distinguish it from an intention tremor, such as is found in multiple sclerosis, in which the tremor appears only as one attempts to carry out a hand movement.

Parkinson's is also notorious for causing difficulty in starting movements, especially when walking, and it is difficult to continue brisk movements such as hand-clapping for any length of time. The impassivity of the face, which may lead the onlooker to assume that there is an inner passivity as well, the stopped forward leaning posture, arms which fail to swing – all these are classed as dyskinesia, difficulty with activity, and in severe cases can lead ultimately to akinesia, loss of activity. These distressing features are markers for the disease and they do not always respond to medication.

Dementia also occurs in some cases of Parkinson's. Sufferers and their families can, in major population centres, usually find information and help through support groups and societies (which also normally provide information leaflets for those who are prevented by distance from attending group meetings) and these measures are of great value in maintaining morale.

We see some people who have survived into old age with multiple sclerosis, or have developed the condition late in life, perhaps with dementia or other cognitive deficits to add to their physical incapacity, creating further insults to their integrity (Mahler 1992). It has been said that those who are most at risk of major disability are those who were elderly at the time of onset (Weinshenker 1995, pp.119–146).

Huntington's disease, a genetic disorder, causes mental and behavioural deterioration as well as the choreiform movements which gave the disorder its old name of 'Huntington's Chorea'. Although it can occur unexpectedly through chromosome mutation, it is normally considered to be strictly an inherited disease, and this creates emotional problems for families; genetic and other counselling is usually available for affected people. Generally it does not affect older people *ab initio*, but people with the disorder can live into old age, and when a family member is afflicted by Huntington's, everyone in the family suffers distress so that elderly people are distressed over the disease in younger family members and friends.

Motor neurone disease too brings increasing feelings of powerlessness, as loss of control over muscle function gradually leads to total dependence.

All of these conditions bring physical and emotional distress to sufferers and their families, and we must not concentrate so intensely upon the physical aspects of the disease that we lose sight of the emotional challenges.

Non-neurological physical challenges of old age

Osteoarthritis is common in middle and later life, and many older people suffer to a lesser or greater degree from its effects on their mobility, hand function and general flexibility, but not all feel themselves to be 'crippled' by it. Occupational therapists provide guidance and equipment to minimise the effects of the condition, and medication also helps many people.

Older people can suffer from the effects of rheumatoid arthritis from earlier in life, and some who were in the past treated with steroids dread fractures caused by the consequent brittleness of the bones (also seen in osteoporosis). It is especially frightening if the neck is affected.

Oliver Sacks has described his loss of wholeness when he was immobilised for many weeks after a skiing accident and lost track of the impaired leg, even though there was no neurological damage. He also described a later event in which the sense of loss of ownership of a limb was again experienced during spinal block anaesthesia and the subsequent encasement of a limb in plaster (Sacks 1991, pp.171–189). Some of the strangeness experienced by older people as they learn to walk again after long immobility may be of similar origin.

Respiratory disorder and heart disease in old age can lead to invalidism, either because of the physical condition itself or, in cardiac disease, because fear leads to invalidism as a way of life.

Cancer is common as we age, some forms being seen mainly in old age, as with cancer of the prostate, which can have wide-spread metastases (secondary cancers in other parts of the body).

All of these and other diseases which affect older people, whether or not the conditions are progressive, bring a potential loss of wholeness and an enormous need for loving support as people search for continuing integrity.

Although the feelings of hopelessness which can lead to suicide may be of strictly psychological and emotional origin, physical factors can also have a strong influence on a decision for death, the more so when they are coupled with a depressive illness.

- An elderly man, depressed and suffering from such severe chronic airways limitation that each breath was a struggle, hanged himself in the hospital bathroom.

- An older medical practitioner, faced with the diagnosis of inoperable cancer, chose to escape through death by suicide.

- An elderly woman, depressed and severely crippled by arthritis, was told that she would not be going to her own home on discharge, and, soon after this decision was made known to her, somehow managed to struggle to a nearby waterway to drown herself.

Could these deaths have been prevented by empathic intervention?

Other losses: hearing and sight

It is important to seek help when we first become aware of difficulties with sight and hearing, and that we encourage others to do the same. We know that persistent depressive symptoms are found in older persons with non-neurological loss of vision, and visual impairment, and we must understand the personal meaning to the individual of such impairment. It has been suggested that affective therapy should be more readily available for older people with low vision in order to diminish the disability which is caused by loss of sight (Rovner, Zusselman and Shmuely-Dulitski 1996).

Hearing loss is particularly hard for us to deal with because it so often happens insidiously and we find ourselves blaming others for not speaking as clearly as they once did, rather than recognising that it is our own auditory loss which is making it hard to hear them! When we have been tested and fitted with an aid, we have to get used to hearing once more sounds we which have forgotten, the normal sounds of everyday life, sounds which deafness has filtered out for us.

If they are available, the modern hearing aids which have a separate controller are excellent because, unlike earlier aids which amplified everything equally, they have different levels of amplification, with switch positions for ordinary conversation, for small groups and for 'supermarket bedlam' as it has been described! They also have the T-switch (for use with the telephone or in buildings which have an induction loop fitted) as a button within easy reach and sight on the controller rather than as a small lever on the ear fitting in such a position that it is difficult to operate.

A personal note: I realised that I needed help when, occasionally, I found it hard to hear what clients said when their speech was inhibited by tears or embarrassment. The few colleagues who noticed that I was wearing an aid expressed surprise that I needed any technical help. The increase in hearing has, to me, been significant and valuable, after I had become used to hearing myself eat, hearing myself talk apparently too loudly and hearing all those background sounds which had, for some time, been inaudible!

Difficulties in hearing can put a strain on marriage, and a Sydney audiologist described to me how the acceptance of hearing aids by both partners has saved the marriage of two elderly people from irretrievable breakdown.

When hearing has deteriorated seriously, it is difficult to adapt to using an aid and, for some, it is (for psychological reasons) impossible. This can cause conflict across generations as well as in a marriage, so that we hear a middle-aged daughter saying angrily 'If you wore your hearing aid, Mum, you *would* be able to hear what I am saying! I'm not mumbling; it's your fault!'

Visual losses too must be investigated immediately. Glaucoma has in many instances caused visual losses before the condition is recognised. Because the chronic (wide-angle) form of the disease is caused by a particular formation of the eyeball, which restricts drainage and is therefore potentially heritable, we must encourage anyone who has glaucoma in the family to have regular checks of intra-ocular pressure, annually or more frequently if necessary.

Another frequent cause of visual loss in older people is macular degeneration, in which the retina is impaired at the macula, the point at which the cells focus, with loss of vision to a greater or lesser extent. It is now known that some forms of the condition are amenable to treatment, if treatment is started early. Haziness of vision must therefore be investigated, if possible within hours of it being noticed, so that, if possible, something can be done to save sight (Sarks 1996, personal communication).

Therapeutic help

Therapy has much to offer in both rehabilitation and in long-term help for those who are left with residual deficits following a stroke or who have on-going disabling conditions such as Parkinson's disease. Sacks (1991, pp.110–13), in the book referred to above, described the return of awareness of his damaged leg as a consequence of moving with music, and similar effective help can be provided for those with neurological impairment from whatever cause. Music therapy is helpful in problems with gait – for example, in Parkinson's disease – or in loss of confidence, as well as for many other practical aspects of rehabilitation. But it is also helpful in facilitating the working-through of grief and anger over losses, whether due to bereavement or to loss of life-control because of disability and illness, and this is so for both patients and those who are significant in their lives.

Alexithymia is an uncommon word, used to describe the difficulty in finding or using words to describe one's emotional responses to life experiences (Nemiah 1985, p.936). It is a concept which we should consider when we work with elderly people who have difficulty expressing their reactions to traumatic events. The problem has been well described in elderly people by Joukamaa and colleagues (1996), who discuss difficulties experienced in symbolic thought with people suffering from this condition. It has been found that it is not associated with major psychiatric illness but is associated with poor somatic health. For this reason, study of alexithymia is highly relevant to older people with physical disabilities (Kirmayer and Robbins 1993), and the nature of the difficulty may help to explain why music therapy, with its emphasis on non-verbal emotional symbolism, is of such value in helping those who find it hard to put things into words. We must not, however, confuse alexithymia with loss of language following a stroke; the word is used only to describe a difficulty occurring in the absence of any neurological problem.

Physical health cannot be separated from emotional well-being. Philp (1996) has suggested that quality of life for elderly people should be routinely measured; it is, he believes, as important as the routine measuring of blood pressure. If a full assessment is too time-consuming, the asking of a single question about quality of life, 'How happy, satisfied, pleased have you been about life in the last month?', will often reveal what life is like for the person in question, since it is time-specific but on a broad scale – not 'today' and not 'in the last year'. The question gives the person the opportunity of opening his or her heart and also offers reassurance that wholeness matters to the questioner.

The disabilities which develop in later life are not accepted without a struggle. Adaptation to change is particularly difficult when that adaptation entails a diminution of our normal quality of life and spells an end to long-cherished plans for retirement or other activities. Yet many are able to adapt to changes, however unwelcome, and find new meaning in life despite its limitations.

CHAPTER 6

Emotional and Psychological Challenges

Introduction

How common are emotional and psychological distress as we get older and how well do we cope with these risks to our wholeness? It seems that there are today greater resources to deal with psychiatric illness. People spend shorter periods of time in hospital, partly because of new medication but also because community care is available for long-term support after discharge. In some sections of society at least, there is clearer understanding so that psychiatric illness no longer carries as heavy a burden of stigma as in the past.

When someone is found to have a psychiatric disorder, what is the balance between organic and environmental causes for the illness? The answer may well affect the treatments which are recommended. In some of these disorders there appears to be no biological cause. But in many (most?) of them, there are some organic factors, so that it is difficult to separate 'environmental' or 'functional' illness from 'biological', 'organic' disorders. So what words do we use?

The editors of the Cambridge University Press publication *Functional Psychiatric Disorders of the Elderly* discuss the problem, accepting that, although 'functional' is not an accurate description, it will have to remain in use temporarily until a better one is evolved (Chiu and Ames 1994, p.xix). Probably the terminology will remain controversial for some time, and we must hope that this leads us not into etymological conflict but into thinking more clearly about the causes and origins of the disorders we meet, considering both biological and emotional factors.

We also meet many elderly people who have a dual diagnosis (Solomon, Zimberg and Shollar 1993, pp.256–258) such as alcohol dependency with dementia, and it is often difficult to establish the weight which should be attached to each condition as rehabilitation proceeds (Hanks and Lichtenberg 1996) and as we try to deal with the person as a whole.

Depression

Feelings of depression and anxiety are major features of late-life dementing illness, but they are also common experiences for many older people who are not dementing. The losses of old age – loneliness, bereavement, loss of self-esteem and of health, sensory impairment, loss of independence, diminishing finances, loss of mobility, isolation – are well-known and it is not surprising that so many people suffer from depression, together with anxiety about the present and the future (Rozzini *et al.* 1988).

How far should we equate feelings of depression with a diagnosis of depressive illness and where is the dividing line between distress and psychiatric illness? The word 'depression' is used widely to denote, at one end of the scale, slight and temporary down-heartedness in everyday life following a minor setback and, at the other end, a major disabling illness which may well lead to suicide. Despite the frequency of its occurrence in older people, family doctors are known to miss many instances of depression (Jorm 1995).

Depressed people do not always appear unhappy, and depression can present as pain (Von Knorring *et al.* 1983) or as 'smiling depression' in which the cheerful face and bright tone of voice hide the true emotional state. In the past, the term 'masked depression' was used to describe the depression which presents as physical symptoms, and 'depressive equivalents' were discussed, ways in which the body's organ systems expressed depression in the absence of superficial signs.

The term 'endogenous' was previously used to describe a depressive illness which arose without any apparent trigger event, perhaps at more-or-less regular intervals. This was presumed to be of biochemical origin because there was no apparent cause, while 'reactive depression' described depression which clearly had a link with a life experience of loss. The latter was generally called 'neurotic' (commonly used with pejorative implications) and was perceived as less damaging to life.

Today the separation into 'reactive' and 'endogenous' depression has largely been allowed to lapse, and no longer appears in DSM IV. The diagnosis is now divided into Major Depressive Disorder, either as a single episode or recurring, and Dysthymic Disorder, colloquially described as 'down in the dumps' but occurring on more days than not for at least two years (American Psychiatric Association 1994, pp.339–349).

Depression occurs also in bipolar disorder in which there are alternating major depressive and manic episodes, and, in less severe form, in cyclothymic disorder in which major mood swings occur but are less disabling than those in bipolar disorder (American Psychiatric Association 1994, pp.350–365).

For some people, depressive episodes are experienced closer together as they get older, so that depression may therefore seem to be more disabling for older people. 'The prevalence of depression remains as high amongst the "old old" as the "young old",' observes Arie (1994, p.xxii).

We speak of psychotic depression when the illness leads to delusions of persecution or total loss of contact with reality. One elderly man, following the death of his grandchild in a car accident caused by a drunken driver, became (for a few days only) highly psychotic and paranoid, claiming to be God and threatening to kill members of the hospital staff, including myself.

Although a depressive state may seem to have had no trigger one sometimes finds this to be untrue. One elderly woman had always been deeply unhappy on the anniversary of the adoption of her illegitimate baby in her early adult life, and, as she became older, these anniversaries caused her to be admitted to hospital each year for several years with a depressive illness, yet the anniversary as the cause for her depression went unrecognised for some time.

It is sometimes difficult to decide what constitutes a 'case' of depression and often we must trust to the context to elucidate the matter. In this book 'depression' is used to refer to an abnormal and disabling degree of low emotional affect, sometimes arising for no apparent reason (possibly for biochemical reasons and perhaps at approximately regular intervals or alternating with a manic state), and for other people it is a state which is possibly linked to loss and grief or to a traumatic life-event. If, however, someone feels low in mood without being disabled, I refer to the person as 'feeling depressed'.

Depression can confuse the diagnosis and assessment of dementia because there appears to be a 'two-way street' with dementia presenting as depression and depression presenting as dementia as well as the many instances in which the two disorders co-exist (Beats 1996). Someone suffering from severe depression can appear demented when there is apathy and concentration is impaired; this condition is sometimes referred to as the dementia syndrome of depression.

Depression may be linked with loss of immune function (Restak 1989), and recent research has pointed to depression as also being a risk factor for osteoporosis (Michelson et al. 1996), a condition prevalent in older women, causing pain and fractures. It is important to note that the study showed that the risk was found in women who had suffered from depression in the past and was not limited to those currently depressed, which has implications for older women with a history of depression.

Snowdon (1991) has discussed low morale in nursing homes and Ames (1994, pp.142–162) described depression in nursing and residential homes. Frail and ill older people are much at risk, especially when living in any institution.

There are links between physical difficulties and psychiatric disturbance. A study of amputees, an average of 17 years post-operatively, showed that amputations increase feelings of being stigmatised and diminish self-esteem. Because this was observed many years after surgery, it is clear that it could not be ascribed simply to early issues of adaptation (Rybarczyk *et al.* 1995). The researchers suggest that the social discomfort should be viewed as a 'marker' for depression (Rybarczyk *et al.* 1982). Loss of self-esteem has long been recognised as a key issue in the aetiology of depression (Ingham *et al.* 1986).

These responses may have their origins in the individual's previous thoughts on amputations as emotionally and socially damaging, and these existing attitudes increase the emotional impact of the procedure. An elderly Greek man, suffering from depression, was able to speak to me (after trust had been established) of his diminished sexual capacity after amputation and this was not due simply to practical difficulties but also by his sense of being less of a man after a leg was amputated. Perhaps even today the cultural ideal of physical beauty and perfection, which is found in so much of Greek classical literature and historical events, intensifies the feelings of Greek people about physical mutilation.

Another elderly person suffering from post-operative depression following bi-lateral amputations was referred for help after suicide attempts. She described herself as having lost control over life, with feelings of emotional impairment as well as of physical mutilation as the basis of her suicidal despair.

Depression is also seen in persons suffering from multiple sclerosis, and although this may result in part from unhappiness over the disability, some writers believe that it has organic causes (Berrios and Quemala 1990). Murray gives the opinion that depression in multiple sclerosis 'is multifactorial, including both psychosocial and neurolgic factors' (Murray 1995, pp.197–223).

Depression, and the anxiety which so often goes with it, must be managed correctly for the sake of physical as well as for emotional and psychological health. We must recognise that depression is life-threatening, either directly through suicide or indirectly in other ways, and we know that unresolved grief is a common cause of suicide in older people (Draper 1996).

Suicide

In antiquity, the suicide of older people aroused a wide variety of feelings (Seidel 1995) but was well-known to occur. Although today rates vary for different countries (Diekstra 1989), suicide is highly prevalent in older people throughout the world (Boxwell 1988).

Although identification and prevention are difficult and complex (Maltsberger 1988), the identified risk factors include depressive illness with its features of hopelessness, powerlessness and helplessness, command hallucinations, some personality disorders (Ladame 1992), extreme pain, a history of previous attempts, and (because impulse control and insight are so often impaired) dependency upon alcohol and other addictive substances (Burch 1994).

The myth, that we can ignore suicide threats as 'mere histrionics', is dangerous. To talk with a seriously depressed person about possible plans for suicide, and to provide empathic counselling, does not increase the risk. It actually decreases it by giving the person a sense of control (Morgan 1994).

The effects of completed suicide upon staff and others are hard to deal with (Little 1992), whether the person is old or young, and we must recognise that de-briefing needs to be done adequately, with all that this implies (Bright 1996, pp.105–118, 174, 177).

Other psychiatric disorders

Some people in old age suffer from a mental disorder (other than depression) which leads to loss of contact with reality in a psychotic illness, with delusions of persecution or feelings of being controlled from outside oneself, or with auditory, tactile or visual hallucinations.

Hallucinations are heard or seen; they consist of false images, perceived by the person as being real, and are usually symptoms of a psychiatric illness. Auditory hallucinations often consist of derogatory statements or commands. Instructions, often telling someone to harm himself or someone else, are called 'command hallucinations'; for example, 'Why don't you kill yourself (or kill a certain person)', 'You're no use to anyone and deserve to die', etc.

Visual hallucinations are often of a person, and we become aware of these by the individual's changes in posture or changes in visual focus, perhaps also by hyper-vigilance in which the person seems always watching, waiting for something to happen.

Quasi-hallucinations are common in bereavement when one feels that the dead person is present, hearing footsteps or the key being turned in the lock on the front door; a meal may be prepared for the deceased and a place set at the table. Whilst worrying to neighbours and friends, these experiences should *not* be regarded as abnormal, and are usually transitory, disappearing over a matter of months or around the first anniversary of the death. This may leave yet another sense of loss in the bereaved person, but it is sometimes a relief to be free of the 'hallucinations'.

It seems that medication can give rise to hallucinations without there being any psychosis. One elderly patient in a rehabilitation unit described the presence of a brass band on the hospital lawn, and had a slight sense of loss when change of medication removed the hallucination!

An elderly childless widow described the night-time visits to her house of a young child who always sat and never spoke, even when a meal was prepared for her. In the mornings, the widow felt bewildered at finding an uneaten meal in the living room, and unsure as to whether or not a child had really been there. Perhaps the figure was the phantom of the child she never had, but, when she was persuaded to tell her doctor of her experiences (she had feared to do so lest he thought her 'mad'), change of medication ended the dream visits.

These case vignettes indicate that it is unwise to try to separate the mind and the body. Nottingham University has a 'Health Care of the Elderly' department, headed with great distinction by Professor Tom Arie, to whom I am grateful for inspiration in my understanding of life in old age. By looking simply at 'health care', it avoids the dangers of treating the body separately from the mind and spirit.

Delusions are false beliefs or ideas which the sufferer believes to be real, usually as a result of psychiatric illness, but they can also result from medication. The beliefs are strongly held and can alter the person's behaviour because the theme is frequently of persecution, plots to harm the individual. There may also be 'ideas of reference', in which ordinary events are believed to have a private meaning, for example, that the television or the way the leaves move in a tree gives special messages.

Delusions may or may not be combined with auditory or visual hallucinations as part of a significant psychiatric illness, or they can be the result of misinterpretation of events, especially in those who are seriously depressed or suffering from dementia.

The losses and stresses of old age may bring a new episode of an illness, so that a disorder which had been in remission, perhaps for some years, flares up again because of crisis or loss. We also know that new psychiatric illness can arise late in life, sometimes complicated by physical frailty or by a dementing condition.

Over recent years there has been ample discussion of the occurrence of psychotic illness which starts in old age, and of how this should be described – as classic schizophrenia of late onset, hebephrenia (now largely out of use) or paraphrenia. The last seems to be currently the term of choice, and is useful in separating schizophrenia, with its (frequently) global-scale hallucinations and delusional beliefs of international plots and dangers, from older people's fantasies of persecution which are usually on a domestic scale – neighbours getting in and running up a large telephone bill, daughters putting them into hospital to get hold of money, microphones in the wall to pick up their thoughts and so on.

Mania in response to loss is not unknown in people of any age (Rosenman and Tayler 1986), but the state of mind in older people during a manic episode seems to be characterised by pressure and anger rather than high spirits. It was interesting to work with a young woman suffering from a manic episode following the sudden death of her much-loved husband, (leaving her with two very small children), observing the apparent happy excitement which pervaded her flirtatious behaviour, and contrasting this with an older patient whose mania following the death of a grand-daughter was characterised by anger and restlessness.

We must distinguish between manic and hypomanic episodes, the first of greater intensity than the second; hypomanic episodes do not necessarily require admission to hospital.

Post-Traumatic Stress Disorder (PTSD) is much discussed today, and is perhaps over-diagnosed. However, one wonders how far the experience of loss in an amputation, a stroke or other life-changing crisis of health for an older person approximates to the stresses associated with PTSD. It is reported that older people who suffer stress from trauma or natural disasters (a) experience more serious physical injury than younger people and (b) suffer a greater risk of depression, because the after-effects often make changes in living situation necessary and because older people may have less emotional resilience (Marmar *et al.* 1993, pp.239–272).

In a review of late paraphrenia and its aetiology (Roth and Cooper 1992, pp.25–42), the writers comment that long-term deafness is a factor in its development, but only one of many. Because deafness is common and paraphrenia uncommon, there must be some pre-disposing factor other than hearing loss. Two further questions raised by Roth and Cooper are: is there a predisposing factor for all late-onset psychotic illness, and do cerebral lesions contribute to some cases of paraphrenia? More research is urgently needed on this as on many other matters (Jeste 1996).

Rare disorders

There are some rare psychiatric syndromes which can affect life in old age, and, despite their rarity, it is useful to have some knowledge of them.

In *Charles Bonnet syndrome* there is an onset (often abruptly) of visual hallucinations, usually in people with visual impairment (often glaucoma). The hallucinations are commonly to the side of the impairment. There is often insight into the illusory nature of the perception and, if surgery corrects the visual impairment, the hallucinations cease. Charles Bonnet syndrome is usually described as an organic hallucination analogous to musical hallucinations (Fuchs and Lauter 1992, pp.187–198). Beats (1989) believes that, when visual hallucinations are a major feature of dementia, we should describe these as being part of Charles Bonnet syndrome and not see them as indicating psychosis.

Musical hallucinations are found in several clinical conditions such as ear disease, toxic states and in both psychiatric and neurological disorders. They may start gradually or abruptly and may be the only complaint or may be part of a group of problems including, for example, tinnitus (Berrios 1990). There is discussion about the nature of the hallucinations, about where one hears the music, and what the implications of the experience are for trained musicians compared with people who are untrained, since some research suggests that the musically trained and the musically naive process music in different areas of the brain (Bever and Chiarello 1974). This difference was discussed in a research report on hemispheric localisation of rhythmic function (Bright 1975).

Content of musical hallucinations is often from childhood, consisting of hymns or music with emotional association, but not necessarily preferred music; one woman described the irritation of hearing music which she hated! Some people grow to recognise the illusory nature of the experience. Psychotherapy and pharmacological treatments do not extinguish the hallucinations, but if correction of deafness is possible, the experiences may cease.

Those who are accustomed to having tunes 'running through the head' may ask what the difference is between that experience and having hallucinations. Does the difference lie only in changed perception caused by emotional disturbance or illness?

When melodies are running through my head, my vocal musculature makes micro-movements to fit the tune although no phonation is occurring, or there is sensation in my fingers as if I were playing a keyboard although no movement occurs. I am experiencing sub-vocal singing and 'piano-playing without movement' rather than listening. There is no hallucinatory quality to the music. How does this differ from the sensations of those who have musical hallucinations – is it only a different perception of reality?

Reduplication syndrome, described originally as reduplicative paramnesia, (Pick 1903) is also rare. An elderly sufferer arrived home by taxi after a family visit but insisted 'This is not *my*...(giving the address) but another (same address).' He believed that it was not his house but another exactly like it in the same place. He slept under the garden hedge because he refused to go into this strange house. He suffered no ill-health as a consequence, but the event led to greater recognition of his early dementia and (not surprisingly!) to the family making other arrangements for his future accommodation.

Capgras syndrome also involves misidentification; in this condition, the individual believes that someone (known to them) has been replaced by another of identical appearance. It is not unlike Pick's 'reduplicative paramnesia' but reduplication syndrome is regarded as being of neurological origin whereas Capgras syndrome is usually classified as of psychiatric origin (Enoch and Trethowan 1991, pp.1–23).

Although the two syndromes are discussed in textbooks as separate entities, they have common features, and Pick's paper describes the patient as being confused about people as well as buildings being duplicated – she insisted that there were two Dr Picks. But duplication is not synonymous with the replacement found in Capgras syndrome.

Graduates of the public hospital system

The concept of 'graduates' of the public psychiatric hospital system has been discussed (Campbell 1991, pp.779–818). Such people were not old when admitted to hospital, but are old now, and Campbell reports that in 1985, in Glenside Hospital, Bristol, England, one-third of the hospital population had been there since 1960.

Most 'graduates' in the study had a diagnosis of schizophrenia, followed by far lower numbers of people with personality disorder and with an organic disease other than Alzheimer's. Campbell disputes the idea that schizophrenia burns itself out, believing that the protected environment of the hospital has reduced the intensity of symptoms, thereby lessening bizarre behaviour, but without changing the underlying pathology.

Who should be responsible for the care of those who have suffered from psychiatric disorders for a long time, whether or not they have been in hospitals? Should they be 'managed' as clients of psychiatric services, geriatric services, psychogeriatric services? Should they be in the community, in long-stay nursing homes or in hospital? Controversy continues.

Sexuality and psychiatry

Persons of homosexual or bisexual orientation who suffer from mental illness often have difficulties in hospital care. They may be faced with stigmatisation (from staff or fellow-patients) and their needs are not always understood (Hellman 1996). We must realise that elderly homosexual people who seek help because of problems arising from their sexual orientation are looking for counselling and not treatment (Post 1982, p.180). They seek help in dealing with the specific problem which has arisen, not with changing their sexual orientation.

It is only relatively recently that homosexuality has ceased to be categorised as a psychiatric disorder (Stein 1996, pp.5–8), so that elderly gay or lesbian people who become psychiatrically ill may be affected by their feelings about past humiliations and treatments, which included not only psychotherapy but aversion techniques. It is important that the gay and lesbian community realise that a member of their community might suffer psychiatric illness without its being in any way related to sexual orientation.

Problems arise for transsexuals, transvestites and persons with hermaphrodite or quasi-hermaphrodite physique, such as Klinefelter's syndrome, when they need to enter a psychiatric hospital. Their emotional needs, as distinct from the needs imposed by their illness, are not always understood and their bedroom accommodation can be difficult if only shared rooms are available.

Life-long burdens

Many conditions have constituted a life-long burden for the sufferer and for the family. Such conditions include bipolar disease, obsessive compulsive disorder, phobias, panic disorders, paranoid disorders and other psychoses (with the accompanying torment of hallucinations and delusional beliefs), psychosexual difficulties, anxieties, substance dependencies. These all cause suffering to older people and often to their families.

Our feelings about ourselves are gravely affected by the losses and disorders from which we suffer, from disturbance of affect, disturbance of thought, disturbance of relationships. As we age we are perhaps more vulnerable to these, as to so many other conditions, and we need not only loving care and support but the highest possible level of clinical skill from professionals involved in our care. Society has far to go before there is sufficient care and appropriate accommodation for older people suffering from psychiatric disorders. We must take note of this – and learn from it!

Recommended Reading

Chui, E. and Ames, E. (eds) (1994) *Functional Psychiatric Disorders of the Elderly*. Cambridge: Cambridge University Press.

This text concentrates on psychiatric disorders which have no major psychosocial component, nevertheless the impact of such factors upon the mental health of older people is not ignored.

Gelder, M., Gath, D., Mayou, R. and Lowen, P. (eds) (1996) *The Oxford Textbook of Psychiatry*. Oxford: Oxford University Press.

This is a general text on psychiatry, written for medical practitioners who are preparing for a career in psychiatry, but the book is also useful as a source of information, references and suggested reading for all professionals who wish to find out and understand more about their patients and clients.

Jacoby, R. and Oppenheimer, C. (eds) (1991) *Psychiatry in the Elderly*. Oxford: Oxford Medical.

An extended general coverage of all psychiatric aspects of life for older people, including psychosocial difficulties.

CHAPTER 7

Dementia and Wholeness

Introduction

Fear of dementia seems almost universal amongst educated people. Those who had no anxiety about their children becoming demented when those children left their school books at home are fearful for their own mental state when, in later life, they themselves suffer from similarly trivial lapses!

In the past, 'Alzheimer's disease' was used only to describe dementia of early onset and 'senile dementia' described dementia in later life. The discovery that, at *post mortem*, the plaques and neurofibrillary tangles in the brain were the same led to the use of Alzheimer's disease or Dementia of Alzheimer Type (DAT) to describe this particular type of dementia at any age, with the modifier of late or early onset. Today we have gone to the other extreme and non-professionals commonly use 'Alzheimer's' as a generic term for dementing illness, perhaps because it is more acceptable than 'dementia'.

What is dementia?

Dementia is not itself a disease entity but a cluster of symptoms and signs found in several diseases including Alzheimer's disease, Pick's disease, normal pressure hydrocephalus, some cases of Parkinson's disease, progressive supra nuclear palsy, alcoholism, AIDS, brain damage from car accidents, brain surgery, and so on.

Dementia usually includes loss of memory and cognitive skill, loss of orientation, changes in capacity for employment and (ultimately) loss of self care, loss of speech, and (for some) loss of body image. Depression is common and can confuse diagnosis. A feared aspect of dementia is that (except for early-onset Alzheimer's, which may have genetic origins) it appears to come 'out of the blue', with no explanation as to who will be affected, so that one feels a loss of control in being unable to prevent its occurrence.

One sometimes hears comments (usually in a 'superior' tone of voice) such as 'I'll never get dementia, I keep my brain active – people who get

80

dementia have just let their minds go!' A defensive bravado born of fear, or does it have some basis of fact? At present there is no clear answer, but recent reports suggest that some people are less vulnerable to severe impairment in DAT. Researchers measured head circumference for almost two thousand subjects and used new methods of brain scanning to estimate their brain size earlier in life. Results suggested that those with larger brain size are less vulnerable to severe impairment in DAT and the authors ask whether good nutrition and a beneficial environment pre-natally and in early childhood enhance brain size, thereby leading to less impairment (Graves *et al.* 1996; Mori *et al.* 1997). If this research is widely accepted and publicised, there are grave social and emotional implications for stigmatisation of dementia sufferers.

So it may be reasonable for some people – endowed with larger brain capacity from birth, and presumably therefore people who (as the comments quoted above indicate) 'keep their brains active' – to see themselves, through fortunate circumstances in infancy, as the invulnerable elite.

Memory loss

Loss of memory is a major feature of dementing illness. We also see confusional states, in which there is not so much loss of memory as loss of clear thinking, and there is some difficulty with terminology between 'acute confusional states' and 'delirium', with the latter being regarded as having high risks (Gelder *et al.* 1996, p.520).

'Memory loss' may sound relatively minor, but the effects on personal life can be catastrophic when daily living competencies are lost and there is:

- ○ failure to cope with household routines because one has forgotten that there is a saucepan on the hot stove, and a fire hazard is created
- ○ failure to remember that perishable food needs to be refrigerated so that food rots on kitchen tables with consequent risks to health
- ○ failure to remember which way to go, so that walking to a local shop becomes a potential source of danger.

There may also be impairment to relationships because there is, for instance:

- ○ failure to remember that bladder and bowel should be emptied only in that part of the house set aside for that purpose, not in the corner of the living room, even if the wastepaper basket does resemble the bowl of the toilet

- ° failure to remember to bathe and change clothes regularly so that
  smells are obvious and people no longer wish to be in close
  proximity, and health may also be impaired

- ° failure to recognise significant others, because their names and faces
  are forgotten, so that visiting becomes painful for families and
  friends, and perhaps ceases

- ° failure to remember why one is in a nursing home, followed by
  desperate confabulation as one attempts to account for apparently
  inexplicable circumstances, so that there are accusations to family and
  friends, which results in grief and perhaps also anger and alienation

- ° failure to remember where one has put things, followed by agitation,
  confabulation and misinterpretation and perhaps accusations as one
  tries to account for the disappearance of items.

In 1985 an elderly Jewish concentration camp survivor was perceived by
some staff as psychotic because he believed that night-time noises in the
hospital indicated the imminent arrival of the Gestapo. After long discussion,
the view prevailed that this was not psychosis but a misinterpretation, caused
by an early dementia coupled with disturbing memories of actual life events.

Today, however, it is more likely that such an explanation would be
readily accepted. I have observed a greater willingness today in professionals
to treat what is otherwise anti-social difficult behaviour as being simply a
consequence of misinterpretation. A male nurse, trying to lead a woman
gently into the dining room for lunch, who is hit or kicked in the process,
is willing to accept that this is the woman's misunderstanding of his action,
she sees it as a threat of coercion from which she must defend herself, perhaps
based upon past experiences. The nurse therefore refuses to think of her as
difficult or bad-tempered.

The personality

Most people truly fear dementia because they believe they would no longer
be 'whole', no longer be the same person. How far is this true? Do we really
become different in personality or is something else happening? And, in this
regard, should there be any universally-applicable perception of all the
dementias?

A man who uses what his wife describes as quite uncharacteristic coarse
language is perceived by staff as living out his work-related habits from the
building trade (where such language on the job and in the pub afterwards
was normal); he has forgotten that there were two styles of speech – one for

his wife and children and the other for his work-mates. And yet his wife, who had not heard him speak in this way earlier in life, perceives the alteration as being a change in personality.

In 1985, at the International Congress on Gerontology in New York, there was a lively discussion as to whether dementia necessarily involved change of personality or whether it consisted only of cognitive loss generally and loss of memory in particular, which caused changes in behaviour. Was it indeed 'dementia' if someone remained essentially the same person, or should it be called 'benign senescent memory loss'?

We need to consider the possible survival of individual personality despite dementia, but this in turn raises the question of what we mean by personality. Is it only the sum total of the individual's observable behaviour or is there something else, the persona, which may be different from the behaviour? Can our behaviour be altered by circumstances beyond our control without this indicating a change in our inward selves?

Despite all the changes in behaviour, it seems that the personality can often remain unchanged, that accusations of theft and other uncharacteristic behaviour have their origin simply in this same problem of misinterpretation.

An aunt of mine, aged 92, on the occasion of one of my infrequent visits to England from Australia, said, 'I'm a silly old thing and I can't remember anything. You'll have to tell me again, dear! Who are you? And why are you here?' In view of the infrequency of my visits the questions seemed not surprising! But a few minutes later she said, 'I've forgotten already, you'll have to tell me again – who are you, dear, and why are you here?'

This was not total failure of memory because the wording in both cases showed an awareness of memory loss, and the empathic style in which she accepted responsibility for the failure to remember was certainly her own. Yet, when she was unable to find the family silver, she had suspected a visiting cleaner of stealing it, because, she said, nobody else would have had access to it. On trying to play the piano, I found the box hidden inside the instrument, presumably for safety!

It is of major interest that, in the 1987 publication *DSM IIIR* (American Psychiatric Association 1987, pp.104–5, 107), the possible criteria to be met in order to make a diagnosis of dementia included a change of personality, but the more recent publication, *DSM IV* (American Psychiatric Association 1994), omits this, and the World Health Organisation's Classification of Mental and Behavioural Disorders, *ICD 10*, gives only change in behaviour as one of the criteria for dementia to be diagnosed (World Health Organisation 1992, p.44).

Two Australian researchers, discussing the prevalence of change of personality in dementia of the Alzheimer type, commented that changes of personality may be a secondary effect of cognitive decline and that significant correlation between dementia and change of personality may indicate that different neural substrates are involved (Jacomb and Jorm 1996).

It may seem surprising that their study showed that, while there is a change in agreeable and neurotic traits with cognitive decline, these changes are not necessarily downward but may demonstrate an increase, including increase in the pleasant characteristics. I have observed this in a family member who, as she became demented late in life, started for the first time to express gratitude for the help she received.

Jacomb and Jorm concluded that the situation is as yet unclear, partly because the persons in their study were from a clinic dealing with problems of dementia, so may have been a sub-sample of those who display more distressing and disruptive behaviours. They ended their study by stating that more longitudinal studies are needed to clarify the relationship between cognitive decline and personality change.

But we cannot ignore the possibility that perceived changes in personality may be artefacts, caused by misunderstanding or misinterpretations by the carer who describes the problem. How many changes in personality described by relatives could, in fact, be ascribed to failure of memory, and perhaps compounded by depression?

For example, someone who has always been co-operative and helpful now fails to respond to requests and continues, for instance, to sit un-moved when asked to change chairs so that one can clean the carpet, or to wash his hands for a meal. This can be perceived as obstinacy, showing a change of personality, yet it can equally reasonably be perceived as memory loss (the request has been immediately forgotten) or as indicating depression or cognitive decline (the request has never truly been registered or understood).

So many features of dementia can be explained thus that one can see why, in the past, the diagnosis of 'Benign Senescent Memory Loss' was attractive rather than 'Dementia', with its (then) diagnostic inclusion of change of personality.

Defining dementia

Historically, dementia was perceived as a condition in which degeneration necessarily occurred, so that there was a progressive and irreversible course. This led to some anomalies. For example, it was thought by some that the brain impairment, with consequent disabilities and handicaps, which is seen in the person with alcohol-related brain damage was not a true dementia because, when the intake of alcohol ceases, the progress of the impairment ceases (Bright 1989, pp.301–314). It was recognised that there remained the possibility of a subsequent dementing condition such as Alzheimer's disease causing further deterioration, but this was seen as separate from the alcohol-related brain damage.

Marsden (1977) discussed the probability and the possible causes of dementia developing in advanced alcoholics, concluding that alcoholism predisposes the sufferer to so many insults to the neurological systems (anoxia, liver damage, hypoglycaemia, malnutrition, head injury and so on) that the precise aetiology of dementia in a person with alcoholism may be difficult to elucidate.

In the first-ever volume of the journal *Brain*, Lawson (1878) described the symptomatology of alcoholic brain disorder as including short-term memory loss and what we now call confabulation: the unconscious invention of complex stories to account for circumstances which the person cannot understand or remember. Things have not changed much!

Since the publication of *DSM IV*, dementia is described on the basis of a pattern of cognitive deficits and is classified as static, remitting or progressive. The inclusion of 'remitting' or 'static' is important because it introduces a healthy doubt as to the hopelessness of dementia when it is diagnosed (American Psychiatric Association 1994, pp.133–139).

We also know from research findings that depression can be the first indication of an incipient dementia, so that a significant number of persons diagnosed as 'depressed but not dementing' were later found at follow-up to have developed dementia. Anxiety too is often observed as an early feature, and this seems to be linked with depression. Depression is a common feature of dementia, affecting probably 50 per cent of persons with Alzheimer's disease, and it is frequently linked with unresolved grief, which poses a suicide risk (Rothschild 1996).

I have seen first-hand evidence of the effects of depression upon dementia when working with people for whom unresolved grief and consequent depression have exacerbated a dementing condition so that the person has appeared to be in a more advanced state than was actually the case. Facilitating the resolution of the grief returned the person to the state imposed by the organic aspects of the condition, a moderate forgetfulness, which, for two such people, was readily managed at home for several years by regular visits from a community nursing service.

These findings have implications for the quality of life in old age because, if reducing depression can reduce the apparent level of a dementing condition, it will also help people to maintain a sense of self and help relatives to maintain their relationship with the affected person. We must remain hopeful about dementing clients!

The possibility of classifying dementia as remitting may encourage clinicians to act more vigorously and therapeutically than in times when there was an attitude of hopelessness, typified by the remark of a Cockney woman on a London bus, who said of her father, 'Senile dementia's set in and you can't do much about *that!*'

Vascular dementia

Failure of the brain's blood supply, for whatever reason, contributes to dementing processes. In the past we spoke of multi-infarct dementia, the brain dysfunction resulting from a series of small strokes, which caused social and cognitive losses. Although it was theoretically possible for the series to cease, this was so unlikely that the condition was regarded as degenerative, even though the deterioration was caused by a continuation of separate insults rather than an on-going illness such as Alzheimer's disease.

Failure of oxygen supply to the brain during sleep apnoea can also contribute to the course of dementia (Culebras 1992); this can be compared with the vascular dementias (Vitiello 1996). Dealing with this problem is an essential part of preventive care. Vitiello states that 40 per cent of older adults are dissatisfied with their sleep, for a variety of reasons.

Both the disorder originally known as multi-infarct dementia and the impairment resulting from a single major cerebro-vascular accident are now included in classification 290.4x, Vascular dementia (American Psychiatric Association 1994, p.143). In the brain impairment caused by trauma or surgery, there is a single insult, or group of simultaneous insults, to brain tissue which leads to disabilities and, usually, to handicaps. But unless further insults are sustained the level of impairment remains the same. In the past this was seen as cognitive and behavioural disability with, in most cases, severe handicap in living and relationships, but not as dementia. The planning for future care was, therefore, based upon expectation of a stable state when restitution of function by natural healing was complete, unless there was, in later life, an additional disorder such as dementia of the Alzheimer type.

Now that DSM IV describes dementia only in terms of a single state, and characteristics of degeneration are no longer key criteria for dementia to be diagnosed (American Psychiatric Association 1994, p.137), there is a wide range of conditions described as dementia, whether or not the condition is intrinsically degenerative.

How far is this helpful? It is useful in bringing together sets of similar or identical observable difficulties in cognition, insight, behaviour, relationships and everyday competence, so that it is possible to provide services which take account of the deficits, whether or not further deterioration occurs. But it is also unhelpful because, by failing to include the probability of deterioration, it fails to alert social planners to the fact that those people who do have a degenerative condition will have higher dependency needs in the future. Others, with a static condition, may not do so unless some other problem arises.

Methods of assessment are still needed, such as the staging approach in the assessment of dementia, which takes account of the degenerative course of so many dementing illnesses (Cohen-Mansfield *et al.* 1996). It has been suggested that cognitive screening of people over the age of 75 should be done routinely by general (family) medical practitioners (McKenzie *et al.* 1996). Potentially reversible dementias can thus be found and appropriate measures set in place for the care of those who have an irreversible disorder. Such procedures may, however, strike fear unnecessarily into the well aged.

Assessment methods must be internationally accepted if we are not to see a perpetuation of the present situation, in which it is possible for one therapist to describe someone as having 'advanced dementia' when another clinician, in a different country and with a different set of criteria, would perceive the person to be only moderately affected.

A disadvantage of the use of 'dementia' to include static and remitting conditions is that the word has, for many, connotations of hopelessness. A diagnosis of dementia, while useful for the clinician, is therefore disheartening for relatives who are trying to maintain a feeling of wholeness about someone who has sustained a major head injury, a single stroke, or some other brain trauma.

It is difficult to balance out the advantages and disadvantages of changed perceptions of progression in dementia, but the omission of the personality change as one of the diagnostic features is helpful to relationships and wholeness. From experience in music therapy with people suffering from dementing illness, we see that the inner self does survive, because behaviour and responses in the music therapy session are positive. Such responses, usually to songs or other items which are familiar from the past, would not be possible if the total personality had disappeared.

This awakening process is moving to observe, and can be enhanced through a well-planned and executed programme. We need to be very clear in our own minds, and to make it clear to relatives, that we cannot cure a true dementia through music therapy but that we can help to reverse a condition which is reversible. The revival of old memories in this positive manner is only temporary; we shall need to embark on the same process the next time we meet the person, but it is still worthwhile. It reassures family members that there is something of the person still there, and it seems to reassure the sufferer by providing something which is familiar, so that he or she can feel still a 'real person'. It can alter staff attitudes because it shows a different, and positive, side of the person compared with what is usually observed.

Coping with dementia

Coping with dementia is difficult, whether one is a sufferer, a family member, or a professional, and it may be the strongest threat of all to the wholeness of family and individual. It is hard enough to cope with the changed circumstances and the exhaustion of looking after a dementing relative when relationships with that person have been happy, but when relationships have been complex because the sufferer has been difficult – autocratic, even bullying, violent and abusive – the emotional response to that person's dementia often requires some measure of professional help. Relatives in this situation need permission to disclose their (frequent) feelings of 'It serves you right' or 'It's your turn now to be told what to do!', and professionals must be aware of these secret feelings and aware too that respite from care is even more important for these carers.

But given appropriate and adequate support, families manage generally to cope with the challenges of dementing illness, and the sufferers themselves also may manage to cope with dementia and retain some feeling of wholeness. The woman in late middle age, coping with her own early dementia and the completion of a PhD thesis, may be unusual, but the determination of herself and her family to retain for as long as possible her integrity of thought and personality is not unique.

CHAPTER 8

Effects in Later Life of Earlier Impairment
Ageing with a Physical Disability

Introduction

In this book the United Nations terminology regarding disability and handicap is used (WHO 1980). The sequence is thus:

1. the *abnormality, defect, disease or injury* which is present at birth or which occurs during life

2. the *impairment* resulting from that abnormality, defect, disease or injury

3. the *disability* resulting from the diminution of functioning which is caused by that impairment. An impairment may or may not cause a disability, depending upon its nature; for example, one might say that a person whose eyes were different colours or who had one finger a little shorter than the corresponding finger on the opposite hand had an abnormality, but it would be improbable that this would be classed as a disability.

4. the *handicap* which may or may not be the effect on the individual of a disability. The extent to which a disability causes handicap will be influenced by the interaction between individual and environment and includes many factors, such as the person's own attitudes (Barker, Wright and Gonick 1946), the attitudes of the person's own family and friends, society's attitudes in the provision of services and facilities and so on.

The concept of handicap as being determined by environment is not new – it permeated Beatrice Wright's (1960) book about attitudes towards disability. A woman in a wheel-chair is both disabled and handicapped if her city has no wheel-chair ramps, no appropriate toilet facilities, and even more so if this lack of facilities indicates apathy or even antagonism towards those who need such special arrangements. Where facilities and attitudes are helpful, she can acknowledge her disability but without feeling handicapped by that disability. Her life retains its quality, even if some things have changed.

Using this commonsense sequence, one does not speak of a person as handicapped unless he or she is disadvantaged by the disability. Nor does one speak of a person who is born with an impairment as being disabled unless or until it is shown that he or she suffers a diminution of function because of that impairment.

The past

Until relatively recently, life expectation was short for persons with a major impairment, and for those who did survive, quality of life was often poor. Those who were born with major congenital defects usually died in infancy or in the earlier years of life. Nothing could be done about cardiac abnormalities in the newly-born; children born with no bowel orifice died very quickly; those with Down syndrome were usually expected to die in middle-age or earlier from one of the disabilities commonly seen in that syndrome, such as respiratory or heart dysfunction.

Acquired disabilities also, in the past, brought a gloomy prognosis. Those who were rescued alive from accidents often died quickly from shock and stress or from infection, and, even if they survived the initial stress, their lives were usually cut short by organ failure or later infections in a matter of months or years.

Diseases which caused an impairment of function such as the paralysis caused by poliomyelitis resulted in handicap and, in the most serious cases, those who survived faced life in an 'iron lung' with extremely limited quality of life, or (for the lucky ones) some mobility but only by the use of cumbersome portable respiratory equipment.

Many of those who lived through the acute phases of polio had an additional problem because, at that time, the idea of involving the patient in his or her case management was unknown, and they found it extremely difficult to assert their needs for independence in the face of the entrenched institutional paternalism of the day (Armstrong 1985).

The present

But today we see people surviving into old age despite major disabilities. Survival is possible because of better initial treatment, surgical innovativeness, more rapid transport to hospital by helicopter or road ambulances equipped with intensive care equipment, advances in pharmacology and medical technology, and a willingness by society to spend money on saving lives. Society's willingness to spend money on improving long-term quality of life for survivors is less certain!

There is an emerging awareness of the need for independence, and group homes are being set up for people whose level of handicap is such that, in the past, they would have faced being in an institution for life. This change in attitude is not without difficulty. Some professionals find it hard to believe that their 'patients' will survive without 24-hour professional care, and it is true that, in a few instances, failures can be seen. However, these do not cancel out the total value to residents of their new-found independence.

The enthusiasm of those who champion the 'normalisation' of disabled people has sometimes moved outside the parameters of practicality. The streets and parks of big cities have in some places become the back wards of large 'chronic' hospitals, because closing hospital wards has not been matched by the provision of professional care in community services (Braceland 1973, pp.7–9). Some of the boarding houses for people discharged from institutions offer a poor quality of life with little support, and we may suspect that many such changes have been for motives of political expediency and cost-cutting rather than any true commitment to normalisation.

Some group homes (mainly, I find, for people who were previously in state institutions and who have both physical and mental handicaps) do not provide quite enough specialised care. There are too many changes of staff so that residents suffer from the failure of continuing relationships, and staff are not sufficiently trained to meet all eventualities nor fully to understand the particular needs of some residents.

But the overall benefits outweigh the occasional mistakes and difficulties and, since society as a whole welcomes the medical prowess and technology which enables the 'normal' un-disabled person to survive infections and trauma, we can hope that there will be not merely a grudging acceptance of responsibility but a welcome to the survival of the disabled as being a measure of the success of medical art and science.

The following sections discuss some of the specific challenges faced by people with disabilities.

Spinal cord injury

We tend to think of spinal cord injuries (SCI) as being a problem of young adults, but this is not necessarily so; in 1991, over 20 per cent of those people in the USA who had spinal cord injury were aged over 61. Injuries newly acquired in old age are also a major area of concern. In 1991, 1.3 per cent of persons with spinal cord injury were between 76 and 98 years of age at the time of their injury (Menter 1993, pp.2–8). This is explained by the narrowness of the spinal cord canal in old age so that permanent paralysis tends to result from what would, in younger people, be only trivial, transient damage.

The extent of handicap tends to increase with age so that there is an add-on effect:

initial trauma + the ageing process = greater degree of handicap

and we then see an accelerated rate of ageing.

To adapt to a new spinal injury in late life is a challenge that few of us would find easy. When we work with older people disabled by SCI, whether they have grown old with the injury or sustained it late in life, we must understand their increased vulnerability as we help them plan activities to enhance their quality of living.

Problems can include:

- shoulder dysfunction and carpal tunnel syndrome, which affect the independence of older paraplegics, because the upper limbs have for many years had to carry the whole weight of the body in transfers from bed to chair, chair to car-seat, and so on

- diminution of respiratory function, leading to decreased stamina as the older person with spinal cord injury copes with the stress of everyday living

- ageing of the skin, which creates special risks; the skin becomes more frail so that sitting for long periods is hazardous. This affects those with spinal cord injury, brain injury from trauma or cerebrovascular accident, or anyone with a major disability which makes it necessary to spend many hours each day seated in a wheel-chair, especially if it is impossible for the person to move sufficiently to alter the pressure areas

- loss of parents, so that the handicapped person loses the person(s) who provided the support necessary to maintain independence. Behaviour may alter as the result of this loss and the changes which it brings.

These exacerbated physical difficulties often lead to admission to a nursing home at an age when non-disabled people are still living independently. This is also true of conditions such as cerebral palsy, spina bifida, polio and head injuries, and it causes great disappointment to those who had only recently achieved independence outside institutions.

Psychosocial needs affect later life for those with major limitations of mobility and independence:

- reduction of employment possibilities or full retirement, bringing a lessening of financial resources

- consequent diminution of social role, with consequent sadness, disappointment, bitterness, depression

- a major social problem when parental support is no longer available, or when an ageing partner is no longer able to provide support because of illness or because of death.

Charlifue writes that limitation of function in old age may result more from a youth-oriented environment than from a willing withdrawal from an active life. 'The role of being "aged" in fact may be thrust upon a person of advanced years!' (Charlifue 1993, pp.9–22). This also applies to many older people who are not disabled. Menter (1993, pp.1–8) comments, however, that a few older persons with spinal cord injury report increased satisfactions in old age. The possible reasons for this include a maturation of attitude, a new sense of purpose and an acceptance of life situation.

Perhaps there is a meeting place for these two paradoxical views. It may be that, because society's expectations of older people are less, it becomes easier in old age for a person with a handicap to reach those expectations and so feel less inadequate than in the past. In the successful ageing of some spinal cord injured persons, we may also be seeing the result of recent community and individual education about coping with handicaps.

'As if' behaviour

Beatrice Wright (1960) described, in a series of vignettes, the dangers of and the toll taken by 'as if' behaviour, that driven approach to life of a disabled person who denies the potential for handicap in a disability and behaves as if there were no need to modify activities and life-style. In writing of his experiences with spinal cord injury, Gerhart (1993, pp.239–249) clearly recognised something of this when he described (amongst other matters) the bitter sadness of realising that, if there had been a less fierce drive towards quasi-total independence in the early stages after injury, a modified independence could have been maintained for longer.

Another long-term survivor wrote 'What price independence?' and discussed the need to balance out what is feasible to accomplish against the price one must pay (Corbet 1993, pp.219–227). Whilst we admire the determination that says 'I won't let this change me', we can also admire those who are able to say 'It is OK to accept help if it means a better quality of life, and for a longer time.'

I have found that those who, before the trauma, had strong interests in affairs of the mind seem to adapt better to life with spinal cord injuries than do those whose life has centred upon physical pursuits such as surfing, football, fast driving and so on. People in the first group were able to enjoy listening to music, listening to radio drama, were able to make use of talking books with mouth-operated switches to turn the page or to operate the tape-playing machine, used creativity in writing or maintained professional interests by dictating into a tape recorder, using a telephone on a stand, and so on. Being a whole person was still notionally possible for them despite paralysis.

Those, however, whose only interests had been in physical activities had major difficulties in finding any source of enjoyment or interest, and felt that they were certainly not whole people. Depression, whether as a feeling of being down-hearted or a clinical depression, seems a probable outcome. Since these observations were not derived from a controlled study but only from two separate convenience samples, it is not possible to draw any general conclusions.

We need to be aware of possible links between depression and impaired immunity, and how this can affect carers. Depression has been described in carers, with possible lessening of immunosuppression caused by the emotional and other stressors connected with their tasks (Nash and Fletcher 1993, pp.159–182).

Depression may be both a psychosocial and a biological response to an acquired life-threatening disability, as indicating a possible impairment of the endocrine system in increased production of cortisol and reduction of endorphines in spinal cord injuries (Ragnarsson 1993, pp.73–92). We must recognise the multi-factorial nature of depression and its aetiology.

Cerebral palsy

The term 'palsied' may date from the sixteenth century, but the problem is as real today as it ever was. The disorder has multiple effects which can include cognitive as well as physical difficulties but, for simplicity, the disorder is dealt with as a whole here rather than shared between two chapters.

Cerebral palsy (CP) has been described as:

> a persistent though not unchanging disorder of movement and posture, appearing early in life, and due to a non-progressive lesion

of the developing brain. It is often associated with other conditions such as mental retardation, epilepsy, and loss of hearing and vision. (Little Club 1959, quoted by Crichton, Mackinnon and White 1995)

What happens in old age to people who suffered cerebral palsy from birth injuries or in the prenatal period? As with many other disabilities, there is much variation in the extent to which people are disabled and handicapped by cerebral palsy. Some have only a minor difficulty with gait or speech. Others are so affected either by spasms (which gives the condition the name commonly used by support groups, 'spastic') or by other movement disorders that they need much physical support and are necessarily looked after by full-time carers, sometimes in an institution or group home if the family cannot cope with the tasks.

Some, but not by any means all, suffer cognitive as well as physical impairment. It is horrifying to hear many children continue to use 'spastic' as an insulting term meaning 'stupid'. One can only begin to imagine the suffering of those people with cerebral palsy who were in fact highly intelligent but who were, in the past, assumed by the onlooker to be severely mentally retarded as well as physically impaired, and who were treated accordingly. Children's use of 'spastic' as an insult may indicate that this misunderstanding is not all in the past.

Some people affected by cerebral palsy have, however, become high achievers and receive general recognition as such, although their personal lives are fraught with challenges and difficulties.

Janicki (1989) commented that literature on cerebral palsy concentrated almost entirely on studies with infants, school-age children and young adults. There is now, however, a growing interest in what happens to older persons suffering from cerebral palsy, and I am indebted to Dr Susan Balandin, of the Spastic Centre of New South Wales, for her help in finding references and in discussing with me new findings on life for older people with the condition. I am also grateful to cerebral palsied residents at Weemala, within the Royal Rehabilitation Service, Ryde, NSW, for the opportunity of sharing a small part of their lives and seeing what challenges they face in coping with the limitations to their quality of life imposed on them by their disability. It is also heartening to share the excitement and hope of those who are able to move into supported group homes.

Discussing life-expectancy of persons with CP, Crichton and colleagues describe studies published between 1985 and 1990 which suggested that the most important factors influencing survival are the presence of severe mental disability and reduced mobility. Their own large study, completed in December 1989, followed up a total of 31,287 cases, divided into birth cohorts depending on whether they were born in the 1950s, 1960s, 1970s or 1980s, and looked at survival rates and the factors influencing it. They found that the strongest association with reduced survival was that of severe to profound mental retardation, followed by cerebral palsy other than hemiplegia, followed by epilepsy (Crichton, Mackinnon and White 1995).

These authors point out that the population of British Columbia, from which the research data was drawn, has a racially mixed population, including persons of Asian origin and many people from the Native American population which is mainly rural, and that they were not able to study these populations separately. Since, however, many countries, such as Australia and Great Britain, have similarly diverse populations, the figures of Crichton are generally relevant.

The authors also comment that survival today is affected by new technical expertise in gastrostomy feeding and management of respiratory infections but that we shall not know, perhaps for many years, what the effects these strategies will have on general survival rates.

How does all this knowledge affect the attitudes of geriatricians and others involved in aged care? We can no longer see cerebral palsy as a young person's, even a child's disease. We must be prepared for the long-term care of people with major support needs which, for various reasons, increase with age. As Crichton's results show, survivors may well be those of higher intelligence than those who died at an earlier age. We cannot, therefore, take the paternalistic path of providing mere institutional custodial care; we must also plan for quality of life, for support within the community in group homes (as is happening in the rehabilitation service with which I am associated) and for maintaining the individuality and the self-esteem of older people with cerebral palsy for as long as possible.

A report from New York commented on the lack of appropriate living resources for older people with gross motor impairments, whether these are to prevent institutional life or to provide for those who are being moved out of institutions. The writer asks that adequate community housing be made available, appropriate in being barrier-free and having adaptive devices, and supported by proper therapeutic and clinical services. In the years since Janicki's plea, we have seen positive changes, such as those mentioned above, but such facilities are far from universal and there are never enough of them (Janicki 1989).

Head injuries and brain-impairment in old age

How do older people cope with head injuries? How do those who suffered brain impairment early in life cope with old age? As with spinal cord injuries, these queries are not merely of academic interest. Those who had brain injuries earlier in life may live on into old age. Car accidents afflict older people, falls are a frequent cause of brain trauma to elderly people, and we can expect that the after-effects will be more serious than for young people because of the loss of plasticity and reduced potential for restitution in the central nervous system as age advances.

Investigation of head injuries of older people (Rakien *et al.* 1995) in which 263 people, all over the age of 65 years, were surveyed, found that most falls were caused by pre-existing cardiovascular disease. These falls had a mortality rate of 17.5 per cent, with concussion and minimal brain injury as the predominant problems.

To prevent falls, simple interventions and the provision of 'gadgets' can be helpful if these are emotionally acceptable. However, this is not always so; some people find that accepting gadgetry increases their feelings of dependence, and long-held habits prevent them making the necessary changes in routine. But some can accept help, and to provide those at risk with long-armed tongs to pick things up from the floor, to teach older people to get up slowly and turn around gently at the end of a conversation or an activity, or to be involved in an activity such as gardening using raised flower beds and long-armed tools is to introduce strategies which may well save our clients from death or disability.

Assessment after head injury from whatever cause will normally be done by a team of people who have expertise in the task and who will recognise when the initial crisis period has passed and acute assessment can be done, when the time has come for the person to move from acute assessment into rehabilitation and when (if the damage to life function is substantial and there is no expectation of further improvement) it is necessary to move into long-term care. In permanent care, it is just as important to maintain the quality of life as to maintain optimum physical well-being.

Those who were young at the time they sustained a brain injury may continue to live for many years, necessarily remaining in long-term care, some of them fed by gastrostomy, some able to take a more active but still restricted part in life. Those who lack speech or other means of communication are at risk of their individuality being forgotten, but there are ways of reaching some of those people who seem to be in a vegetative state. When there is some capacity for interaction our goal is to find out how to use this in an appropriate way, whether there is an interest in painting, sculpting of a simple kind, listening to music or other activities.

We have a responsibility when working in geriatrics to be empathic to the problems facing older people with traumatic brain injury, new or old, whatever its cause. We must think about quality of life, considering social and neurological impairments as they affect this, since after-effects are known to be long-term (Dawson and Chipman 1995).

It is difficult for families to maintain regular visiting when they receive no response from their visits, and we need to avoid, if we can, being angry about those relatives who do gradually stop visiting. In such situations the staff tend to take over the role of 'family'. We need to understand that it is difficult for families to resolve their grief when the person is still physically alive but when there is no apparent awareness of, or capacity for, emotion and interaction, or when brain damage has caused such changes in behaviour that the person no longer seems the same. This has been described under the heading 'mourners without a death' (Gosling 1985).

Staff and relatives experience grief and loss when a resident or patient of any long-term facility dies, and they may need help in resolving these feelings because there is commonly a combination of sadness and relief that the suffering of the individual and the family is over. For staff there will often also be feelings of personal relief that the stress of providing care for that person is at an end.

Older survivors of polio

What of the quality of life for elderly people living with the after-effects of polio? They had less benefits of technology and medical expertise, things that today we take for granted. At one time it was thought that their disability did not increase once the acute stage of the illness was over, but new research tells us that this is not so, that they suffer increasing handicap as a consequence of their initial disabilities (Menter 1993, pp.1–5). Professionals involved in their support need to recognise the emotional responses to any unexpected deterioration in function and capacity for ordinary living.

Menter comments that it was in the 1980s (when most of them were 40 years post-deficit) that the post-polio cohort found themselves facing the changes happening to them as the result of ageing and they were, he said, totally unprepared for these. Nor were they prepared for the changes in life-style which ageing forced upon them, which often included admission to a nursing home.

There may be an additional problem because (as was noted earlier) at the time polio was common patients were not considered to be competent in making decisions about their own rehabilitation goals, and it may be difficult later in life to accept shared responsibility in making decisions. One may speculate that today's victims of trauma and illness have the advantage that they are encouraged to help in making decisions about their own treatment and well-being, which must impart some feeling of wholeness.

Those who had a polio infection earlier in life have experienced in recent years what has seemed like a revival of the original condition, suffering from muscle pain, fatigue and weakness, and nobody, it seems, had expected this would occur. There are various theories as to causes (Dalakas *et al.* 1986; Currie, Gershkoff and Cifu 1993; Treischmann 1987, pp.90–94) but, whatever the reason for the phenomenon, it is extremely disappointing for post-polio sufferers to experience further disability, and possibly lose again the independence they strived for in the past.

Dyslexia

There are many other special needs of organic origin, arising in youth and continuing, perhaps in a modified form, into old age, which bring challenges for professionals and clients alike. One of these, dyslexia, may seem trivial because the person looks normal, speaks normally, acts normally (unless so affected by depression and hopelessness that this is apparent in behaviour, posture and gait). But we need to consider what old age is like for people who suffered from dyslexia earlier in life, many years before the condition was identified. Probably nothing was done to help them, and they went through school labelled as 'lazy', 'stupid', 'lacking concentration', 'not trying', so that their self-esteem has been damaged (Hampshire 1990, pp.1–2).

If they have depended upon their spouse to help them cope with everyday or special needs which involve reading, what happens when that spouse dies? Do they suffer additional medical hazards, even death, when they cannot read instructions for medication? A story, possibly true, circulated in Sydney about a man who died because he was unable to read the instructions as to how to remove the child-proof cap on his newly-dispensed heart medication ('Push cap down and twist in a clockwise direction').

Because of the shame engendered by unsympathetic teachers in their childhood, older people are often reluctant to admit that they cannot read, and, sadly, become expert in ways around the problem: 'Please read this for me, I have left my glasses at home.' But when an emergency arises with chest pain and the medication is in a new package, what then? Or what happens when they cannot read the telephone book to summon help in an emergency? Older people are particularly at risk and, as one person commented, the condition seems to get worse as you get older (Hampshire 1990, pp.133–134). Many people suffering from dyslexia manage to cope and triumph over their disability, but what of the many others who did not achieve this? What happens to them? Perhaps some of them are our sad nursing home patients who make excuses not to take part in Bingo, in word games, in newspaper discussion groups.

We need an empathic awareness of possible difficulties with reading, not assuming that anyone in our care who seems intelligent can therefore cope with written instructions. I have personally confronted a well-known evangelistic American outreach programme on behalf of dyslexic people because the programme failed to meet the needs of non-readers, assuming that everyone who was not blind could read the booklets which were handed out!

What constitutes 'home' in later life?

Homelessness is an especial hazard for older people, and although there are those who take a judgmental view of this life-style, it remains for some men and women the only answer to what seem to be insuperable emotional and social problems. Some homeless people seem to age prematurely, either because of substance abuse (here included as an organic rather than a psychiatric disability), the life difficulties from which the homelessness sprang or because of the problems associated with the life itself.

For someone who has lived a nomadic life, either for cultural reasons or because of social and psychiatric difficulties, an acquired disability presents added stress in the change from the state of homelessness to residence in a structured environment.

A man from a nomadic Australia Aboriginal tribe, whose spinal cord was severed at the C4–5 level, found it bewildering to be in a city teaching hospital and later confided to a staff member that he had thought perhaps he had died! Although the numbness of his body contributed, his perplexity was in large part due to the strangeness of being in a large institutional building with hundreds of people moving around, all of them dressed in unfamiliar clothing, which at that time included the white veils of nurses, whom he thought must be the angels seen in picture books on the mission station of his childhood.

An elderly woman had enormous difficulties, both practical and emotional, when a stroke forced her out of the railway station precinct which she had made her living-base for some years, into a rehabilitation hospital and thence to a nursing home.

Those who work in substance abuse, who have homeless people amongst their clients, may describe such people as 'heart sink' people, because one's heart sinks on hearing of their difficulties. However, some positive changes can be made with some people, even with those seen as 'elderly', if helpers are willing to adopt an empathic and non-judgmental attitude and have appropriate resources to provide support (Reeson 1991).

My own work in counselling and music therapy, as part of a team approach for substance abuse, has revealed some surprisingly positive outcomes. Although most of the clients have been only in middle age, they are aged physically and emotionally because of their life-experiences and multiple illnesses or traumas.

Nursing homes can be seen as 'homes away from home' but do not always live up to this description. They usually have a varied population, and there is frequently a wide discrepancy in levels of cognitive functioning between the different residents. We see in the same home, sometimes even in the same room, a person with major dementing illness and others who are dependent only because of physical disability.

A highly intelligent woman, living in a nursing home because of the effects of life-long rheumatoid arthritis, said that life was not worth living and that she longed to be able to kill herself because of the invasion of her room and her belongings by a dementing patient from the next room, an invasion which she was powerless to prevent except by (usually fruitlessly) pressing her buzzer in the hope that someone would come promptly. And yet this invasion could be seen as the consequence of failure to provide sufficient activities for the wandering demented patient, and failure to provide her with appropriate accommodation.

The needs of those who have retained their full cognitive function and those whose consciousness of the world around them is clouded are quite different. The differences are accentuated when there is a wide discrepancy in age, as happens when a younger person has to be in permanent care because of a major disability. Yet they all share common needs: to feel that they are individuals of worth, to be helped to retain personal dignity, to be allowed to make decisions, and to have activities which are appropriate to their ages, which give fulfilment and do not merely fill in the hours of the day.

The nature of those activities is necessarily based upon the level of awareness and life function of the individual concerned, but one should never assume that someone is so impaired that the only requirements are nutrition and physical care.

Residents who have previously had long-term care from parents, spouse or siblings will have a double grief in admission to a nursing home: grief at what may feel like abandonment (especially for those who have an intellectual deficit) and grief at loss of independence, with a possible re-experiencing of the emotional trauma of the original accident or illness, and further realisation of the extent of handicap. Those who are involved in aged care must be aware of this emotional trauma.

All who unwillingly give up their independence grieve over this loss, and the consequent sense of powerlessness which that loss engenders. If personal individual care is given and appropriate and achievable activities are provided, the effects may be lessened, but the grief response to loss of familiar people and territory may be such that difficult behaviour is caused despite loving care from staff and the provision of activity programmes.

Those who suffer only from a physical handicap will recognise the practical need for a move to supported living, but their emotional responses may not match that intellectual recognition, so that we see indications of depression. These may include anger and irritability in addition to the more easily recognised signs of depression such as changes of appetite, sadness, changes of sleeping patterns, and so on. But these should be seen as symptoms of grief and loss, perhaps as a form of adjustment disorder (American Psychiatric Association 1994, pp.623–627), rather than just 'being difficult'.

It may be that people are particularly vulnerable to depression on moving to nursing homes if, in the early stages of an acquired disability, they have denied the effects of that disability in 'as if' behaviour, and driven themselves unrealistically, or if (even without having any disability) they have lived life in an attitude of such fierce independence that they have rejected all concepts of inter-dependence.

We all have to strike a balance between denial and acceptance: on the one hand we must refuse to accept the stereotypes of others about old age if these tend to relegate us to the role of spectators in life. But on the other hand we must be willing to modify our actions if, by so doing, we are able to have more years of contributing to life.

We also need to strike a balance between independence and dependence or inter-dependence. We see this in young children who swing between 'I'll do it myself!' and 'Do it for me!' We observe it also in ourselves as we go through life, and in later life that balance may be of crucial importance to our happiness.

Summary

There are so many long-term organic disabilities that it is impossible to discuss each of them in detail, but the general principles for the helping professions who seek to nurture a sense of 'wholeness' remain the same, whether we work with those who are chronologically 'aged' or those whose disabilities have accelerated the ageing process.

- We need to understand as much as possible of the physical nature of the disability so that we understand what people are coping with in everyday living. Only by so doing can we walk successfully that therapeutic tightrope which seeks to achieve a healthy balance between asking too little of someone, thereby diminishing individual worth, and asking too much, thereby setting up a situation in which failure is inevitable, which also diminishes personal worth.

- We need to develop an empathic insight into the emotional impact of the condition.

- We need to develop creative and imaginative strategies to minimise the impact of the handicap and make use of the capabilities of each person.

- We must involve the person as much as possible in discussions of future plans, treating each person as an individual who has a past, a present and (even if limited) a future, so that we avoid an atmosphere of paternalism.

In *Ageing with a Spinal Cord Injury*, Menter ends the chapter written by himself and Whiteneck with the following words:

> Grace means many things to many people. For many, grace is that state of being which arises out of suffering and adversity…may we all sense and realise the grace that can come from it. (Menter 1993, p.397)

Although the writers were referring only to spinal cord injury, the same words could apply to many similarly devastating disabilities and to the process of growing older. We must never demand that disabled people should accept the added challenges of the ageing process with grace, but we should recognise and admire grace when it is present.

Recommended reading

Bright, R. (1996) *Grief and Powerlessness*. London: Jessica Kingsley Publishers.

Although this is a general text on grief and powerlessness, it includes chapters specifically on old age, on disability and on the grief of the helper.

Hampshire, S. (1990) *Every Letter Counts*. London: Bantam Press.

This moving, encouraging, and surprisingly entertaining book gives a number of interviews with dyslexic people which reveal both the cruelty they have suffered and their courage and enterprise in dealing with their difficulties.

Treischmann, R.B. (1987) *Aging with a Disability*. New York: Demos.

In the opening sections of this book Treischmann describes the fight for life, liberty and the pursuit of happiness of people who are facing old age with the added challenge of a disability from earlier life. She then goes on to demonstrate the general challenges of disability by describing case histories of people with various disabilities and the way each has fought his or her particular battle either with society or with personal difficulties. She reminds us that life is influenced by psychosocial, organic and environmental factors.

Treischmann discusses ageing with multiple sclerosis (p.94) and says that there is no typical pattern of ageing, but that it is more likely to have a progressive than a yo-yo course. No references are, however, given to support this statement. She also discusses stress as a factor which changes our response to infections and disease organisms, saying that we only succumb to infections when our resistance is weakened. Thus, stress may be *the* factor affecting our health (pp.99–102).

Although the book is not new, it provides interesting case histories and encourages us to think empathically of the quality of later life for those with disabilities.

Whiteneck, G.G., Charlifue, S.W., Gerhart, K.A., Lammertse, D.P., Mauley, S., Menter, R.R. and Seedroff, K.R. (1993) *Aging with a Spinal Cord Injury*. New York: Demos.

A number of professionals from various fields have written this useful book on what it is like to be getting older when one has a spinal cord injury It is a valuable resource for those who are interested in the new challenges facing us in the provision of aged care, and it should be required reading for all physicians, psychiatrists and other professionals in this field. It includes wide-ranging topics, covering not only all of the organ systems, but also the psychosocial needs of older people with long-standing SCI.

The book reminds us that being quadriplegic or paraplegic causes difficulties to every system of the body, although at the same time it may bring what is described as a bittersweet mixture of wisdom and maturity, with the satisfactions of having survived.

CHAPTER 9

Effects in Later Life of Earlier Impairment
Ageing with Genetic and Congenital Impairments

Introduction

As we have seen in the previous chapter, society is challenged to accept the rightness of what may be seen as the 'survival of the unfit', with consequent needs for financial resources and supportive social structures. This chapter is concerned with the problems and needs of ageing people suffering from mental retardation and pervasive developmental disabilities. I use the term 'mental retardation' (rather than one of the many euphemisms for those who suffer from cognitive impairment) without any adverse implications. I use it simply because the word is universally understood and is used in publications of the United Nations World Health Organisation and of the American Psychiatric Association as well as in *Index Medicus*. Although many autistic children do have a lower-than-average intelligence, this is not a necessary criterion for the syndrome to be diagnosed, and some autistic people have areas of normal intelligence; to use totally different nomenclature for the conditions makes for clarity when one writes about various disorders.

Those who are responsible for the care for older disabled people must understand the particular problems of those who have a dual diagnosis, with psychiatric or cognitive disabilities in addition to disorders more commonly associated with old age (Shah 1994). We must see the person as a whole being, and all health professionals are responsible for finding out as much as possible about the condition, about the individual's life circumstances, their joys, problems, griefs, frustrations, all the emotions which are experienced by the human race, disabled or not. The emotional responses to life do not cease because the person is elderly. Indeed the needs of someone who is both ageing and disabled will be greater.

The trend towards community care for a wide range of disorders and disabilities, including pervasive developmental disabilities and the various manifestations of mental retardation, has been part of our accepted responsibility for the quality of life. It also has some advantages in saving money to the tax-payer as we are move away from the vast state institutions in which custodial care was available in the past.

Unfortunately, however, some people with these disabilities either can never be moved into the community because of their support needs or must return to institutional care later in life because their support needs have increased. A study of the daily lives of four young adults who were mentally retarded (Raynes *et al.* 1987) showed that there are variations in the quality of service provided in community hostels, with (one assumes) corresponding differences in the quality of life of the residents. The authors also note the essential need for staff training so that a satisfying quality of life is available for people living in hostels. Even more care is needed when older disabled people move into hostels because of the diminished flexibility of attitude and thought of those who have long-term cognitive impairment.

The classic indications of depression may occur following admission into residential care of an elderly person who has a psychiatric disability, mental retardation, dementia or a developmental disorder. But, as with similar responses seen in those with physical disability, we should perceive the behaviour as indicating grief and loss and difficulty in adjustment, and not as 'bad' (American Psychiatric Association 1994, pp.623–27).

Down syndrome

There are various questions we need to consider about survivors of those impairments which are apparent at birth, in genetic and inherited disorders. People with the genetic disorder known as Down syndrome are today far less likely than in the past to die from the cardiac dysfunction or from the respiratory diseases which so often accompany the genetic disorder. Young children with the syndrome can be (and often are) operated on to change blood supply to the heart, or to correct other physical abnormalities. Medication is available to deal with respiratory and other illness, so that we now see elderly people who have lived all their lives with Down syndrome.

Since the probability of a child being born with this particular genetic defect was estimated in the 1970s as being 1.0–1.2 per 1000 in live births, with variations due to various factors, such as the number of births to older women or racial differences (Hook 1981), there is a very large number of elderly people with Down syndrome.

We know that, as with some other genetic defects, there are wide discrepancies in the extent of disability experienced. In Down syndrome, in which there is an extra chromosome on the 21/22 group or a translocation abnormality of chromosomes, the extent of the consequent disability depends upon the number of affected chromosomes. Some people function at a high level and work in open employment, but others have very great support needs, requiring substantial levels of care and protection.

Because of the characteristic facial features, finger spacing and size, and other physical manifestations, the impairment of the syndrome is readily seen (Holmes *et al.* 1972, p.150). But again, there are differences in the extent to which people's appearance is affected, and this alters the extent to which a person may be perceived as 'normal' or 'abnormal' when travelling on public transport or going to the shops. Those who suffer from less visible disorders have their own problems in that people expect of them a higher level of competence than is actually possible.

Those who work with people suffering from Down syndrome and other syndromes involving mental retardation know that some of them develop difficult behaviours, but we must realise that the behaviour is not part of the syndrome (Szymanski and Kaplan 1991, p.161). Einfeld (1992) gave similar warning when he wrote about the prevalence and assessment of psychiatric illness in persons with mental retardation.

We must recognise that retardation does not protect against psychiatric illness, and professional intervention is needed with mentally retarded people just as it is with the rest of the population, when there are indications of depression, schizophrenia and other disorders.

The social environment, such as changes in staff or being moved from one institution to another, can give rise to depression, hallucinations and delusions, grief reactions to bereavement or other losses and disturbed behaviour. It is important, for humane and other reasons, that these are recognised for what they are and not ignored simply because the person is mentally retarded or, which is worse, regarded in a punitive manner and dealt with accordingly.

In some who have cognitive and behavioural problems, we observe aggression towards others or self-injurious behaviour. We may see the person bashing his or her head against a wall, or hitting the face or other parts of the body with the fist or the flat of the hand. We may see destructive behaviour with ripping of clothes or bedding, or self-care may diminish with incontinence of bladder or bowel (O'Brien 1996).

Winchell and Stanley (1991), in a review article on self-injurious behaviours, discussed the problem both as it relates to psychiatric illness and to mental retardation. They state that, apart from that seen in syndromes such as 'Lesch-Nyhan' and 'Cornelia de Lange' (which include self-mutilation as part of the characteristic behaviour), self-injury usually only occurs in mentally retarded people after admission to a chronic care institution.

The writers also point out that prison is known to elicit self-injurious behaviour in some individuals, as a consequence of confinement, and it may well be that it is the loss of their customary sense of freedom, in addition to loss of familiar loving faces, which elicits the behaviour in mentally retarded individuals when they are admitted to an institution.

I have found, however, that established self-mutilating behaviour continues even in those who have been moved from an institution to a small group home in the community. The same is true of aggressive and violent behaviour towards others, and, as O'Brien (1996) described in autistic people, one particular fellow-resident may be the regular target.

This is indeed an indictment of the quality of life which is available to mentally retarded persons when their own families cannot care for them. Because we still have a long way to go before the goal of universal care in group homes is reached, difficult behaviour is something we must be aware of when older retarded persons face changes – from home to institution, from home to group home or from institution to group home.

There is a strong probability of persons with Down syndrome going on to develop dementia in later life, and there has been research to investigate the links between this and dementia of the Alzheimer type. In one study it was found that the average age of onset of clinically-diagnosed dementia in persons with Down syndrome was 51.7 (a range of 31–68 with a standard deviation of 7.1), with significantly earlier onset in women (Prasher and Krishnan 1993).

Regarding the known association between Down syndrome and Alzheimer's disease, DSM IV includes a comment that, at *post mortem*, evidence of brain abnormalities associated with dementia are found in the brains of (all?) Down syndrome people by the time they are in their early forties (American Psychiatric Association 1994, p.141). But another study concludes that, despite this association, the matter must be more complex than simply a trisomy of chromosome 21, since not all persons with Down syndrome go on to develop Alzheimer-type dementia. It suggests that possible factors include family history and the precise location of the gene on the chromosome (Crapper-McLachlan, Wen and Wis 1985).

Because Down syndrome is no longer a sentence of death in middle age, and because of our knowledge about the prevalence of dementia in older people with the condition, many families have a dread of what is to happen to their adult child or other relative when they themselves are no longer able to support that child.

Furthermore, epileptic seizures occur in many Down syndrome people and are a significant cause of ill health, occurring in 46 per cent of persons over the age of 50 (McVicker, Shanks and McLelland 1994). Nursing homes and other long-term facilities such as group homes within the community must therefore be prepared not only for transfer grief and possible epilepsy but also for the changes which dementia causes. They must have appropriate programmes in place to enable the people concerned to retain dignity and function to the best possible level in their new environment.

Fragile X syndrome

As with other genetic disorders, there is a strong chance of the people with Fragile X syndrome reaching old age, or at least living on into late middle-age. The syndrome is caused by a constricted site on a chromosome, at Xq27–28, and this abnormality starts at the onset of mitosis in the cell division. Fragile X syndrome has been estimated as the second most common cause of mental retardation, after Down syndrome, with a probability of 1 in 2000 live male births (Desai *et al.* 1990).

Desai and colleagues comment that there are 70 different mental retardation syndromes linked to the X chromosome, and Fragile X accounts for approximately half of the affected people. As with Down syndrome, there is significant difference between the impairment and disability of different individuals due to the different proportion of affected chromosomes. One may see two full brothers, one of whom is severely affected and the other only to a minor degree. There is increasing interest in the status of female carriers of the condition, and whether they are strictly carriers or whether they are perhaps affected in some degree by the syndrome, but these are outside the scope of this book.

As with Down syndrome, we are looking at the needs of a large number of older people with such a chromosomal abnormality. But a literature search in 1996 revealed no available information about the quality of later life for persons with Fragile X. One difficulty in reporting such work may lie in the wide differences of impairment which make it impossible to say authoritatively 'All or *n* per cent of persons with Fragile X syndrome are able to survive in the community', or other generalisations.

But it is clear that, for all levels of disability, the capacity for life and relationships is made more difficult. Difficulties may lie in the individual's inability to tolerate physical contact (which can be profoundly disabling in everyday life and relationships), difficulties with eye-contact, misinterpretation of circumstances, problems with frustration tolerance (which can lead to anti-social and aggressive behaviour), and so on.

Some of the behaviours, such as hand-flapping and difficult eye-contact, can lead to a misinterpretation of the condition as autism, but the similarity lies only in the minor details of some behaviours. Autistic-type mannerisms can occur without there being any of the major difficulties in relationships which are the *sine qua non* of the pervasive developmental disorder of autism (Einfeld, Moloney and Hall 1989).

Nevertheless, the physical appearance and behaviours characteristic of Fragile X can be seen by the community as making the person unacceptable. One such young man, travelling home from his sheltered workshop, was severely teased by a group of teenagers in the train because his long facial features and unusual ears reminded them of an unpleasant character from a television cartoon. Although he was able to contain his unhappiness and anger on the train, he was not able to control an outburst of destructive anger when he returned to the safety of his (supervised) group home. Life in the open world is not necessarily easier than life in the protected world of an institution.

Autism

We notice that most people speak of autistic children and never of autistic adults (Sacks 1995, p.235). But what happens to older autistic people? There is an increasing number of older people with autism, even though, since the condition was only described by Kanner some 50 years ago, the first of those who were formally diagnosed as autistic in early childhood are still only in middle-age. But we know that there must be many others who were autistic before the condition was officially recognised and named and who are now elderly. A long-term study into autism has been in progress at the Institute of Psychiatry in London since the subjects were children, and the results of this now extend into middle age. The most recent findings have, however, not yet been published (Rutter 1996, personal communication).

Ever since it was first described, autism has challenged professionals to evaluate causes and evolve methods of management (Rutter 1970; Wing and Gould 1979) and support groups have been established in many places to help both child and family.

One assumes that, in the past, autistic people were perceived as insane, as retarded or perhaps (because of their failures of communication) as deaf, and placed in state institutions. Probably there are many such elderly people still surviving in state psychiatric hospitals, suffering from add-on handicaps of institutionalisation and, for some at least, organic dementias.

Autism today is classified as a pervasive developmental disorder (American Psychiatric Association 1994, pp.66–71) and by definition is necessarily present before the age of 3, although in the past it escaped detection until far later, and may still do so in places where paediatric psychiatry is under-staffed or undeveloped.

Some autistic children function at a higher level as they get older, and it is said that 10–20 per cent of affected children begin to improve around the age of 4 to 6 and are able to go to an ordinary school. A further 10–20 per cent can live at home but need to attend special schools or training centres, but the remaining 60 per cent show little improvement, requiring long-term and full-time care. Those who do improve tend nevertheless to remain emotionally cold and have unusual use of language (Russell, quoted by Gelder et al. 1996, p.692).

There is overall ignorance about the condition despite the continuing presence in the popular press of items about autistic people. The film *Rainman,* in which Dustin Hoffman portrayed what was generally described as autism, but which could be perceived as Asperger's disorder (Wing 1981), brought more understanding to those who saw it.

A recent Australian trial for tragic multiple murders brought deep grief and anxiety to at least one set of parents when the young man on trial was described as possibly suffering from Asperger's syndrome (Beale 1996). They wondered whether their son would be ostracised by society because of publicity and fears about the disorder, and it is unfortunate that reports on those persons who do go on in adult life to develop psychiatric disorders predominate over reports on those who do not (Clarke et al. 1989).

Some who work with autistic children have noted unusual or absent responses to pain, not because they do not feel pain but because they lack appropriate behaviour to indicate this. Yet the comprehensive volume *Text-book of Pain* (Wall and Melzack 1994) includes no entry on atypical pain behaviour, nor any entries on either autism or mental retardation as being areas of concern to those involved in pain management.

One autistic man now aged 62, whom I have known for some 35 years, has changed very little, and he has not deteriorated in his general behaviour. Because he has moved from a large state institution to a group home in the community, it is hard to decide whether his current level of apparent contentment would have been less had he stayed in the hospital ward where he first began music therapy. He is, however, still bound by rituals, and staff say that he lets them know, in a way that leaves them in no doubt, of how disturbed he is if something is moved or a change is made in routine.

In childhood he had been classified simply as 'retarded', but his file revealed quasi-normal development until the age of two, followed by increasingly difficult behaviour and a failure to develop relationships and speech. His parents had placed him in a state institution for retarded children and, although he had been moved from one institution to another, no further investigations took place.

His early history, combined with observations of his behaviour during music therapy sessions, led me to assume that he was affected by (unrecognised) autism. Work with him in music therapy was based upon this assumption, and I challenged the existing diagnosis in his file. His behaviour included failure to communicate by speech, a strong positive response to music, a fascination with rotating objects and parts of objects, a need for ritual and patterns in activities, and a wide range of extraordinary vocal sounds which seemed to have no communicative function, in that no sound was apparently linked with a particular event or object.

One cannot, of course, extrapolate observations from one individual to the whole population of older autistic people, and the uneven presentation of persons with autism is a constant challenge, but it has been interesting to have the opportunity of following this man for so many years.

In working with a young man described as autistic but having speech, I have on a few occasions asked him (after singing a song together) what he thinks the person in the song was feeling, but the question is impossible for him to answer. One of these songs was the Beatles' composition which starts with the words, 'What would you do if I sang out of tune' and has a repeated line: 'I need somebody to love'.

He was unable to indicate any understanding of what this repeated phrase means; is it reasonable to assume therefore that he failed to understand the meaning – or was it simply that he lacked the behaviour and the communication skills to convey his understanding to me?

The same young man composed the words and melody of a song which says that music makes him glad when he is feeling sad. Again, he appeared to have no concept of the emotional meaning of the words, and perhaps chose them simply because they rhymed, yet he is always waiting my arrival outside the hostel where he lives, and, presumably, this is because the music does, in some sense at least, make him happy! He also sings the 'good-bye' song at the end of our session, which includes the name of the person addressed and ends with 'thank you for the music'. He decided one week that he wished to sing this to me, and he used the pronouns correctly for 'you' and 'me' (another usage which many autistic people find difficult). His wish to sing it must, it seems, indicate enjoyment and perhaps a quality of human relationship, yet his voice and facial expression remain affect-less.

Usually he greets me in the car-park with another song he composed for us to sing as a duet, half of each line for each of us; after we have sung this, he laughs. But it is a strange sound, lacking any real feeling of amusement, and reminding me of the 'Ha Ha' sometimes used in print as an indication of ironic laughter.

This man is well on into adult life. His present style of communication and interaction remains a conundrum and it is impossible to know whether (or how) he will change, or what he will be like as he enters old age.

The links between autism and Asperger's syndrome, in which there are similar characteristic behaviours but with command of speech communication (American Psychiatric Association 1994, pp.75–77), are unclear. Are they entirely separate conditions, or should they be perceived as being at different ends of the same continuum of pervasive disorder?

Parental support

For disabilities which cause mental retardation, physical handicap or both together, parental support can be a 'plus' and a 'minus', often simultaneously. Children who have lived for many years with good parental support grow up with a sense of self-worth which was denied those who, in the past, received physical care in large institutions but without any emotional bonding.

But it can be difficult for parents to let go, to acknowledge that the child is growing into some measure of independence. One young woman, suffering from mental retardation as a consequence of severe childhood encephalitis, was not able, on entering a supervised group home, to change her own sanitary protection pads during menstruation, yet only a year afterwards she was not only doing this but helping to clean the house and to plan the weekly shopping list.

The smaller establishments seen today, as long as they have adequate continuity of trained staff, often provide excellent levels of loving care which provide quasi-parental involvement. The child, adolescent or adult then lives with a clear sense of individual value and a capacity for relationships, especially when the parents are encouraged to remain concerned and involved in the person's life.

In a major study of the life of older people with intellectual disability (Ashman, Suttie and Bramley 1993), the authors comment on the expected increases in the numbers of older people in the latter years of the twentieth and the early years of the twenty-first centuries. The inference is clear: we must plan ahead for greater needs of older people with mental retardation, both because there will be more older people and because those with disabilities have survival rates which are greater today than in the past.

In planning programmes for mentally retarded people, we must realise that older people who have lived outside the institutional or state-run system may turn to that system for help as they get older because of the loss of parents or their own increasing frailty (Ashman *et al.* 1995, p.35). The numbers needing help may therefore be far higher than if one merely extrapolates to the future the numbers of people currently receiving care and support.

Ashman and colleagues reported that, in the USA, de-institutionalisation often involved moving to a nursing home rather than to a supported group home, but this is not true for all countries. In the process of survey, they found that some of the people interviewed were apprehensive lest the questionnaire was part of a plan to move them out of the institution which they saw as their home, the place where they shared life with their friends and where the staff were seen as family. Clearly the major changes entailed in de-institutionalisation are not without emotional pain and practical difficulties.

One point made by Ashman and colleagues is of great importance as we consider the need to be a whole person in old age, and this is the need to retain individuality. Our work towards normalisation must not be restricted to the negative, such as training people to avoid 'labelling behaviour' (actions such as masturbation which contravene normal social mores and label the person as 'different'); we must also look at positive intervention, helping people to develop their skills and strengths.

For too long, government planning all over the world seems to have taken a simplistic approach, based on a belief that so many people who are aged, disabled (or both) means so many beds, so many meals, so many sets of clothes, so many attendants, and that this is all. We need far more than this de-humanising approach. My own work (limited as it is), within the community group homes of a disability service on the outskirts of Sydney, demonstrates how the previously unrecognised talents for music of pro-foundly intellectually and physically disabled residents can alter staff perceptions and improve their quality of life and relationships.

We must also ensure that quality of life does not consist simply of recreational facilities. We must ensure that proper medical care is available, that carers do not ignore minor illness, do not ignore the need for dentures, hearing aids and spectacles on the grounds that 'they couldn't cope with them anyway'.

Dentures assist nutrition, hearing aids assist communication, spectacles assist both safety and relationships. Hearing aids have particular significance because auditory capacity, or lack of it, influences behaviour. It is reported that there is an increased risk of paranoid ideation in those with hearing loss in the non-handicapped elderly population, and that a high percentage of deviant behaviour is observed in patients who are deaf. Cooke (1989) comments that not only is hearing impairment more common in those who are mentally retarded than in the population as a whole, but that hearing impairment is likely to lead to hearing handicap in mentally retarded persons because of their inability to compensate by utilisation of the other strategies of the 'normal' population.

Because of the increasing number of retarded persons surviving into old age, the community must accept responsibility for providing prosthetic aids of all kinds, as well as training in the use of these aids, in order to enhance the quality of life. If we ourselves wish to be seen as whole people despite advanced age, we must give others the same dignity.

Summary

Only a few genetic and developmental disorders have been mentioned here, but the general principles are common to all:

- The effects of disability for many genetic impairments, forms of mental retardation and developmental disorders result in varying levels of handicap.
- The capacity for independent living is thus also variable.
- People with mental impairments need strong support in all aspects of life.
- The capacity for independence is influence by physical, intellectual and behavioural factors, but usually people can cope with life better than outsiders would expect.
- Community acceptance is still uneven, and may depend upon the level of education of the onlookers.

Lastly, we must never stop trying!

Recommended reading

Sacks, O. (1995) *An Anthropologist on Mars*. London: Picador.

The surprising title comes from the remark of a high-functioning and intelligent autistic woman described by Sacks who said that when she observed complex human emotions and the (relationship) games that people play, she was so unable to understand what was going on that she felt like an anthropologist on Mars.

Although other topics are included in the book, much of it is on autism; Sacks has written at length on what life is like for autistic people, including some of those who have a very high level of functioning and about whom there could be controversy as to whether they suffer from autism or Asperger's syndrome. His empathic discussion of their challenges and achievements inspires us, and the book is strongly recommended for all who work with people who suffer from autism.

PART II

CHAPTER 10

The Practicalities of Music Therapy in Later Life

Introduction

Why use music? How can music contribute to our wholeness as we age? The concept of music therapy is based upon the belief that music is an experience as well as a 'thing'.

The nature of music is hard to define and it is also hard to describe our responses to it, apart from knowing whether we like or dislike a particular piece, and (very occasionally) knowing why! Taste varies tremendously from one person to another because of educational and cultural background, family preference, associations from the past with particular compositions, and so on.

Except for people with a significant hearing defect, there is an almost universal interest in music amongst people of widely different backgrounds. Beside this universal interest we must, however, set the certainty that there is no universal music. What is pleasing to one is displeasing to another, a composition which calms or satisfies one person may stir another to anger or bewilderment. This depends as much upon our associations with the music as on its style, although some of us do have feelings (for or against) about a particular genre of music or a particular tonal and harmonic system.

Even improvised music elicits strong feelings of pleasure or displeasure, and its meaning can be interpreted very differently by different people, either because of individual cultural background or because of underlying emotional bias. This difference in interpretation often amounts to the psychological phenomenon of projection, which is the foundation for part of my own methods in grief counselling. Projection takes place when we ascribe to other events, experiences or people those aspects of ourselves which we find difficult or impossible to acknowledge and deal with.

We may listen to music receptively, either passively or with lively interest. We may listen to it with bodily involvement by swaying the trunk or tapping our feet in time to it. We may participate in making music by playing alone on an instrument or by singing in a choir, playing in a group. Music can be a profession or it can be a hobby; we can make music solely for our own enjoyment or we can make music for others.

Music can be the means of energising our movements in dancing or keep-fit work, or (through cheerful songs) it can help to get a disheartened scout troop on the move again. Music is involved in many of society's rituals, from solemn and happy music for the bride arriving at her wedding, to sad and spiritual music for funerals, from marches to mark the entry of a football team to the arena to quiet music sung or played during religious worship to enhance meditation.

Music can consist of bagpipes or angry drumming which incite us to ferocity in war, or lullabies which soothe a baby to sleep. Music can remind us of the growth of love when we hear the song associated with courtship. It can bring sadness and anger if that same music reminds us of the breaking of that relationship or its failure to flourish.

Music is also a source of happiness and interest. Older people enjoy listening to music of all kinds. Concert managers should be pleased that so many of us go to concerts, ballets, operas and recitals. They should be glad that we find the interest and pleasure of music far more important than the challenges of travel by public transport or the parking of our cars because, if we did not, concert halls would be less well-filled than they are!

Music in therapy

Words may be inadequate to describe our inner responses to music we hear or music in which we share, and yet, ironically, music may help us to express through words problems we are facing which have previously been inexpressible. Music can help us to externalise the hidden feelings associated with loss and grief, the anger or fear, guilt or relief, so that these can be resolved. It can stir us to renewed effort in any rehabilitation work which tires us, and it gives rhythm to our efforts at mobilisation when gait is impaired. It can help to reconstruct our communication with others when speech is impaired from a stroke. It helps to build social bridges between those who are isolated and lonely because of bereavement or disability, and so on. And therein is music therapy!

The idea of music being linked with healing goes back to classical Greece, where the same deity was patron of both music and healing. It is, however, only in the twentieth century that there have been efforts to investigate the reason why music is useful as a therapeutic medium, how it works, for whom it is suitable, for whom it is unsuitable. And it is only relatively recently that educational programmes have been set up in universities and other institutions in many places across the world.

Codes of ethics and criteria for professional accreditation have been drawn up in many countries. There is a World Federation of Music Therapy which recommends (but does not administer) standards of professional work, ethics and conduct. Thus the profession is, in most places, self-regulating. Conferences take place nationally and internationally, so that there is a constant exchange of ideas and experiences.

Researchers have looked at and measured outcome in a variety of programmes and in a diversity of clinical areas. Music therapists are employed in psychiatry and substance abuse, in children's hospitals (for example, in units for burns, oncology, cardiac surgery and rehabilitation). They work in units or community centres for mental retardation and pervasive developmental disabilities such as autism, in centres for physical disabilities such as spinal cord injuries, cerebral palsy, muscular dystrophy, in the 'well population' for specific events such as childbirth, and with the 'at risk' population such as homeless young people, children of dysfunctional families.

Music therapists also work with families in which there is a child with a disability, whether this is an impairment of body or of intellect, enhancing parenting skills in order to minimise the probability of a major handicap developing (Oldfield 1996).

Last in this general list of people for whom music therapy is appropriate, but most important for the present book, is the population of older people, whether 'young old', 'old' or 'old old'. Music therapists work with elderly people in geriatric rehabilitation, in psychogeriatrics, in social group-work, and with those who suffer from an on-going problem such as Alzheimer's disease, Parkinson's disease, and others.

Work is usually preceded by a written referral from another health professional, who is aware of what we have to offer as a member of the clinical team, Those of us who work individually as well as in groups also practise 'case-finding'. When we observe responses in a group session which suggest that the person needs individual work, we then talk with the person's case manager, explaining our observations and asking that a referral be written.

When we work with clients or patients, we:

o explain what we are hoping to achieve

o answer their questions

- listen to their stories

- assess their needs by observation and (often) by asking questions

- carry out music interaction and counselling or other interventions which are required.

After an individual music therapy session is over, we write a brief account of what has taken place in the patient's file so that our comments are available to all staff members. This is important in order that music therapy does not proceed in a vacuum but is part of team approach to the individual. When we believe that we have done all that is possible, at least for the time being and usually after several sessions, we discuss this with the referring person, if possible at a case review meeting. Finally we have a session at which we separate from the client, reviewing what we have achieved together and (a key issue) ensuring that the person is not left feeling abandoned or rejected.

Music therapists who work in private practice use less clear-cut procedures, and the way of finding clients will depend upon communication with other professionals in our area and perhaps on whether or not advertising is considered ethical.

We must also decide whether or not to accept unreservedly those people who come of their own accord. Generally there is little risk attached to this, but it may be advisable either for our own protection or for other reasons to consider carefully the possibility of there being an undisclosed capacity for violence because of delusional or other illness. In one such instance, in which my initial assessment was that there was a significant risk to myself and I did not undertake any interventions, I later received very disturbing anonymous mail. This was unpleasant, and led to my contacting the police, but it reinforced the wisdom of my having refused treatment.

I have found that it is useless to accept a referral for an elderly person from a relative; for any real benefit to accrue the wish for help must come from the individual concerned. I routinely ask any private client who comes without a formal referral for the name and address of the family doctor or some other professional in case I need to communicate with that person because, for example, an intervention is needed which I am not competent to give, a suicide risk and for support and consultation.

The general principles of accountability under the 'Duty of Care' (which over-rides confidentiality) demand that we communicate with the appropriate person(s) if it seems that there are plans for suicide or for harming another person, and to ensure that a psychiatric or other significant illness receives appropriate treatment.

Summary

Music therapy is a combination of theoretical knowledge and practical skills, added to empathic communication through music and through words so that a therapeutic alliance is established. The ideas in this second half of the book are intended to be a starting point for the interested music therapist who works with older people, and not the ultimate definitive description. The ideas presented may be of interest to others, who are searching for new and positive ways of communicating with older people.

CHAPTER 11

Individual Work with Elderly People

Why do some older people need individual work in music therapy? The reasons vary as much as one person differs from another.

Problems of ageing

- Some people need help because unresolved griefs affecting their general happiness and stability, even to the extent of planning suicide, are causing a substance dependency or are otherwise interfering with daily life. For a tragic few, the failure to deal with personal needs or losses leads to hospital addiction, in which the sufferer yearns for individual care and attention, finding a spurious form of it in hospital treatment. The additional tragedy is that such people are stigmatised and rejected by a busy health care system so that their needs remain unmet and the search becomes the more intense.

- Others suffer as a result of losses from the past: sad memories of the death of a baby, the loss of the spouse through death or divorce. Or there may be new losses: of health and independence, of spouse, friends or relatives, loss of hope for the future in the diagnosis of a terminal or chronically-disabling illness.

- Other recent losses include having to relinquish the support of an adult disabled relative because of personal frailty or illness. An elderly person is stressed by caring for a disabled or dementing spouse, even to the extent of reduced immunity (Nash and Fletcher 1993, pp.159–182), but grieves when he or she can no longer provide that care. Elderly parents may re-live the grief when the child with a disability was born or when the adult child became disabled as the result of illness or accident.

○ Others need individual help when social conflicts arise with family or neighbours, sources of grief but not in themselves grief 'scenarios' except that they indicate a failure of affection. The help needed may be to provide support in making decisions, an ally who will help the person gain their 'rights' or an intermediary to facilitate the resolution of the conflict.

○ Some people go through an existential crisis as they look back at their lives and think about the end of life. For them, the opportunity to talk about the issues of the meaning of life, death, eternity and the universe can bring comfort or, at the very least, an opportunity for deep discussion on topics which have arisen in their thoughts.

○ Some are suffering from a depressive illness or other psychiatric disorder and need support in accepting the necessary care and treatment. Some, without ever having been labelled a 'case', are dysthymic, having had a life-long pattern of low spirits. Their outlook on life is impaired by feelings of sadness and worthlessness, and sometimes further complicated by anger and difficult behaviour which alienates others.

○ As we get nearer to the end of life, many of us yearn to know that something of ourselves will live on into the future, either because of genetic inheritance, or through the values we have instilled into our children and other descendants. Those who die childless can have no such expectation of indirect immortality. Some childless people wish they had done something which would be remembered or which would have an influence on future generations, and are sad that they leave behind no such legacy because (as they see it) their lives were humdrum and useless.

○ Parents who have lost a child think with regret of how much better life would be if they had a son or daughter not simply to inherit tangible and intangible gifts but to visit them, care for them, be interested in them. This realisation of loss becomes still more painful if the person is in a hospital or nursing home where other patients have families to visit them and their own loneliness is underlined.

○ Parents (especially mothers) who have lost a child describe how they have always kept track of the milestones of life which that child would have reached, thinking with sadness or anger 'He would have started school this year', 'She would have been starting to think of having a boyfriend about this age', 'That young man next door is the same age as my son would have been, I bet my son would have been better looking!'

- If the parents see their friends and contemporaries being cared for and visited by their adult children, and they themselves are greatly in need of such support, they are constantly reminded of the death of their child, which deprived them of the possibility of filial care. If they have moved away from the town where a loved person was buried, or if they are now too frail to visit the grave, they may mourn again and re-live the circumstances of the death.

- Modern medical advances may re-awaken old griefs as people look back and realise that today the fatal illness of someone close to them could have been dealt with by medication or surgical operations. Some people in this situation insist that they are 'just glad' that people today do not go through the sadness they had to endure, but this is often only part of the truth.

- Those who were bereaved by death of the spouse earlier in life and who did not re-marry are increasingly aware of their own solitude if they become too frail or disabled to be able to travel and meet friends or to take part in activities which kept their loneliness at bay earlier in life.

- Those who never married may re-experience a grief that they have been without a mate all their lives; this is particularly painful if a fiancé was killed in the 1939–1945 war, or died from an illness which today could have been cured.

- Those whose marriage was a failure, whether it ended in divorce or remained as a legal entity but without love or support between the partners, may grieve for the relationship that never was, for the hopes that were never fulfilled. As the end of life draws near, there is a recognition that it is now too late, the hopes for a loving partnership can never be realised.

- Other people are simply lonely and of a personality type which does not fit well into senior citizens' clubs or day centres. They may or may not feel guilty at not wanting to join a group but they do need visitors, not necessarily for therapy but for some level of intimacy in occasional companionship and the sharing of common interests.

- Some elderly people have been for many years, or have become recently, dependent upon alcohol or other substances. Although this may be a consequence of a grief or loss, it is in itself a source of further losses, of health or relationships, and there is an additional problem that alcohol-related brain damage inhibits both insight and the capacity for change. Substance dependency impedes progress in rehabilitation, and the difficulties it imposes are often unrecognised.

Even this list of losses and difficulties, substantial though it is, covers only some of the causes for grief in later life, and only some of the possible ill-effects when that grief remains unresolved.

Counselling older people

The topic of counselling older people through a combination of music and an eclectic therapeutic approach has been discussed elsewhere (Bright 1996, Chapters 3, 11 and 12). But the topic warrants further discussion, and this section also includes recent clinical work that illustrates various points.

We know that in old age we may suffer loss of health or loss of relationships. We may go through experiences which sap our self-confidence and we may live in an atmosphere of denigration in which destructive stereotypes of old age lead us to doubt our own integrity. The loss of health may include loss of reality in a major psychiatric illness, and our thinking is distorted. So many and so frequent are the losses of later life that it is a matter for self-congratulation and perhaps of amazement that so many of us survive, continue to be creative, continue to enjoy life!

Many of those who become ill or emotionally disturbed as a consequence of loss are found to be people who have lacked self-confidence since early life. They have lacked emotional support either since childhood or for a major part of their lives, and may have been dysthymic for many years. There may be a built-in sense of guilt, engendered by authority figures in their lives, that anything that goes wrong is their fault, and they often describe being told 'You'll never be good at anything you do' and 'Anything you touch goes wrong.' Rutter's paper on resilience in the face of adversity is cogent to this sad situation (Rutter 1985).

Grief therapy

The general aims of music therapy for grief counselling can be summarised thus:

- to establish a non-judgmental atmosphere of trust in which the therapeutic relationship can develop

- ◦ to give permission to acknowledge the difficulties of the past, sometimes using music which has been significant in those relationships to enhance disclosure

- ◦ to deal with difficulties, past and present, by assisting insight into the manner in which others have contributed to the present situation

- ◦ to validate the emotional content of what has been disclosed through improvised music

- ◦ to achieve self-acceptance, self-forgiveness and (often) forgiveness of others

- ◦ to look realistically into the future, discussing possibilities for change

- ◦ to provide a musical mnemonic, a familiar song with appropriate words which can be used as a form of 'self-talk' to reinforce changed behaviour in the future.

The lasting nature of grief

One might expect, as we get older and events are separated from us by an increasing number of years, that our grief over past losses would become less vivid and less painful, but this is not so. In many instances the grief becomes more poignant and more painful, and the capacity to deal with painful feelings is diminished to the extent that, perhaps for the first time, an admission for psychiatric treatment is needed.

There seem to be several possible reasons why the losses become more and not less painful with the passage of time. Not all are applicable to all people but all are worth bearing in mind when working with grieving older people:

- ◦ We may lose some of our emotional resilience as we age

- ◦ We are increasingly aware of lost companionship as our world shrinks because of frailty or disability, and there is sadness over the companionship which was lost as we mourn each new loss of friend or relative

- ◦ Because of these losses, there are fewer people with whom we have an intimate relationship, people who in the past supported us in times of difficulty

- ◦ Increasing deafness makes it difficult to use the telephone or lost mobility makes travel impossible so that we cannot receive comfort and support from friends at a distance

- If substance dependency has been the preferred method of dulling emotional pain, the brain impairment which occurs as the result of alcohol abuse makes it ever more difficult to deal with our feelings of anger and sadness

- Thoughts and fears of our own mortality tend to lead us into thoughts of the past, with possible regrets and remorse, and these are the more poignant because it is now, generally, too late to put anything right

- The anniversary of a loss can re-ignite the pain of that loss, often for many years, as the anniversary recurs.

Substance misuse

The possibility of change in substance abuse is unpredictable but it is worth trying to achieve change by whatever means are available. Ticehurst (1994, pp.269–284) comments that alcoholic elderly people often present indirectly, and that clinical suspicion must remain high when dealing with certain elderly patients whose problems could well be explained by substance misuse. He also says that some elderly people, usually late-onset misusers who are recently-widowed, are well-motivated for change and show long-term benefits from properly planned programmes.

The therapeutic uses of behavioural and cognitive approaches have been shown to be effective for some people in the management of alcohol abuse. But, because the population is not uniform, no single approach is universally appropriate and it is essential to match the treatment method to the needs of the individual (Mattick and Heather 1993). Music therapy combined with counselling makes use of cognitive and behavioural methods and, for those who are capable of insight and abstract thought, also makes use of approaches based upon those skills.

Other aspects of individual work

In psychogeriatric work in hospital we may be able to work at greater depth sooner than with someone who is living at home because, in hospital, support is available if painful feelings emerge after the session is over, support which is unavailable to the person living at home.

For work in the community, the risks of decompensation are greater and we must be aware of this.

Agitated restless people may not initially be accessible to our work until medication has reduced stress levels, and those suffering from manic disorder may also be difficult to reach at first for similar reasons. I find that persons

suffering from paraphrenia can sometimes be given peace from their delusions and hallucinations by appropriate music and conversation which takes
their thoughts in a different direction.

Case studies

In several publications, I have given various extended case histories which
describe the ways in which grief can remain unresolved, and the reasons for
this blocking, together with discussion of the problems which arise and the
methods used to facilitate resolution. Brief summaries of these are as follows:

- A woman had felt great anger with her dead husband for 'causing'
  his own needless death by not having the car repaired, but found it
  impossible to voice that anger because of family expectation that she
  would simply be sad. This had led to nineteen years of alcohol
  dependency but a series of six intensive sessions, including a visit to
  the cemetery, led to satisfactory resolution and lasting sobriety
  (Bright 1994, pp.584–7).

- Two layers of grief were disclosed by a patient, one concerned with
  the death of her abusive husband and the other the death of a
  much-loved sister. These had caused agitated depression, but
  responded satisfactorily to a series of six sessions, including a visit to
  the cemetery (Bright 1995, pp.318–320).

- An elderly woman came to hospital only for pain management but
  was found to be suffering from guilty feelings about what was
  perceived as a discreditable relationship, ended by death of the
  partner, so that she felt forbidden to grieve over the loss. A single
  session lasting well over an hour, with a shorter follow-up interview,
  facilitated resolution of both pain and emotional difficulties, and this
  was confirmed at 12-month follow-up (Bright 1995, pp.316–317).

- Another elderly woman who came to hospital for pain management
  was found to be suffering from repressed anger with her recently
  deceased daughter because the daughter had kept her cardiac illness
  a secret from her mother. Five sessions were required to facilitate the
  resolution of both the grief and the pain, but both the immediate and
  the long-term outcome were good (Bright 1994, pp.587–9).

- A woman had suffered a major disappointment because of a failed
  surgical intervention which had led to loss of power in her hands.
  She showed, however, no signs of her inner grief and anger, and I
  described her as suffering from 'smiling' depression. Reassurance and

permission to speak openly of her sadness and disappointment proved helpful to her inner emotions, although she continued to protect relatives and others from knowledge of her true feelings (Bright 1996, pp.153–6).

The following vignettes are of more recent work and again illustrate the diversity of the use of music therapy with elderly people.

Vignette 1

Ann was in her early seventies when she was admitted with a depressive illness and her doctor noted that she had had several admission over the last six or seven years and that, each time she became ill, it was at the same time of year. This time factor aroused the doctor's interest and she referred Ann for music and grief therapy.

Despite her hyper-vigilance and hyper-acuity, which complicated the establishment of trust in the initial interview, Ann was eventually able to speak of what that particular time of year meant for her. The date was the anniversary of the adoption of her illegitimate son over fifty years before. (Did the hyper-vigilance have its origin in the need for secrecy during her pregnancy because of family shame? This necessarily remained a matter for speculation.)

She described the circumstances in great detail. The child's father had been of a different denomination from herself and the family forbade the marriage, even though the young man genuinely, she said, wanted to marry her. She gave birth to the baby in a maternity home and, when the baby was a few days old, she had to go by taxi to a home in a distant suburb for him to await adoption. She described sitting in the taxi trying to cope with her feelings that this was the only time she would have him to herself.

She said that all her life since that time she had continually wondered what had happened to her son, what his life had been like and, on the basis of his age, kept track of what he might be doing. She looked at men of the same age in shopping centres and elsewhere, wondering 'Is that him? Is that what he looks like now?'

Later she was persuaded into a marriage with a man substantially older than herself, whom she found not really loveable. The son born of that marriage was, she said, exactly like his father and, not surprisingly, the mother–son relationship had been an unhappy one.

It was, of course, impossible to know whether her husband had really been autocratic and difficult and how much he suffered by comparison with the lost love. Nor could I know whether the son was as 'bossy', as she described, or whether the conflict arose because no son could ever have matched the perfection of the idealised lost child. But this was irrelevant to the therapeutic process. Arguing someone out of false beliefs is not part of one's task except in certain circumstances where cognitive approaches are required.

Music of two types was used in the short series of interviews which were arranged during Ann's brief admission:

○ Improvised music was played to express for her the guilt, anger and sadness she felt, even so many years afterwards. In particular it expressed anger with her mother for her religious bigotry in forbidding the marriage. It had been difficult for Ann to acknowledge her anger because it was masked by her own sense of guilt at having become pregnant without being married. There was perhaps also anger with herself and the child's father for accepting the prohibition, although this acceptance was understandable in the milieu of the time.

○ Significant and familiar pieces of music were played and she was encouraged to sing the lullabies and other children's music she would have sung to her son had she been permitted to keep him and bring him up herself.

There was an unequal balance between time spent on music and on counselling, but it was the music which provided the unique key to resolution of that long-held grief. The improvised music, which was played as the first step towards resolution, was effective in reflecting back to Ann her feelings of sadness, regret and anger, and validated those feelings, giving her permission to feel that it was all right to have had these emotions.

This musical intervention and her response to it then provided the way to the next stage, which was to ask her to sing to that baby as she wished she had been able to do. By imagining that she was singing to the baby, she was able at last to cry and grieve in a way which she had, quite literally, been forbidden to do at the time of the birth and adoption, because of the social stigma attached to the situation at the time.

Ann was discharged quite soon, and has apparently remained in good health despite the passing of a further anniversary of that adoption.

Vignette 2

Bruce was a man in the early years of old age who had made a suicide attempt and had been admitted to a psychiatric hospital for assessment and treatment. His life story revealed a satisfying early life in the Navy, where his technical prowess had earned him high esteem. Subsequently, however, he experienced in civilian life a series of losses caused by the changes in technology which affected his employment and led to job after job being 'phased out' as his particular skills ceased to be needed.

Although he knew that the series of 'sackings' was impersonal, it had, he said, felt like rejection and also reminded him constantly of his increasing uselessness in today's world. He knew, however, that there was no point in trying to be re-trained and learn new skills because he was at retiring age.

His marriage provided him with no support because his wife was engrossed in their daughter and grandchildren, who shared the house. She made it clear that he was in the way by being at home instead of at work, and he felt increasingly unwanted, so that death seemed the only logical solution to an otherwise insoluble problem.

Bruce was allowed to speak freely of what was happening to him and how he felt, and he was later able to cry about his sadness and loneliness when this was expressed in music. To do this I played improvised music using the Dorian mode (approximating to the key of D Minor) with discords and unresolved progressions to symbolise uncertainty, and chord blocks which had a slow, heavy quality to symbolise hopelessness. Composed music was also used, Tchaikowsky's 'None but the lonely heart', and this he said symbolised his loneliness, although he had not previously known the song. Bruce knew from this verbal and musical interaction that his emotions were validated and accepted.

Visualisation was then used, based on a bush track in the Blue Mountains West of Sydney, where the Bowen's Creek track zig-zags down into a steep valley and up the other side. To climb the track demands determination and a belief that, although one feels one is making no progress, one is actually getting nearer to the top!

For the effective use of visualisation it is essential to use a familiar musical composition since the aim is for the music and visual images to be used after the session is over and in the future as mnemonics symbolising progress in an apparently impossible situation. Improvised music is useless for this purpose because the person can only recall the content in the most general way and certainly cannot sing it privately in time of need! Because of his age, the well-known 'Climb every mountain' was used for Bruce, as it has been with several people of the same age.

He had only a brief admission of a few days so that only a single music therapy session was possible. Because of today's changes in hospital admissions and the emphasis on community care, it is not uncommon to meet someone only once. Whilst this is not ideal, even a single session can provide an impetus for insight, self-acceptance and change.

Clinical teamwork was essential because it seemed probable that Bruce's wife was a major cause of his suicidal despair. Regaining for him the financial control of his Navy pension was an important issue. This had been assigned to his wife during an admission for a very slight stroke so that Bruce had no personal money available to him, and family interviews were needed to restore his overall autonomy.

The hazard of a professional taking on the role of champion to a patient who is in a destructive relationship was recognised, and there was discussion amongst the clinicians involved in the case as to whether we were 'taking sides' on the basis of inadequate information – a risky procedure and one which all too easily merges into 'rescuing'. But after analysis of available information it seemed that Bruce was indeed being badly treated, that his suicide attempt was an understandable response to an impossible situation rather than a manifestation of a depressive illness, and that the approach being used to try to resolve the situation was correct. The team view was that the insight and understanding gained through the complexities of grief therapy and music therapy would arm him to face the future.

As often, there were doubts as to the eventual outcome for this sad and lonely man, but follow-up indicated that things had indeed changed for him as a consequence of the admission and that he probably would not again 'need' to make a suicide attempt.

Vignette 3

Clare, aged 85, had lived for six years in a nursing home. She was confined to a wheel-chair and required regular physiotherapy. Her life was limited to the facility and its immediate surroundings, although she did have some adult family and friends, who visited and, on rare occasions, arranged an outing.

She was referred for music therapy because of a perceived loss of autonomy. Although she was permitted and encouraged to make decisions for herself (understandably on relatively minor matters), she had difficulty in doing so for fear of 'doing the wrong thing', of being unpopular, of being a nuisance to staff and so on. In fact her inability to make decisions was far more irritating to staff than if she had made the occasional inconvenient request.

Music therapy did include some level of counselling, by giving her the opportunity of talking about the death of her husband, her disappointment at being dependent upon others for daily living, and her disgust with what she described as her ugly skin (fragile skin in which purple bruising appeared after even trivial mishaps).

Most of the therapy consisted, however, in giving her an opportunity for choice, helping her to feel that it was fun to make decisions about what music to hear next. The diverse programme (in which I was helped by students) included:

- encouraging Clare in her choice of songs, using songbooks of appropriate eras to match her early life and her years of courtship and marriage. Using song books made it easy for her to make a decision, and easy to join in with the words of some songs because two of the books were in large print.

- playing favourite instrumental items for her. This was a difficult challenge for students who, at first (literally!), did not have at their fingertips the repertoire which was required but who gradually learned by example from me the favourite items, such as songs sung by Richard Tauber, songs from 'The Land of Smiles', 'The Desert Song', and so on.

The music trolley was brought beside Clare's bed or chair and she was encouraged to play some of the instruments within the limits imposed by her hand function, which was impaired by arthritis. The possible risks of extending joint damage were discussed and the programme was planned jointly with the occupational therapist. Although she tried several instruments such as tambourine and slit drum, Clare's favourite was a set of chime bars in the pentatonic scale; the beaters for these had the handles built up so that they were large enough to be held, but because foam plastic was used, there was no perceptible increase in weight.

Playing the chime bars correctly was at first a challenge but Clare soon learned the technique of letting the beater bounce back from the bar, rather than hitting and holding, which produces a dull 'clunk' instead of a ringing tone. As accompaniment, sometimes a portable keyboard was used, sometimes an autoharp or a guitar while the melody was sung in the tonality of the chime bars so that Clare could join in by playing instead of singing. Sometimes music was improvised (again in the key of the chime bars) with or without a specific theme for the improvisation.

Clare was encouraged to reminisce about her life, to speak of her happy marriage and her grief at her husband's death. This reminiscence led to the composition of a song, the melody and words devised by Clare (after substantial encouragement) and harmonised by the student. Thanks to computer technology it was possible to print the words and the music of the song in a highly professional manner, with Clare's name as composer of words and melody, and the title, which referred to what her life was like in old age and disability.

The song gave permanence to Clare's memories of past happiness but also expressed a philosophical acceptance of the present, in which acceptance her Christian faith was significant. Because the words of the song were highly personal and emotional, there was discussion with the nursing staff and the social worker about issues of confidentiality and ethics, as to whether or not a copy of this song should be placed in Clare's clinical file. She had been given several other copies for her own use as gifts or simply to keep in her drawer.

It was decided that Clare should make the decision, and it was seen as significant that she was able to reach a decision without difficulty or delay, that she would like the song to be placed in her file and that it was all right for people who had access to that file to read it.

We found that staff perceptions of Clare changed somewhat after the song was placed in the file. She was seen as a person with a history of happy relationships and achievements in bringing up her family successfully, someone who had seen much of the world when travelling with her husband. All of these helped to make her a person, rather than just someone who needed help for various activities, and who had an irritating difficulty in making her mind up about things. She continued to have difficulty in making decisions, but this seemed to be somewhat more accepted by staff than in the past.

This work is similar to song-writing for people in palliative care units, which can bring comfort and satisfaction to those facing the end of their lives (Bailey 1984; O'Callaghan 1990). Although the care of elderly people with chronic ill-health is not synonymous with palliative care, many older frail or disabled people do see themselves as 'dying' even though there is no definite idea that death will occur in the immediate future, so song-writing is equally appropriate for both populations.

On one occasion when I was alone with Clare, I used visualisation techniques, with bell-chimes on the keyboard matching the sounds of the chime bars mentioned above. Clare was asked to imagine herself on one of the bush walks which she and her husband had enjoyed so much, and we imagined ourselves sitting near a waterfall, and, in the trees overhead, bell-birds calling. (These are Australian birds of unexciting appearance but with strong and beautiful bell-like calls which ring through the sky.)

I suggested that when she was feeling a bit down-hearted, frustrated by being confined to bed and missing those most dear to her, she could imagine herself in the bush, hear in her mind the sound of the waterfall and the bird calls, and feel at peace. This worked well and she has since found it possible to reproduce the same peaceful atmosphere inwardly even in the absence of the musical stimulus to the imagination.

This detailed description of the various music therapy interactions with Clare illustrates the complexities and the paradoxical simplicities of what can be done for lonely and disabled people through the empathic use of music, when this is backed up by knowledge of the disability, the emotional needs of the individual client and what is (and what is not) possible for that person.

The nature of music therapy

We must not perceive improvised music as the only 'real' music therapy. For one person or group the use of improvisation may be indicated, but for someone suffering from delirium or major cognitive impairment with anxiety, it is vitally important, both musically and ethically, that we do not add to the confusion by playing music which is unknown and strange.

We do not promote or encourage the catharsis of terrifying emotions through musical improvisation, no matter what the age of the person, without recognising that decompensation may occur, so that there is a total breakdown of the defence mechanisms by which he or she has previously managed to keep going. If we allow this to happen, the individual is forced into a counter-productive emotional crisis and a deteriorating state of mental health, and even stirred to suicide.

This can occur in individual work but can also happen in group work when the music has particular effects on one member of that group. It may seem that such a situation is more likely to arise with young people rather than with the elderly, but this is by no means certain. It can occur at any age if a specific item of music evokes painful memories from the past.

In using improvisation, I have found that one may need to adapt the music to the age of the person; a young person can often cope with extraordinarily strong discords and unexpected harmonies which can leave an older person merely bewildered. One young woman who had spoken of the uncertainties of the future became distressed by the playing of unresolved discords to symbolise her uncertainty because the image evoked was so powerful. (The disturbing music consisted of a major scale, harmonised with highly conventional chords but stopping on the dominant seventh chord in second inversion with the leading note at the top.)

A change of mood, mediated through a change of improvised music, was essential in order to avoid a dangerous decompensation crisis. But her insight into life problems was enhanced by discussion as to why that music was so disturbing. She had often heard the harmonised scale before, but the abrupt ending with the final discord unresolved symbolised for her the fact that her life had seemed to be going smoothly until a sudden crisis had taken away her certainty of the future. This incident shows clearly why verbal interaction must be included in music therapy. Although this took place with a young person, the principles remain the same for all ages. Music can express those feelings and responses which we find hard to face, and we must assess and meet the needs of each individual.

Short-term intervention, in particular, poses a problem with the use of improvisation because it may take time to establish sufficient trust so that patients will see the playing of musical instruments, alone or in a group, as an adult and a therapeutic experience and not as childish foolery which achieves nothing except to use up valuable therapy time.

We need ways of establishing trust in the first session, and I find that listening to the person's story is essential as a first step, followed by my own improvisation to reflect the emotional content of that story. This gives reassurance that the story has been understood and the emotions accepted without judgement, and the improvisation usually moves the interaction into further trust and greater depth. Some people like to join in, either sharing the keyboard or using another instrument, but usually older people do not wish to do this unless they have a background of music-making.

The opportunity of telling one's life story – of being heard and understood by someone who is neither shocked nor judgmental – is therapeutic in itself, and the reflective musical improvisation adds a powerful new dimension to the experience.

Despite the value of group-work, there are matters which are difficult to discuss in the presence of others, particularly by older people who are usually reticent about personal difficulties, and individual work is essential because of its gift of privacy. The background knowledge of the therapist is of great importance, whatever our professional role, as we try to facilitate the resolution of griefs, whether these are recent or long-held.

Links between hospital and community

Today we need to see a hospital in-patient facility as part of the community rather than as a separate and perhaps even a rival system. This can be seen either as a problem or a challenge, depending upon our own attitude and the support we receive in our work. We may see hospital patients for only a short time before they are discharged and it may or may not be possible to continue to see them in the community. We need to bring each session to a close in such a way that, if it proves to be the last, there will be a sense of closure and completeness.

The situation differs for different places. In some instances when a patient has been discharged, I continue to see that person as an 'out-patient', which means that they do not have to pay fees since this is regarded as part of my professional responsibility to the Area Health Service. Some of the in-patient referrals are arranged with this plan in mind, that the person will be seen in hospital until the acute phase of the illness has passed and then will continue to be seen in a room on the hospital campus but as a 'visitor'.

Some music therapists are employed exclusively in community work, and clients from their own homes or from sheltered accommodation are seen for music therapy without having been resident in the hospital or, for those who have intermittent need for hospital admission, in their times of remission from illness.

Each country, each town, each facility has its own mode of working, its own structural links between hospital and community care. Each of us has to adapt our approach to fit in with the particular methods used in our own geographical area. Adaptability and a capacity for change are necessary for both therapists and patients.

CHAPTER 12

Music Therapy For Those
With Physical Disorders

Various physical difficulties can affect us as we get older, and many of these are dealt with by medication such as eye-drops, equipment such as walking sticks and hearing aids, and measures such as taking more care to protect our joints, avoiding certain movements, reducing our stress levels and so on. We follow instructions, have regular check-ups and diagnostic tests to make sure nothing has deteriorated, and we are then able to ignore the problems. But some difficulties, particularly neurological problems, are less readily dealt with and require extended professional help from therapists; some of these are discussed in this chapter.

Neurological disorders are not unique to older people. Multiple sclerosis, for example, although not restricted to younger people is more common in earlier than in later life. Cerebral haemorrhage is often called 'the young person's stroke' because it arises from a blood-vessel malformation which was present at birth and the rupture usually occurs before middle-age.

It is more common, however, for neurological disorders to affect our lives in old age, when we may suffer from the effect of strokes, dementia of the Alzheimer type, Parkinson's disease or other conditions. (Because dementing illness affects the nervous system and is of organic origin, it is included in this list.)

Music and the other therapies

It is helpful to combine music therapy with other forms of treatment, whether in physiotherapy, occupational therapy or speech pathology; this is so for both neurological and non-neurological disorders.

Someone whose pain, fatigue or apprehension (for example about weight-bearing after repair of a fractured femur) limits the work in physio-therapy can sometimes be helped to greater persistence by appropriate rhythmic music. This needs to be of their own choosing or, if they are unable to make a choice, chosen as suitable to their age and the nature of the work being done. For this work, the music therapist must be able to play a portable instrument, to move along with the patient. Singing can also be useful, when a strongly rhythmic tune is used, particularly for people whose walking will be difficult in the future because of long-term effects of a stroke or other disability.

The advantage of singing with someone as one walks side-by-side is that the patient can sing too; it is then possible to suggest that he or she uses the same tune when practising walking between sessions and also when going home. One person suffering from multiple sclerosis, who had unequal muscle strength in the two legs, was found to walk better if she led with the right foot and said to herself '*right*-left, *right*-left' instead of the more usual '*left*-right, *left*-right'.

To this was added the Scots song 'The Keel Row', a long-standing favourite of hers, which she sang, first of all with me and then alone. She said, 'You can sing as you walk down the street to the shops and nobody thinks you are very odd!' We later decided that, even if they did think she was odd, it was worth it if it helped her to walk better!

Music also assists those who suffer from anxiety about their ability to walk, which may occur without physical cause but can happen after a long illness, and some people are immobilised by their anxiety. I have found it useful in this situation to adopt a behavioural approach, singing with the person as a distraction from anxiety and fear.

One woman who had this difficulty was helped by our singing together as we walked down the hospital corridor, making each picture on the wall our goal for the next segment of the journey. We looked ahead at the pictures and talked about what song might be appropriate, so that she kept her head up instead of gazing at the floor as was her habit. At first I walked with my arm linked in hers, as a substitute for her usual method of clutching at walls and furniture, but as she gained confidence I was able to hold her arm less tightly until eventually she was walking alone.

The next phase of the programme, in the third session, was to walk ahead of her when we came to a step or the threshold of a door; previously she had not been able to step over the junction of tiled floor to carpet, or from one carpet design to another even when there was no change in level, but when I stood on the other side of the doorway and continued singing, she was able to make the move and to laugh at her own fears. The final stage in the treatment was to encourage her to sing alone as she walked so that there would be transfer of training to the home situation, and this proved successful.

This is similar to the methods described for the woman with multiple sclerosis, but the main hazard in the second case was loss of confidence in a person who had suffered a prolonged illness and was prone to anxiety.

Other, non-neurological, difficulties which affect our physical functioning include arthritis, and support groups are found in some places. Because joint protection is of major importance, it is impossible to give recommendations for the use of music to assist movement, except to say that some people do find that rhythmic music of an appropriate type, played at the appropriate speed, does help them to move more easily. But there must be consultation with occupational and physical therapists to ensure that the movements will help and not harm joints already impaired by the disease.

People who suffer from long-term effects of rheumatoid arthritis and who were treated with steroids (so that there has been demineralisation of bone structure) require extreme care in movement lest a transection of the spinal cord occur in the cervical or other section of the spine, and should not be included in any programme for music with movement.

Stroke

After a stroke, music therapy is useful in changing the cycle of fear and pain. Early on in my work for stroke patients, I saw a woman who was having passive movements of the affected arm to prevent the shoulder from becoming 'frozen' and painful. As she saw the physiotherapist lift the arm she screamed, but when music was played to her on the other side, so that she looked towards the piano accordion instead of at her arm, the arm could be lifted level with her shoulder without any awareness of pain.

A bongo drum (with its paired drums) has helped persons with hemiparesis. By resting the paralysed hand on one drum and using the intact hand to beat out a strong rhythm on the other drum, there is (a) transfer of vibration, which stimulates the affected hand and provides proprioceptive feedback of the position of the hands in space, and (b) often an associated movement so that the affected hand makes some movements, enhancing re-education and reassuring the patient. This was part of a combined programme with the occupational therapist, as also was some work using pairs of cymbals of diminishing sizes to enhance the hand co-ordination of a person who was unco-ordinated because of brain damage to the cerebellum.

When, after a stroke, there is a loss of part of the visual field (hemianopia), musical instruments and activities can encourage people to use head-scanning movements to compensate for loss of visual field, contributing to occupational therapy programmes. One can, for example, encourage some-one to play the notes for the full length of a keyboard, watching the fingers whilst playing, and this assists in the re-training process.

There are some situations in which the use of music for stroke patients is contra-indicated:

- Emotional lability (laughter and tears occurring without any emotional affect as a result of stroke) can occur, and it may or may not be appropriate to persist with the music. One such patient said 'Don't take any notice, I'm really enjoying it!' as tears ran down his face while music was played.

- Recruitment is found in some forms of deafness such as Meniére's disease, and following some forms of brain damage. In recruitment, loud sounds cause physical pain and are intolerable. The differential in volume between sounds which cannot be heard and those which cause pain is surprisingly small, and many of us have met people who fail to hear our first comment because it is too soft but, after very little increase in volume, flinch and say 'There's no need to shout!'.

- Perseveration can cause difficulties because the person 'gets stuck' on a particular word or movement, repeating the activity or the words until something happens or is done to achieve change. It also occurs conceptually, when a person sticks at one idea.

Physiotherapy for aphasic patients

Usually an aphasic person does not suffer from loss of body image, although this can occur, and there may be major difficulties in co-operating in physiotherapy because the patient does not understand verbal instructions or practical demonstrations. Music has proved useful for many aphasic people in helping them to understand what movement is required.

Good communication between therapists is essential. The physiotherapist must be able to describe or demonstrate what type of movement is needed and the music therapist must be able to play, on a portable instrument, music which is appropriate, normally by playing a pre-composed item which is familiar to the patient so that it can be remembered in the future if necessary.

If the only instrument available is the guitar, then the rhythmic basis may be helped by having a song to fit the movements, which the patient may eventually learn to sing and which will then become a memory aid when he practises at home or in the ward between sessions with the physiotherapist. The piano accordion is particularly useful because it gives a strong rhythm as well as the melody, and with it one can walk along beside the patient or (with care!) walk backwards facing him, adjusting the speed of the music as necessary.

Recorded music is useless and even counter-productive for such work because the speed cannot be adjusted. As someone's gait improves, the music must be changed both to match and to encourage increased speed and rhythmic certainty.

For movements made whilst lying on the treatment couch or wide plinth, the therapist can stand next to the patient or, for preference, sit on a stool so that eye contact can be maintained both with the client and with the other therapist. However, after the initial explanations, the music therapist may well be left alone with the patient to continue the work for however many minutes are required.

A separate group may be set up for those who require prompts from music to enable them to participate in physiotherapy. In the work described, a physiotherapist planned what was required and an assistant, who was partly trained but not professionally qualified, assisted in the sessions.

In one case, the physiotherapist wished a woman (suffering from global aphasia following a massive stroke affecting the right side of the body) to lift her paralysed right arm with her left hand as high as she could, so that passive movements might prevent shoulder dysfunction. The patient had no idea of what was expected of her even when this was demonstrated to her, until we sang the children's action song 'You push the damper in, and you push the damper out, and the smoke goes up the chimney just the same...'. As this started and the rest of the group began to sing and move, she took the affected arm in the other hand and carried out all the necessary movements, singing the words as she did so, thereby promoting her own well-being and remaining in command of her own actions.

Selection of music

One needs a repertoire of various types of music. These must be played from memory because it is not practical to have to have a music stand. One needs to be able to move around a large area to watch the work in progress and adjust the speed of the music as required.

For brisk walking, a march can be played at the appropriate speed, gradually increasing the speed if it is planned to help the patient to walk more briskly. For slow walking, however, a waltz is more useful, with one step to a measure (bar), and the speed can be adjusted as one becomes familiar with the patient's gait.

Swinging movements are best performed to music in either 3/4 or 6/8 time; this has proved useful for people who are regaining their balance by swinging one foot at a time to and fro. It is also useful with a group which is holding hands in a circle for mutual support while each person swings each leg in turn.

Wheelchair people who are redeveloping their quadriceps, the muscles above the knee which waste so rapidly after bed-rest but which are essential for effective walking, have enjoyed doing the dance 'The Can-Can' to music. The legs are straight and are moved up and down as high as possible in time to Offenbach's music, so that the exercise is performed against the pull of gravity.

The musical accompaniment helps people to persist for a longer time than if the exercise is done silently, and it also interprets for them what type of action they are intended to perform. The music can be gradually played more slowly so that there is an increasing challenge in working against gravity and muscle strength is built up. As with all other work in physical mobility, this must be discussed with the physiotherapist in case there is a group member for whom any given exertion or type of movement would be harmful.

Because treatment methods vary from one patient to another, no firm recommendations can be given. We have to adapt, improvise, develop the music to suit the needs of the moment, and always allow the physiotherapist to take the lead because, in this work, he or she alone knows what exactly is required for maximum treatment effectiveness.

Parkinson's disease: how can music therapy help?

It is not difficult to see whether or not someone suffers from Parkinson's disease. The forward-leaning posture, the difficulty in getting started as one tries to move, the tiny steps, the tremor and (often) the rigidity, the expressionless face and monotonous speaking voice, all tell us that the person is suffering from Parkinson's disease. Depression, loss of motivation and emotional numbness are common, and, for some people, dementia may occur, which adds to the physical problems. Those who are elderly at the time of onset are more at risk of dementia (Reid *et al.* 1996), and this may affect their response to interactions of all kinds, including music or other thera-peutic programmes. Although medication may bring some relief from physical problems, it is not always a complete answer, and therapists need to be aware of the complex nature of the disorder.

Parkinson's sufferers have difficulty in getting started in any activity. Their movements are slow (bradykinesia), and this may finally result in inability to move at all without major support (akinesia). Yet they are able to step quite briskly over objects or white lines on the floor because of the visual stimulus (Hurwitz 1964/1975, pp.93–98). Music has the same effect and, although the initial effect may wear off so that walking starts briskly but slows down, one can, by changing the style and volume of the music, assist the person to keep moving and even to walk faster as the music increases in speed. Music must be played or sung 'live'; no recorded music can be adjusted in this way. This approach may be used at home or in a nursing home if the family or staff are willing to sing clearly and enthusiastically to support the person's walking.

A consultant neurologist working extensively in Parkinson's disease has written of the value of music in walking, the music therapist picking up the patient's natural gait and then enhancing this, as demonstrating the phenomenon of entrainment (Swallow 1996). A few people have been able to sing 'inside their own heads' to achieve the same end but not everyone is able to do this. Dementia or depression and loss of motivation will make such an extended plan impossible to put into effect.

A somewhat similar approach, in which the patient's wife danced with him in a gentle waltz, was used with a man suffering from progressive supranuclear palsy (PSP, also known as Steele-Richardson-Olszewski syndrome), a disorder which has been mistaken for Parkinson's because there are some similarities. But in PSP, in addition to other problems, there is loss of upward and downward gaze. Because of the progressive nature of the condition no lasting change in function was expected, but it gave to both the patient and his wife the opportunity and the pleasure of holding each other and moving together without anxiety, which was otherwise impossible.

A Parkinson's support group on the outskirts of Sydney arranged for a tape of exercises with appropriate music to be recorded. I prepared it with a physiotherapist who specialised in Parkinson's, so that the benefit of group activities could be transferred to home use.

To make the speaking voice sound more normal and less monotonous, a few people have been able to think their sentences in music, with both melody and pitch, so that their speech has normal prosody. This is, of course, suited only to formal sentences which the person is able to plan ahead and the method cannot be used for spontaneous 'chit-chat', but it is useful if the affected person needs to make a brief speech at a wedding or other formal occasion.

Although initially individual work is needed, these activities are also effective in a group because there is mutual encouragement.

Huntington's disease

This inherited disease, usually becoming obvious only in adult life and characterised by jerky movements and impairment of mind and behaviour, has intense emotional implications. This is especially true for those sufferers who married without knowing that a near relative had suffered from the disease because it is often 'hidden' as Parkinson's. They know that their adult children may well develop the condition, and when those adult children have themselves had children, there is fear of the outcome for grandchildren too. Recently, the discovery of the responsible gene and the possible identification of carriers has produced new ethical dilemmas for sufferers and their families (Martin and Gusella 1986).

In Huntington's disease, music seems to have value only in emotional support. Although I have worked with many people suffering from the disorder, I have not found that music has significantly reduced the choreiform movements, although it may help the person to be less anxious.

The dementia of Huntington's is not uniform in its effects; some people appear to have more physical than cognitive disability, and others have more cognitive than physical manifestations. The disease affects people of advanced age, whether as sufferers or as relatives of sufferers, and we should encourage them to join a support group in addition to giving empathic help to the best of our ability. Sharing in a music activity may be a useful part of that support, especially because there are, in many places throughout the world, nursing homes specifically planned for Huntington's sufferers and their families, and appropriately-planned group music activities can be included in the programme.

Summary

General mobility work is often combined with a social group because it is most needed in groups of people who are demotivated or depressed but who have no specific need for physiotherapy. Because of the lack of motivation and because the people need stimulation, to incorporate segments of physical activity in a general programme is more acceptable than to have a group specifically for physical movements.

Music therapy as combined with physiotherapy is useful as a physical stimulus, especially for rhythmic work, and also as a motivating force to encourage people to persist, to deal with pain threshold, and to make their treatment procedures enjoyable rather than drudgery.

CHAPTER 13

Music for a Social Support Group Programme

Introduction

There are some special advantages in doing something with a group of other people. The human race, in general, seeks group contact. Groups can be primary, in which numbers are fairly small and there is personal contact and (often) mutual support, or secondary, in which a large membership is bound by common interests or ideals but without, usually, much personal contact between members. There may be sub-sections of such a group, such as branches of large organisations, which offer personal contact and friendship. Large hospitals or health facilities are usually secondary groups, bringing status and some feeling of solidarity, but it is only in specific units or teams that primary group bonding and support occurs.

Our membership of groups changes as life progresses, and mature people's group membership is usually of professional associations, service or social clubs and religious or informal family groups. Those who enter hospitals and nursing homes have often belonged for many years to clubs and societies, so that group relationships are familiar to them.

The group is not necessarily the universal ideal, and for those who live entirely in a herd situation, perhaps in a large institution or a nursing home with shared rooms, privacy is a rare privilege.

For those, however, who have isolation forced upon them or wish to make bonds with others but find this difficult, a special-interest group has much to offer. It also gives a sense of familiarity to those whose earlier life experiences included membership of a group of some kind. Cognitive and sensory losses increase isolation because people with hearing loss, visual loss or dementing conditions, or with combinations of these, find it difficult to achieve close relationships. Even family relationships can be impaired, so that encouragement to join in group activities can be both necessary and helpful, and it may be possible to include family members or friends.

Australia has developed a system of 'clusters', nursing homes which improve the quality of life of non-English-speaking frail elderly people. In these homes, staff and patients have a common culture, so that language, food, festivals and other customs are shared.

The group life of older people can take place in the ordinary community, in retirement communities, in day centres which have a semi-therapeutic purpose, in rehabilitation units where people remain for an extended period, in hostels (protected accommodation for the frail aged) and in extended care facilities such as nursing homes. Most retirement villages have a three-tiered system: independent living; hostel; nursing home.

People often grieve when a move from one level to the next is considered necessary because of illness or increasing frailty, and the move is made more difficult when the person, because of increasing memory loss, cannot recognise the need for greater support and believes that he or she has been managing well.

Music groups

Music is a common *raison d'etre* for groups to be established, and older people may have for many years belonged to choirs, orchestras or other music groups, so that music as a basis for group life is a normal part of their lives.

Day centres, whether these are clubs for 'seniors' or centres which provide care for elderly people in order to give respite for families, almost always include therapeutic or recreational music in their programmes, as also do some day hospitals, to which patients come for specific treatment. Hospitals and nursing homes where a music therapist is employed, or where diversional therapy is part of the programme, almost invariably include music groups in their regular programmes, although the aims and the methods used in diversional and therapeutic music groups will be somewhat different.

In retirement villages, the group may initially form spontaneously from the interests, shared by a number of residents, in study or performance, and one sees 'music appreciation' groups, choirs, chamber music groups and so on. The group will have an on-going existence and new residents will be invited to participate. In some villages, a staff member is involved in initiating and running music groups; this is helpful so long as it does not destroy the autonomy of more able residents.

In day centres, rehabilitation units and hospitals or nursing home, music may be included when the establishment is first set up, or may be added later on. Music therapists work in these settings, and volunteers or other staff may also provide help.

In psychiatric hospitals, music forms a satisfactory basis for group work, although (as described for individual work) people who suffer from manic disorder, or who are agitated, depressed or restless may not initially take part, or may participate on an 'in-and-out' basis, which we are wise to accept as part of the illness. We must again be careful lest people's defences are overwhelmed by music which elicits fears and extreme anger, but the therapist will be aware of such risks and plan sessions accordingly.

The number of people in the group affects the agenda for the group:

- In a small closed group in which trust is established, difficult topics can be openly discussed
- Groups of ten to twelve people can have programmes which are therapeutic in aim, although meeting some of those aims will be difficult if there is no permanency of membership
- In a larger open group, recreational activities and entertainment will predominate, but the trained therapist will take note of people whose responses indicate that individual work is needed.

The aims of a social group programme include:

- building of social bridges between people
- discovery of common interests so that friendships may develop outside the group
- noticing the needs of others, to avoid the self-centredness which can mar later life and its relationships
- opportunity to work together for a common goal, so that participants gain an increase in their self-esteem
- problem solving, in the context of a shared task, whether this is a musical team game or the preparation of a concert
- sharing of memories and reminiscences, tears, jokes and laughter in a supportive atmosphere
- opportunity to talk of grandchildren, adult children, friends, even though there may be competition for the opportunity to boast of grandchildren!
- increasing mobility, co-ordination and flexibility through movement with music; supporting movements through music sometimes

diminishes the psychological pain and so encourages greater range of
movement than is otherwise possible

○ increasing awareness of body-image in those who have lost this
image, or whose self-image is impaired because of brain-damage in
stroke or trauma

○ opportunity for informal physical contact between friends, holding
hands whilst doing a dance in a circle, games which involve
touching hands and so on. This is included because the opportunity
for such contact is often lost to those whose spouse has died, when
touching is restricted to nursing procedures or the occasional formal
kiss on the cheek or formal handshake.

○ inviting relatives to music group allows the family to enjoy an
activity together. This should be planned with colleagues in case
there are any personal problems.

'Case-finding' will also be part of the professional therapist's agenda. Music
has extraordinary power to elicit hidden or repressed emotions about past
experiences and present losses and, even in a group planned for socialising,
it is not uncommon to see someone crying when others are smiling. Except
in rare circumstances, we should make arrangements for private discussion
and, if necessary, formal therapeutic intervention.

The atmosphere in music therapy group work contributes to the atmosphere of a unit as a whole, so that newcomers feel generally hopeful about
the outcome. I have found, for example, that 'old' patients tell newcomers
about the weekly music group as something to look forward to. A geriatric
unit made a video about the activities and work of the unit, including music
therapy, and the excitement of the patients in seeing themselves on the screen
was significant.

Another group in the same hospital, many of whom were slightly
impaired cognitively, agreed to take part in a video about sexuality in old
age. This too was useful for the morale of those who took part. It was
interesting to see their responses to the film when it was shown to them
before being publicly released; interest seemed to be entirely focused on their
own performance rather than on the topic of the film, although the matter
had been discussed with them before filming took place.

One of the items used in the film was the Irish song 'Danny Boy', sung
to the Londonderry Air, and for technical reasons we had to sing it through
at least ten times. It was heartening to see how the group's motivation helped
them to do this when asked. To be asked to sing the same song ten or more
times in the weekly session would probably have caused a revolution!

Some cautions

The following points indicate the care which must be taken when setting up music groups:

- One should have separate groups for those with major cognitive losses and for those who are mentally alert, otherwise programme planning is difficult and the atmosphere unhelpful for participants.

- Rehabilitation patients may only want formal treatment, perceiving enjoyable activities as a waste of time, presumably on the 'No pain, no gain' principle. Cultural attitudes also influence this; some European migrants perceive the only 'real' treatment as consisting of surgical operations or of medication, administered by injections, by tablets or (in some countries) by suppositories. Occupational therapy and speech pathology are commonly seen by these migrants as mere recreation because the underlying purposes are not understood, and there are even stronger doubts when music therapy is in question. Such unwilling participants will need to have the therapeutic aims of the work explained to them privately, with reassurance that it is all right to enjoy oneself.

- It is better to have separate groups for people with major language impairment, but those with only minor problems may benefit from the stimulation of the general group.

- In arranging group work in a facility where there is a team of clinicians, we must discuss plans with our colleagues. If, for instance, we plan to do exercises to music, our duty of care demands that we discuss these with a physiotherapist who knows of any special hazards for the participants. For example:

  - Some people suffer from feelings of faintness when the arms are raised above the head because of what is called 'the sub-clavian steal'
  - A strong twisting of the ankle in a seated exercise with music can cause pain to someone who has severe arthritis in the feet and ankles
  - It is not good practice to ask an older person to perform strong, rapid head movements from side to side because of the risk of dislodging an embolus from a blood vessel in the neck and thus causing a stroke.

- We usually assume that reminiscence is enjoyable, and for many people it is a positive experience to look back at past achievements.

The confidentiality of the group must be emphasised to all participants because difficult memories may also emerge, of sadness, disappointment, frustration, regret, remorse. These too must be acknowledged, the speaker supported and given the opportunity to withdraw from the group with a supportive person available. Memories may in themselves be happy but bring sadness because they are only memories. Group work gives the opportunity for case-finding, identifying those people who need additional work on an individual basis.

○ The music group may also reveal non-emotional problems which have otherwise escaped notice, such as changes in memory status or the start of paranoid or bizarre ideas, indicating the onset of a psychiatric disorder or perhaps the presence of an infection. The music therapist will observe such changes and make appropriate recommendations after consultation with colleagues.

○ In retirement communities, the success of any music group depends upon individual temperament and intellectual capacity of members. Quarrelling is not unknown, with leadership rivalries, arguments as to what music is prepared, judgmental attitudes about music chosen by others, and other clashes. Such clashes may hinge upon diverse musical preference but also indicate lack of frustration tolerance and the beginnings of disinhibited behaviour. These do not always arise *de novo* in old age; some people have been difficult and intolerant all their lives, and it may be necessary for a professional staff member to intervene in order that others are not damaged by the conflict. I have also seen the patronising attitude of some older people who sang in the community's own nursing home, and who argued with each others as to what they should perform, speaking condescendingly of 'these poor old things' – perhaps dealing with their own fears of decrepitude by distancing themselves from the nursing home residents? Intervention may be needed.

○ If one plans a programme with a theme, this should not include matters which will causes confusion to participants who are suffering in any way from a dementing illness. I have heard of one group where a mock wedding was used as a theme, the 'bride' and 'groom' dressed accordingly. I consider this to be unethical because of the possible confusion for those whose cognitive function is impaired, who may be uncertain of the boundaries between fact and fantasy in such a situation.

○ The size and selection of the group is important. A rigorous research programme examined the outcome of reminiscence therapy in small groups, concluding that a maximum of ten people should participate, three of whom would be therapists or co-therapists (Head, Portnoy and Woods 1990). Music therapy often stimulates reminiscence, and some sessions are planned deliberately to achieve this, so that the conclusions described are relevant to our own work, although few therapists will achieve the luxury of a 1:3 ratio of staff to patients. It was found in the study cited above that most interactions were between patients and therapist rather than from patient to patient. Does this behaviour have its origins in school experiences when, at the time the subjects of the research were children, conversation between fellow pupils was forbidden and only verbal interactions with the teacher were countenanced?

○ It is useful for an observer to note the interactions which take place in a group. The form I have used, modified from Cox (1978, p.44), uses a ring of smaller circles showing the seating position of each participant in the circle, each small circle marked with the participant's initials. Arrows are drawn to symbolise interactions, the head of the arrow indicating whether, for example, A contacts B or B contacts A, or whether it is a two-way process, with also an indication of type of interaction: smile, touch, wave, verbal exchange. We need to know how many interactions there were. Was there just a fleeting glance between C and D or a series of friendly or unfriendly verbal exchanges? In an established and a balanced group, the lines between people will indicate approximately equal numbers of interactions between all group members. These will not be exclusively therapist to client or client to therapist but will include a significant number from client to client. People with special needs may stand out in such an evaluation, either as demanding more than the average share of attention or as not participating fully for some reason, which may or may not be known and may need investigation.

○ The group size is important because each member must see and hear what is happening, and also feel confident that, if he or she contributes verbally, others will hear what was said. To do this, the group should be no larger than ten people, seated in a circle. There can be recreational value in a large group, as when a concert is held, but for therapy to be achieved, in which the session is planned in order to meet the particular needs of each individual, a small group is essential. For some people, even ten is too large a number; I believe that the size of the group should be proportional to the level of cognitive functioning of the participants.

Planning the programmes

The following thoughts may be useful for those establishing a programme in different surroundings:

- For extended care in day centres and hostels, one needs variety to maintain interest, with regular features which give stability. If a group identity can be established, this survives changes of membership when some patients move or die and others are admitted. Enthusiasm about attendance carries over to newcomers so that one starts off with a 'plus' each time rather than having to explain each week, as if for the first time, what the session is all about.

- For day centres or hospitals, concerts presented by visiting musicians will be successful and enjoyable, especially if a group of young children comes to sing. The programme should be examined beforehand to ensure that the music is appropriate to the listeners and the programme not too long, especially if there are those who have problems with incontinence. As mentioned above, we must be available to support in private conversation those for whom music elicits unhappy memories.

- In rehabilitation units and psychiatric hospitals, it is generally easier to set up a small closed group which can have therapeutic aims, but when admissions are brief, one has to accept a changing membership and hope that the core participants give cohesion to the programme. The session should last not more than 45 minutes, so that an hour is needed on the timetable to allow time for gathering people together in the same room, placing them appropriately in the circle, and for preliminary toilet visits if necessary. The placement of people in the group can be important. We would not place someone who suffered from recruitment (in which loud sounds cause physical pain) next to someone with a loud drum, nor would we place someone who only speaks Italian next to someone who only speaks German!

Music chosen should be familiar to most people, selected according to their age by using resource books which give copyright dates. One should also allow for request items which may be outside that range, such as songs sung by grandchildren or heard on television and radio.

A possible pattern for a social music session is as follows:

1. Greeting of participants by name, introductions of new people to each other.

2. Music to reflect the day's weather and season of the year, encouraging people to be aware of the outside world and look out of the window.

3. Segment for mobility: one or two of the following – tapping feet, clapping hands, moving shoulders to a jazz rhythm, joining hands around the circle for a seated waltz.

4. Theme for the day: draw sketch on whiteboard, or have it already prepared; pass an item around the room which can elicit ideas for music; use a large picture or map, depending on the chosen theme. For example a rose passed around enhances tactile communication and awareness of neighbours, elicits suggestions of songs about the rose in particular or flowers in general, leads to reminiscence about growing roses, having them in a wedding bouquet or a funeral wreath, and so on.

   A map of the world leads into talk of travel, music of the homeland for migrants, memories of films seen, popular musicians and their repertoire, world events.

   Perhaps a discussion may be promoted, reminiscence about challenges one has faced and conquered in life, using music of a particular era as a stimulus to this. For instance, a song of the depression era can elicit memories of difficulties surmounted at that time.

   In one group of only five people, problems of bladder incontinence were discussed, arising from conversation about going to concerts and the fact that some people cannot go to shows or concerts because of fears that their bladder control will be inadequate. The mutual exchange of anxieties, with some laughter, led naturally into discussion of exercising of sphincter muscles, and we all practised this whilst music was played. My willingness to say 'I had this problem following childbirth so I know what it is like' added to the openness of the conversation. The following week, a woman who had spoken about the awfulness of having a leakage of urine announced proudly that she had been using her sphincter muscles several times each hour and had not had one 'accident' since the previous week.

5. Request section, either played immediately, if the therapist has sufficient repertoire and skill, or as a planning exercise for the subsequent session. The decision-making and planning is in itself therapeutic, as also is the dominant position of the group when their requests are played by the therapist, either at the time or at the next session.

    A man suffering from depression and early dementia, who had made many suicide attempts and was constantly under close observation, asked one morning for the parody on the 1912 song 'Pretty Redwing', the words of which he and his friends had sung as little children around 1916:

> O the moon shines tonight on Charlie Chaplin,
> His boots are cracking
> For want of blacking.
> And his baggy little trousers they want mending,
> Before they send him
> To the Dardanelles.

This marked a turning point in the lifting of his depression, and although his singing and the enjoyment of the group probably did not cause the change in mood, it did underline its occurrence and reinforced his feeling of well-being, giving him a changed status in the group.

6. A short section of instrumental work can be used in addition to or instead of a theme. Percussion instruments, which can be played with recorded or (better) live music, should not be the backbone of a music therapy session. Such work should occupy only a part of each session and not necessarily take place on every occasion. The distribution of instruments must be a matter of choice, whether people wish to play an instrument at all and, if so, which one.

7. Individual farewells, with thanks for particular achievements; usually each person has done something which can be commented upon as one shakes hands all round the circle.

Instrumental resources should include tambourines, maracas, chime bars tuned to a pentatonic or diatonic scale, bongo drums played by hand, drums with drumsticks. Sleigh bells on a loop of braid or plastic are useful for people with impaired hand-function or for those with tremors because the constant ringing does not impair the musical rhythms, as may occur with a strongly rhythmic instruments such as a drum. Triangles are of uncertain value because good co-ordination is needed if the instrument is not to swing wildly as the player attempts to hit it. It may be possible to hang a triangle from a stand on a table or wheelchair tray so that only one hand is needed and the instrument is fairly stable.

Instruments can be used in free creative improvisation, but it is helpful to have a theme as a starting point. Themes such as a storm, a summer day, windy days at sea, springtime, leaves in the autumn, a seed growing to maturity, have all provided a stimulus for free group improvisation, with the inclusion of movement, instrumental work and vocalisation. They have worked well for wheelchair groups as well as for those who are better able to move spontaneously. The therapist may provide instrumental backing on keyboard or guitar, or may play one of the available percussion instruments so as to avoid dominating the group's work.

Group music therapy as an adjunct to other therapies

Some people benefit from the communal therapy area in a rehabilitation unit, where several patients are having physiotherapy and occupational therapy at the same time. Although this is not a group in the true sense, since there is no shared activity, it is encouraging to see others who are having similar battles to regain mobility, or to share a large treatment plinth with someone who is working on pulleys to strengthen muscles of arms and legs. There is a feeling of companionship and shared adversity, with shared triumph when things go well. People who are self-conscious about their disabilities can be gently introduced to others with similar problems and, often, go on to adopt a new and more hopeful attitude towards rehabilitation.

I was privileged to work for several years in a hospital where music was welcomed in the rehabilitation gymnasium, usually for specific patients with particular problems where music was useful in individual therapy, but at the same time creating a cheerful positive general atmosphere which approximated to a group situation. There were, of course, times when quietness was needed because of hyper-distractibility of certain individuals, but these occurred rarely.

The observed benefits included work with:

- persons who needed the rhythm of walking emphasised
- those who had lost confidence in mobility and needed to see walking as enjoyable and not as an ordeal

- people with a global aphasia who had no comprehension of what was required of them and whose anxiety worked against successful treatment, such as passive movements of paralysed limbs

- people who found it hard to persist with pulley work and the like, and were more likely to continue if appropriate rhythmic music was played

- people suffering from pain and anxiety, e.g. after hip or knee replacement surgery, for whom music constituted a distraction, something which diverted their attention from fear and pain to the task of walking

- the creation of a cheerful atmosphere.

Benefits were also seen in a combined music therapy and physiotherapy session for the maintenance mobility group in a psychogeriatric assessment unit. The music encouraged patients to participate in the exercises and activities, and a co-operative effort between music therapist and physiotherapists proved highly successful over many years.

In rehabilitation we walk a tightrope, trying to achieve a balance between asking too much of our clients, so that they fail and experience despair and depression, and not asking enough, so that they feel humiliated, hopeless or bored. This is as true of music therapy as it is of other therapeutic interventions.

Group work should be included in any music therapy programme for geriatric patients since it provides useful social and psychological stimulus. The presence of others can reassure us, spur us on to greater efforts, provide support and comfort, and stimulate the return of awareness when this is impaired following brain damage. Group music therapy encourages the use of impaired limbs, with re-orientation and awareness of the world outside.

Should we put pressure on people to attend group activities?

There are those who never wish to be involved with any programme, and for some of them we must look for the presence of a depressive illness, sensory or cognitive losses, etc. For some people persuasion is appropriate, because even with minor depressive states there is a useful elevation of mood in a cheerful activity, once people have participated.

But group work is not universally appropriate. Those who wish to avoid participation should be allowed to do so, at least until we have if possible found out their reasons for not wishing to attend. Some may yearn for solitude, others may dislike playing percussion instruments. This is often, unwisely, made a more prominent part of the programme than is advisable, and people refuse to attend because they fear that the session is childish. For those who are frightened and depressed by an early dementing condition, any activity which seems to confirm their worst fears of entering second childhood is, understandably, anathema.

The diversity of musical taste can be responsible for many 'refusals', so that when we plan a music therapy group we must take account of this, perhaps having separate sessions in order to cater for all tastes.

Most patients in hospital or nursing home are happy to listen to other people's preferred music for a limited time because they are themselves so deeply aware of the need for individuals to be allowed their own choices in life, but we need to talk openly and explain how the session runs.

Summary

Music therapy can enhance human communication, whether this is resident to resident, patient to relative, patient or resident to staff. Group work in music therapy or recreation is a powerful tool to that end. But our groups must be small, creating an atmosphere in which persons suffering from illness can give each other mutual support and comfort, with supportive reminiscence or helping the creation of a life review.

The skills the therapist needs include understanding the underlying pathology whether of mind or body, the musical skills to meet whatever need arises in social relationships that are under strain, and empathy to present our work for maximum benefit to each individual.

Recommended reading

Bright, R. (1997) *Music Therapy in the Dementias. Improving the Quality of Life. Second Edition.* St Louis, MO: MMB Music Inc.

This textbook discusses specifically and in detail the uses of music therapy for those who have a dementing illness. This new edition includes extensive discussion of music therapy for younger persons suffering from the AIDS-dementia complex.

CHAPTER 14

Music Therapy
in the Management of Aphasia

If we wish to have a combined programme of music and speech therapy, we need to observe speech assessment sessions, to read as much as possible about this complex matter and, if possible, to talk with our speech pathologist colleagues and to observe treatment sessions so as to grasp the most effective mode of communication with aphasic persons.

Representation in the brain

For most people, even those who are left-handed, speech is organised by the left half of the brain, the dominant hemisphere, and so (because of the cross-over of nerve communication) it is a stroke affecting the right side of the body which often involves impairment of speech and communication. If we see someone who has recently had a stroke and who has a 'puffy' right hand with the arm in a sling or resting on a pillow, it is probable that there will be speech problems of some kind.

Nevertheless one observes that those with non-dominant (right) hemisphere damage also show impairment of speech communication and this has various implications:

- It indicates that the non-dominant hemisphere is involved in speech communication, although this involvement may be in matters of perception, synthesis of ideas, and the ability to perform purposive acts, which are known to lie in that side of the brain.

- It is possible that there are previously unused speech centres in the right hemisphere, which permit some recovery of speech after a left-hemisphere stroke.

○ This may help to explain the usefulness of therapy based upon music in the recovery of speech communication (Albert, Sparks and Helm 1973; Sparks, Helm and Albert 1974).

Although adaptability of the brain decreases with age, a certain amount of restitution is possible, and the role of the non-dominant hemisphere in this has been discussed, together with all other aspects of aphasia, by Kertesz (1985, pp.287–331).

Children who have had normal speech centres in the dominant hemisphere obliterated in infancy by trauma or tumours do go on to develop adequate speech, and this is further indication that there are centres in the non-dominant hemisphere at birth which have potential for development. The precise nature of cerebral dominance continues to be discussed (Gaincotti 1993).

Although it is common to refer to 'speech' impairment, in fact it is not merely the ability to speak which is impaired but, in some instances, the whole of language processing. There may be:

○ loss of speech

○ loss of comprehension of heard speech

○ loss of reading (alexia)

○ loss of writing (agraphia).

When some of these functions are damaged but language communication and processing is not completely lost, 'dysphasia' (impaired speech) is the correct descriptive word. But 'dysphasia' sounds so much like 'dysphagia' (difficulty in swallowing) that the word 'aphasia' is usually employed, even though it really means 'absence of speech'.

Stroke does not always cause loss of communicative language, but, because large areas of the brain are involved in the use and processing of words, it is common for at least some aspects of communication to be affected by damage to the dominant hemisphere, whether by stroke, tumour, accidental injury or in advanced stages of dementing illness.

The dominant, left, hemisphere is involved not only in the motor function of the right side of the body but in many other matters of cognition, of music and art, and of 'putting one's world together'.

But there is sharing of function; we do not live with total separation of the two hemispheres. Those who are compelled to do so because it has been necessary to cut through the tissue joining the hemispheres (in a commisurectomy procedure) suffer many and complex disabilities. Consequently a variety of problems can arise following a stroke, in addition to muscular weakness. Many of these are seen after damage to the non-dominant hemisphere:

- ○ loss of awareness of body image
- ○ loss of awareness of people who are sitting on one side of us (neglect)
- ○ inability to process numbers (acalculia)
- ○ difficulty in recognising objects and their use (agnosia)
- ○ difficulty in carrying out planned or requested actions (apraxia).

Because there is not complete separation of function, it is not uncommon for someone to suffer from apraxia and speech difficulties.

Some people suffer amusia (loss of understanding of music) because of damage to the music centres in the non-dominant hemisphere. It is tragic and confusing for those who have previously enjoyed music to find that music no longer makes sense but is just confused noise. One such man, a keen opera- and concert-goer said that music had become a meaningless jangle which he could not recognise at all. His anger and grief were almost intolerable to him, and caused disruption to his marriage because his wife felt she could no longer sit at home in the evenings listening to broadcast concerts or recorded music, as had been their shared habit. She either denied herself that pleasure or went for a short time to another room and listened with headphones.

Levels of speech impairment

Depending on the extent of the brain damage, there may be only a little difficulty in putting sentences together or finding the right word, 'anomia' or 'nominal aphasia'. In major ('global') impairment, however, the person can neither speak nor understand either the spoken or the written word. In the worst instances the concepts of affirmation and denial and the links with gesture are lost, and the person can no longer use meaningful gestures such as nodding for 'OK' or shaking the head 'Not OK'.

To lose even this simple form of communication severely diminishes one's capacity to control one's life, since one can no longer exercise choice in the simplest of decisions – 'Do you want a cup of tea?' Would you like a cup of coffee?' Do you want milk in it?' 'Are you cold?' 'Do you want another blanket on your bed?' One can only guess what the effects of global aphasia may be upon the personal integrity of the sufferer. It must, surely, be extraordinarily difficult or even impossible to feel oneself a whole person in this situation.

When working with aphasic patients, staff must learn to use single-phase questions which need only a nod or a shake of the head, 'Would you like some tea?' How does one indicate by gesture the answer to a two-phase question such as 'Do you want tea or coffee today?'

An unusual problem is that of jargon aphasia, in which the impaired person thinks that he is speaking normally but what emerges are unintelligible pseudo-words. The person may not realise that what he says makes no sense, and becomes confused and angry when people fail to understand him. One man hit his wife for (as he thought) refusing to do what he had asked of her.

As mentioned above, music is, in general terms, represented in the non-dominant (right) hemisphere, and is intact even when there is damage to the dominant side. People who have lost speech communication as a consequence of a stroke can therefore still enjoy music and sing songs. Sometimes this includes the words, although this is often an automatic response to hearing the melody rather than intentional. This capacity for singing was described over a century ago as a well-known phenomenon, with discussion as to whether the individual can sing the tune only or words also (Knoblauch 1890).

Music and speech

The preservation of music, despite loss of speech, can be the basis for a joint programme in music and speech, and our general aims are to:

- enhance as far as possible the return of propositional speech
- give ways of expressing emotions and make decisions by gesture or other non-verbal means for those who are unable to communicate verbally
- enhance human relationships, including inter-disciplinary work, such as consulting the occupational therapist about teaching head-scanning movements to those who are unaware of the presence of people on the affected side because of loss of part of the normal field of vision
- importantly, give an experience of success, enhance self-worth.

If we plan to use singing to give confidence to an aphasic person, the words must already be familiar. One severely speech-impaired woman named Mary (whose only speech was a meaningless 'yes') loved to sing the song 'Her name was Mary', gaining (or regaining?) a sense of identity by doing so. Home visits by the music therapist to the nursing home also helped her, because the staff realised for the first time that there was a sense of humour and a capacity for enjoyment which had not been suspected as long as she was seen only as 'that aphasic who can only say "yes", and it never means anything anyway!'

Although singing for aphasic people may be an automatic process without comprehension of the words used, some people are able to recognise the meaning of the words they are using. They can monitor their own verbal communication and, in rare instances, can use singing to convey information. One such man sang spontaneously 'Happy Birthday to You' to a fellow-patient when they met in the combined speech therapy and music therapy group, pointing so that the rest of the group would know to whom he was singing.

On another occasion, when group members were choosing songs for each other, the same man pointed to another patient who came from Scotland and sang the first line of 'I belong to Glasgow' as his way of asking the group to sing for that man.

Speech pathology assessment will reveal the nature and the severity of impairment to the many skills involved in the use of word and language. The extent of impairment to language and communication skills varies greatly, depending upon the degree and extent of brain damage; some have only a minor impairment, others have a major difficulty. From the assessment we shall know whether, and to what extent, a person is able to understand what is said, is able to speak, able to read and understand the written or printed word, able to write, to name objects which are seen and to understand their use, and so on. (When a person is given a comb, for example, we see whether he or she looks at it blankly or uses words or gesture to indicate combing the hair.)

One unusual physician tested aphasic patients for the ability to read and understand the written word by writing on a piece of paper the words 'Kiss me'. He said that he knew, from the expression on the person's face, whether or not the words had been understood. He explained, however, that nobody had ever actually complied with the instruction!

Most aphasic people who attend music therapy in a rehabilitation unit will have already been assessed by a speech pathologist, or are awaiting assessment. However, if we are working in a nursing home, this assessment may be long past, and improvement in communication may or may not have occurred in the meantime. If this is so, we shall need to carry out our own pragmatic procedure, based on what we observe in ordinary situations, so that we can find out whether or not the person understands what we say, whether the person has any expressive speech, and, if so, whether it is useful speech – whether the person understands the meaning of the words that he or she is using.

We must be on the look-out for the condition called apraxia, in which a severely affected person hears the words but cannot carry out any planned movement when asked or instructed to do so. The condition is bewildering to the onlooker:

- An apraxic person who feels a fly on the face will brush it away automatically (an unthinking, unplanned gesture), yet if asked to place the same finger on the same area of the face, will not be able to do so because an instruction has been given and the movement has become a planned response.

- An apraxic person will pick up a grape and put it in the mouth if it is there on the lunch tray, but if instructed 'Pick up that grape and put it onto your tongue' will not be able to do so.

A simple test of the capacity to understand words in someone who lacks expressive speech is to say something which would normally elicit a bodily response, but at the same time being careful to avoid giving any actual instructions (because of apraxia) or any visual cues which may be used to work out the meaning of what one has said.

One might, for example, say (without looking towards the window as a cue), 'I think it looks very much like rain from that grey sky outside', to which the normal response would be to look out of the window. Because we made a statement rather than asking a question, we are less likely to be misled by the person who, unable to understand the words, tends to reply to anything which sounds like a question with a meaningless 'Yes' or 'No'.

The person whose comprehension is intact and who has retained some expressive speech will turn the head to look out of the window and then use words to give an opinion, so that we know whether speech is understood and what capacity there is for expressive speech. The person who has lost the power to speak but whose comprehension is more or less intact will respond physically by looking out of the window, and then indicate an opinion by gesture (nod in agreement, shake the head in disagreement or even mime surprise).

The person suffering from global aphasia will not make any physical effort to look out of the window and, if there is a change of facial expression, it is likely to be a change to confusion or anxiety. Because we have not given a direct instruction, so that any response is automatic rather than planned, the apraxic person will probably look out of the window in response to our remarks. (See comments above on apraxia.) Whether there will also be a verbal or gestural response will depend on the extent of speech impairment, but at least one knows whether basic comprehension is intact.

Many other ideas could be used, but this suggestion stresses the need for simplicity and the avoidance of both non-verbal cues and verbal instructions.

One of the reasons that relatives often become confused about an aphasic person's comprehension is that family members, without realising it, are using visual cues by gesture to support their speech. When the aphasic person interprets correctly what that gesture means, relatives assume that the words themselves have been understood. For example 'Would you like another cup of tea?' is often (unconsciously) supported by the gesture of tipping up the teapot and holding out one's hand for the empty cup. The responses confuse relatives who think that it is their speaking rather than the gesture which has been understood, and then wonder why the person seems to understand one sentence but not another.

Those who do not understand the complexities of aphasia and assume that the only difficulty is in articulation sometimes ask, 'If he can't speak, why don't you give him a pen and paper and he can write what he wants to say?' Although it is not completely unknown, it is very rare for someone with major language dysfunction to be able to express thoughts clearly in writing.

Difficulty with naming objects can produce surprising results. A man who wanted his reading spectacles but could not think of the correct word described them as 'those things you put on your ears to help you see better.' It seemed amusing that he could produce this complicated sentence yet not the name of the object, but to him it was far from humorous.

Expressive aphasia, in which one understands heard speech but cannot put thoughts into words, can be cruelly frustrating to the sufferer and Ritchie (1960) describes the horror of being addressed in baby talk by a nurse who assumed that, because he could not speak, he should be addressed in childish words. As his speech started to return he sometimes used the wrong word and could hear himself doing so; this was distressing but, as his diary shows, the capacity to express himself did return, and with it his feelings of being once more a whole person.

Supporting and giving explanations to relatives of those who have suffered any kind of disability through a stroke, and especially to relatives of those whose communication skills are impaired, is important. By giving this help, we make it more likely that new relationships will be established, and less likely that relationships will break down because of the strangeness of the new behaviour and the acquired disabilities.

Aphasic migrants may lose acquired skills and comprehend only the speech of their original homeland, though this is not universally true. I have seen people for whom the reverse has occurred – the native language has been lost and the communication skills which are retained are in the acquired language. This may perhaps depend upon the length of time the person has been speaking the 'new' language.

Confusion also arises when an aphasic person is able to use automatic speech, the phrases and words which are mediated from the non-dominant hemisphere. These are usually not strongly communicative and consist of expletives or of cliches such as 'how are you' when seeing a familiar face, but to the uninformed family member these words can seem to indicate a rapid return of speech. Sadly, this hope is sometimes misplaced and the extent of recovery does not match the expectations.

Some aphasic persons have difficulty with the meaning of speech; although they understand the separate words, they do not understand the total meaning of the entire sentence. Consider the sentence: 'The man killed the dog.' In which 'direction' is the sentence going? Did the dog kill the man or the man kill the dog? To the unimpaired person the order of words gives that information, but the aphasic person is frequently unable to sort this out – even though he knows the meaning of the separate components of 'man', 'dog' and 'killed', who killed whom remains a mystery.

We cannot know fully the difficulties experienced by people with extreme communication difficulties. Failure to develop language in those who are congenitally deaf can lead to a form of functional retardation (Sacks 1990, p.8), so we know that abstract and complex thought processes probably require a use of language.

Some people think naturally in pictures and symbols and it may be that, for such people, dominant hemisphere stroke is less destructive than for the person who has always thought in words. But at present we have no accurate way of entering the world of global aphasia.

Bridging the communication gap

There is a difference between aphasia and dysarthria; the latter involves difficulty in speaking but without any loss of language, and this can happen after a stroke. (Someone who is intoxicated has a temporary dysarthria with slurred speech and so on, but knows what the words are that he is trying to say.) There is also a condition called aphonia, in which the vocal chords are paralysed and no sounds can be produced. For dysarthric or aphonic persons, writing or using the keyboard of a typewriter or computer, using a mouthstick if the hands are without function, enhances communication by printed words, because language itself is intact.

Melodic intonation therapy (MIT) makes use of the representation of music in the non-dominant hemisphere, by teaching aphasic persons who have good auditory comprehension and who understand the meaning of the words they hear or sing, first to sing sentences, then to chant them and, finally, to change to normal speech prosody – speech with normal emphasis, rhythm and pitch.

The approach was proposed in the mid-1970s (Sparks, Helm and Albert 1974) and is still in use, but the initial excitement experienced by speech specialists and others when this method was first propounded has not, it seems, been generally maintained, although considerable success was reported from the Veterans Affairs Hospital in Topeka, Kansas, USA (Krauss and Galloway 1982).

The reasons for the uneven success rate are probably varied:

- Not all aphasic persons are suitable subjects because of the need for auditory discrimination and comprehension
- There is a need for constant drilling and repetition, and this is not always possible outside a research unit or a laboratory situation
- It is essential that the singing-chanting approach be used consistently by all staff and relatives. Not all are able or willing to do this, because of lack of time, embarrassment and so on.

I worked for a time with a man who was the ideal subject; he was unable to speak but had perfect auditory comprehension. He was thus able to follow the MIT method, was able first to sing and then to chant and finally to speak fairly normally a number of useful phrases, with comprehension as to what those phrases meant and how they would be used in conversation.

Unfortunately, however, the staff in the unit where he was living said that they 'felt utter nongs' (Australian slang for feeling stupid) when they were asked to encourage him to sing sentences like 'I need to go to the toilet' or 'I'd like some sugar in my tea' and were not able to maintain the work. One can sympathise with them and their feelings. Their difficulties underline the problems of working in the melodic intonation method in the ordinary hospital or nursing home situation. I have, however, had some limited success with a few people who have found satisfaction in singing a 'Hullo' song to visiting relatives, as part of a total music therapy and speech pathology programme.

The programme

At one time I worked at War Memorial Hospital in Sydney in a small rehabilitation unit. In this unit, working with two successive speech pathologists, Mary Minns and Carmel Moore (to whom I express my gratitude), a one-hour programme was devised, which might be adapted and used by others. (In the description that follows, I use male pronouns simply to avoid clumsy circumlocutions like 'he or she'.)

In the session, run jointly by the speech pathologist and me, we used music to enhance social relationships and general communication, including the expression of feelings. The specific aims were:

- to provide some means of communication for emotions in an acceptable way, through appropriate gestures
- to stimulate comprehension of communication through the sensory pathways of sight, hearing, touch and smell
- to encourage social interaction between group members through eye contact, touch and, if possible, through some level of verbal communication
- to enhance physical movement and a sense of the total body, despite the weakness or paralysis of one side
- for some people, to enhance the understanding of what was required of them in physiotherapy programmes
- to enhance the use of language, to the extent possible for each individual
- to enhance the use of gesture to express emotion. (It is difficult to express one's emotions, and a man suffering from jargon aphasia who attacked his wife for not understanding what his speech meant was greatly helped by being taught gestures to express anger in a socially acceptable manner.)
- to provide an experience of success and fun.

Although there were usually six participants in the sessions, all without expressive speech but retaining substantial comprehension of heard speech, on rare occasions there were one or two extra, who were accepted only if their level of communication matched that of the existing members. (In hindsight it would have been better to maintain a closed group.)

Of the six members, usually two or three of them were in-patients and four or three were day-hospital patients. The mixture of populations was helpful in that those who were still in-patients saw and were encouraged by the progress achieved by those who had graduated to day-hospital treatment. With two therapists, six is a workable size for this type of work. All patients had received speech assessment on admission and at intervals subsequently, and these assessments were discussed by both therapists.

Assessment of music skills had been carried out to determine how many participants were able to sing words despite their aphasia, and their auditory comprehension was assessed. This was done by choosing songs (assumed to be familiar to the participants and verified by discussion with relatives) which mentioned colours, and the person was offered a fan of colour slips (such as are used in choice of paint colours for decorating houses) to see whether he could pick out the appropriate colour to match the words of a song, such as 'Two Little Girls in Blue' 'The Blue Danube', 'My World is Blue', depending upon the age of the client.

Other songs were used with appropriate pictures, to see whether the person could pick out the picture to match the words he had been singing. Results of these assessments were always the same as those which the speech pathologist had done for auditory comprehension, but the method was originally devised when I was working alone and is still of value to the music therapist working in isolation.

The perception of rhythm and pitch were also assessed because they affect speech prosody, the 'music' of language. The person with severe rhythmic and pitch impairment gives atypical emphasis to parts of words, words and sentences. This rarely affects comprehension by relatives but it affects comprehension by those who are unfamiliar with the peculiarities of that person's speech.

Rhythm was tested by giving a person a tambour and (by gesture) encouraging him to bang it while music was played on the piano. This test is necessarily simple to allow for the inability of the aphasic person to comprehend instructions, and to allow for the possible presence of agnosia and apraxia. Some people were able to follow complex rhythmic patterns, familiar and unfamiliar, but others were not.

Pitch was tested by encouraging the person to sing a song at several different pitches in turn, to see whether he could match any of these and, secondly, where his comfortable vocal range lay, since to have a song played impossibly high or low will discourage even an enthusiast from trying to join in. (Many song-books have the music pitched incorrectly, suited only to a cathedral choirboy, and the therapist must be able to transpose music to a comfortable pitch.)

Nobody was rejected from participation in the work because of lack of auditory comprehension, but, in planning the programmes, assessment of all aspects was necessary in order to avoid setting up a failure situation for any clients and also to allow us to evaluate improvements which took place.

The presence of apraxia was also evaluated, since this condition makes it difficult for the sufferer to copy movements, whether these are in playing musical instruments or in the capacity to reproduce movements of mouth and tongue, which is normally tested as part of speech pathology assessment.

Lateral agnosia or neglect is seen mainly in persons with non-dominant hemisphere lesions, and unlikely in speech-impaired persons, but this was verified. The presence of hemianopia (loss of part of the visual field) was checked by reading clinical reports from the orthoptist (if available) or from other records, and by testing in the speech therapy department. It was important to avoid placing anyone in such a position that he was unaware of his neighbour in the circle because of lateral agnosia or neglect or because of loss of visual fields.

Organising the sessions

For each session the room was set up with the seats placed in a horseshoe shape, with spaces left for persons who would arrive in wheelchairs. Placement of patients in the group can affect the atmosphere and outcome of the group, so that one would not place as neighbours two people with global aphasia but rather place them alternately with those who have a fair level of comprehension.

When clients arrived, their names were written on the whiteboard, using normal upper and lower case letters, since people do not learn to read with capitals and we might have caused confusion by using them inappropriately. Each person was reminded of the names of other participants and then, in turn, was encouraged to count the names on the board and match each name with each face.

A basket of percussion instruments was placed in the room where the session was to take place, and sketches were sometimes prepared on the whiteboard, ready for a quiz section. Ulverscroft large-print songbooks were on a table ready for use, and even those persons who were, at that stage, unable to read were helped to follow the printed words by one of the therapists running her finger along under the words as songs were sung. The session lasted a total of one hour, including gathering people together, so that the time in therapy was approximately 45 minutes. The session varied in content so that there was no rigid routine.

It was of vital importance for much of the work that music to be included should be known to the participants. In general it can be assumed that one will recall songs or other items of music which were popular in one's early adult life, but there are some songs, still popular and well-remembered, which far predate one's own adult life, presumably because parents or grandparents sang them, or because they are part of the traditional culture. Thus many songs which date from World War I or earlier are still well-known and can be sung by those of British or Australian descent. These include 'Daisy Daisy, give me your answer, do!' from the late nineteenth century; 'It's a long way to Tipperary' from 1912; 'Pack up your troubles in your old kitbag!' from World War I, and so on.

The programme included such components as:

- sentence (song-title) completion. This was helpful for persons with severe impairment and was gradually made more difficult as improvement was observed. At first, for example, one might say, 'How about we have that song, 'It's a long way to Tipper...', and the client was often able immediately to complete the missing part of the word, finishing it as Tipperary. The task was made gradually more complex and it contributed markedly to the use of language with comprehension.

- moving to music of different types, wiggling shoulders and hips to a jazz rhythm; raising the impaired right hand with the intact left hand to give passive movement and sensory stimulation; holding hands around the circle for a waltz. This was planned with care, since most participants had severely impaired function in the right hand. By careful placement it was possible for each person to use his own left hand to hold and perhaps to move the inactive right hand of his neighbour so that a complete contact around the circle was possible. This physical contact and movement encouraged a whole-body image.

- singing well-known songs, with gestures. 'My Blue Heaven' was one of the songs which proved highly successful, with much laughter as different people produced different gestures to represent words of the song. Those whose comprehension was impaired were able to enjoy copying the actions of others, even if, because of apraxia, some of the actions were a little unusual!

- quiz sessions involving pictures on the white board. This quiz section of the programme proved to be the most important of all the components of the therapy. To save time, the pictures were sometimes prepared beforehand, but to have one of the therapists draw whilst participants watched was far more stimulating, and worth the extra minutes it took. There was always laughter as the sketches were drawn because neither of us was very good at drawing, and the apparent sense of superiority was valuable. How seldom do hospital patients get the chance to laugh at the staff's incompetence!

As the first step of the therapy, only pictures were drawn, and the group members had to work out what song was intended. We drew, for example, a horse and cart, a church with a spire, a rose, a dog, an umbrella, a boat. On one occasion I drew what was intended to be the crescent of the new moon, but one participant assumed it was something else and began to sing the song 'Yes we have no bananas!' The laughter which followed was probably more therapeutic than any other event of that day's programme. Music was then played which matched the pictures, and participants were encouraged to sing the words, and to point to the picture which was appropriate to the song.

Each part of the world has its own songs which are known to local people. Those suggested here may be inappropriate for the therapist working in the USA or Canada, but the approach is still valid. Note that most of the songs should be appropriate to the preference, age and experience of the participants, not necessarily the preference of the therapist.

Picture	Songs
A rose	Yellow Rose of Texas
	Roses are Blooming in Picardy
	Rambling Rose
	Paper Roses
	The Rose (film theme)
Church	Get Me to the Church on Time
	Little Church around the Corner
	In the Chapel in the Moonlight
	Hymn tunes
Dog	How Much is that Doggie in the Window?
	Daddy Wouldn't Buy Me a Bow-wow
	Television advertisement jingles for dog food
Horse and cart	The Surrey with the Fringe on the Top
	Horsey, Horsey, Don't You Stop
Horse only	Any cowboy songs
Umbrella	September in the Rain
	Raindrops Keep Falling on My Head
	Singing in the Rain

Boat   Cruising down the River on a Sunday Afternoon
                              Moonlight Bay
                              Michael, Row the Boat Ashore
                              The Skye Boat Song

Although television jingles are songs of the moment, their constant repetition leads people to recall them fairly easily, and it is helpful to use some up-to-date tune to make use of more recent memory traces with the visual stimuli to match, in addition to the well-known items discussed above.

The challenge is to recognise the words one is singing, perhaps by automatic verbal output, and then to match it with the picture which those words describe. As participants in the group became more aware of the connections between what they saw, what they heard and what they sang, the quiz was extended by writing on the board the titles or first lines of the songs, but not in the same order that the pictures appeared. Usually the titles were written in a block in the centre of the board with the pictures around the edge, and numbered.

As the music was played, a group member who could walk and knew the answer would walk to the board and draw a line from the words to the picture, or someone who was unable to walk could either point to the words or hold up the correct number of fingers to match the number of the picture when the song was played and sung, or be wheeled in his wheelchair up to the board to point it out without help.

This programme proved highly effective in linking the words which were sung, the sounds which were heard from other people's singing and the music itself with the picture which symbolised the song's theme.

Objects with particular texture or aroma were also used to link with songs, and sometimes, instead of pictures on the board, real objects were used, which could be passed around the circle. Suitable objects included:

- a teabag for the song 'Tea for Two'

- a packet of sugar for the song 'Ain't She Sweet', or any song which talks about 'My sugar' or the Disney film song 'A Spoonful of Sugar Makes the Medicine Go Down'

- an old straw hat, to link with the Shirley Temple song of that name; trying this on in turn proved a source of fun! And so on.

The programme was highly therapeutic because it stimulated awareness of the presence of other people and the social exercise of passing things on in turn, with all that this involves: looking at each other, smiling, being willing to relinquish the object, the touch of hands as the exchange is made and, for some, gestures or spoken comments. All of these are of value to an aphasic person, especially if wheelchair bound, when social contacts may otherwise be restricted.

Ideas for this aspect of work in aphasia are limited only by the therapist's imagination and the local knowledge of songs, and there is a strong feeling of success amongst group members when the session has been carefully planned. It is important to make sure that all these activities are acceptable to participants – that they are not seen as childish but as challenges to be met in an atmosphere of laughter and achievement.

Expressing difficult feelings

In the expression of emotions, sketches again proved helpful. On some occasions, three faces were drawn – one happy, one sad, and one angry. These were used in different ways.

- I improvised music to symbolise these three basic emotions, the speech pathologist pointing to the facial expression and emotion which was being demonstrated
- The appropriate sketch was pointed out, and (whilst the improvised music continued) the speech pathologist modelled actions which could be used to communicate these emotions to others in a socially acceptable manner:

    (a) for anger: a fist with the thumb firmly pointed down and a slight thump on the arm of the wheelchair or table

    (b) for sadness: chiefly a modelling of the facial expression with some hand gestures to support this such as handkerchief to the eyes

    (c) for happiness: the hand with the thumb up, perhaps an arm wave and a broad smile.

Gestures for 'yes' and 'no' were also taught with appropriate improvised music to reinforce the feeling of affirmation or refusal. The gestures used were both the thumb up and thumb down, and the nod or shake of the head.

The next more advanced and complex step was to improvise music for the three faces without pointing to the selected emotion, and in a different order from that of the pictures on the white board. Participants were asked both to point at the picture which matched the music, then to adopt a facial expression which corresponded with the picture. Actions were also encouraged and each person was allowed to do his own thing, rather than copying the stereotypic action initially presented by the therapists.

This education as to how one can express feelings, especially sadness and anger, in a socially acceptable way was one of the chief aims of this programme. Some aphasic people appear to feel that they must always be pleasant and cheerful in order to be acceptable to relatives and staff, but the pretence which this may entail causes great strain. Others are frankly aggressive and even physically violent towards those who care for them, although this is more commonly towards relatives than towards staff.

To be able to express feelings of sadness, frustration and anger in a way which will be understood and accepted can prevent episodes of aggression or utter despair. Thumping the arms of the wheelchair was commonly used as a way of externalising anger, and grunts of rage were also used. Even if these gestures were in fact only used in the therapy session, they brought relief because they were permitted as representing normal and acceptable feelings. This is reassuring to those who fear that anger will lead to rejection.

This work made a useful introduction to musical instruments – participants were encouraged to choose an instrument and improvise on it to express the emotions selected. Drums and cymbals were usually chosen for anger, chime bars or bells were often played softly for sadness, tambourines and maracas for happiness, but there is no set pattern for people's choice and much depends upon how the instrument is used as to what emotional effect is produced.

The session then went on to other music; participants were encouraged to improvise on the instruments, not merely to thump away in time with the music being played. To increase auditory awareness, an essential feature of re-education in verbal communication, the speed and the volume of the music were altered without warning and people were expected to play accordingly. This brought laughter, but there was an underlying therapeutic purpose, that of encouraging people to listen to sounds carefully and monitor their own performance so as to match what was being played.

Sometimes familiar tunes were played, but sometimes I improvised pictorial music, group members being encouraged to play or to move in accordance with the theme, which might be expressed on the whiteboard as a picture or in words which were then carefully enunciated.

Some movements with imagery were greatly enjoyed. One such case consisted of a picture being drawn and described in spoken words, of seeds lying dormant in the ground, and then growing as Spring arrives. Upward stretching movements of the body accompanied the improvised music to represent that growth. This possibly had symbolic meaning for participants, who were encouraged to see the movement as typifying the development of themselves in the total rehabilitation and adjustment process.

Evaluation

Video records of a series of six sessions following the programme design were assessed by independent observers. Their observations noted that, over the series of sessions, there were improvements in:

- eye contact between members of the group
- touch between members of the group
- facial expressiveness of individuals
- sharing of jokes between members of the group; when something interesting or amusing happened, there was an increasing tendency for group members to turn towards each other to share the joke rather than looking only at one or other of the therapists
- willingness to join in the activities
- efforts to speak
- helpfulness to group members; when the more mobile members of the group were dancing together in a simple folk dance, one man reached out to a man in a wheelchair and held his hand so that the couple became a threesome.

Each session was preceded by morning coffee and followed by lunch in the Day Hospital dining room and participants were observed by independent observers during these social times. Although the observations were not consistent it appeared that, in the first two sessions, there was greater freedom of communication through gesture and attempted speech during lunch after the session than at the coffee break which preceded it. As the series of sessions continued, however, this differential effect diminished because people felt comfortable with each other straight away while they had coffee together, as the result of previous sessions, and no longer required the music and speech therapy session to achieve feelings of friendship towards each other.

Although it was not possible to transform the group members from non-talkers to skilled conversationalists, there was a clear improvement in several communication skills, and, more particularly, in the morale of the participants. Even if speech did not change dramatically, their willingness to try to speak, to enjoy the communication that was open to them and their sharing of human experiences with other group members was valuable.

The work is open to enormous development depending upon the imagination and musical skills of the therapist, and upon the extent of improvement by the aphasic persons. One can embark upon such a programme of combined therapy in the expectation that there will be substantial benefits in a wide range of behaviours and communication skills. Hurwitz (1971, pp.56–65) wrote of the joy which music brings to the aphasic person, and this has indeed been my experience.

Resources

Large-print song books. Published by Ulverscroft Large Print Books Ltd., Leicester LE7 7FU, UK.

Music and words or words-only editions.

Signorelli, R. (ed) (1997) *Exploring Our World with Song: A Multicultural Songbook*. Leichandt, Australia: Uniting Church Homes.

Music and words, or words-only editions (both have words in English and from the original languages), large print.

CHAPTER 15

Terminal Care
Can We Retain our Wholeness?

Perceptions about death and dying

Although no health professional would share their perception, people who have suffered a major disability and lost their independence may perceive themselves as dying. Some people who feel like this have had a life-long belief in the work ethic, and think that someone who is no longer productive, no longer able to help his fellow beings, is unworthy of continued existence. But others who share those feelings are depressed, and need professional help because their thoughts can lead to a wish for death either by suicide or euthanasia. We know, however, that in terminal illness the desire for death is significantly diminished when depression is dealt with (Chochinov *et al.* 1994). Cheering-up and distraction must be used only when depression and real causes for sadness and grief have been acknowledged and, if possible, dealt with.

The person who has been in hospital for a long time with a terminal illness may become out-of-touch with relatives, partly because his or her life becomes centred upon the institution. A middle-aged woman said of visits to her dying father, 'When I go to see Dad he seems more interested in whether his nurse will have a nice night out with her boyfriend than in what I have been doing!'

Visitors may be overawed by equipment around the bed. There is a feeling that someone with oxygen mask, drips or monitors is no longer the person with whom one shared everyday life. Relatives also have difficulty in knowing what to do or say to the dying person, and sometimes we see pretence on both sides in an attempt to protect each other. In one such instance the man knew that he was dying and really wanted to discuss his will and other plans for the future with his wife but did not know how to start the conversation because he did not want to upset her. She did not want to discuss his impending death, ostensibly to save him distress, but, probably, because she had no idea how to talk about it to him and was frightened of saying the wrong thing.

Music therapy facilitated openness so that they were able to drop the pretence, allowing the man to talk about his hopes for his wife's future and that of their adult sons, and to renew the emotional closeness which had been strained by his long fight against cancer. Such mutual pretence is not restricted to elderly people; it happens in terminal care at all ages, especially between parents and dying children.

The person who is dying and the person who is severely disabled share a need to come to terms with what life has been like, acknowledging both failure and success as they seek self-acceptance and closure. We must facilitate without forcing, giving each person the opportunity to look back if he so wishes but allowing privacy and even secrecy if that is what the individual asks. The shared music from the past is particularly valuable because it puts people back into the past relationship, to the time before illness led to strain.

Music is associated with so many life events that it gives form and shape to a life review. Items of music which have associations with events or stages of life are played, and the person then talks about the events and memories evoked by the music. This can be recorded on tape so that it can be left to the family as a concrete memento of that person's life, and some have also included photographs, sketches or collage. Collage consists of pictures of all kinds fixed to sheets of paper, often with addition of sketches and words, and can become an intensely personal document.

Conversation takes place while working on recordings and collage so that we have an opportunity for informal counselling, as patient and therapist gain fresh insights into the life-story, its battles, relationships, achievements and failures.

One man, dying from an inoperable malignancy in the cervical spine, put together a total of nine hours taping of music and reminiscence (partly working with the therapist and partly working alone), and this became a legacy to his daughters. As the work progressed, his attitude toward illness and death changed from extreme anger to some measure of acceptance.

Another patient who had worked at a collage over several days had selected the music to accompany the art-work; she wished to die whilst listening to that music, and in fact was able to do so. (I am grateful to Kirstin Robertson-Gillam, RMT, for describing this case and for other thoughts, and also to Meg Toon, RMT, for shared discussion on hospice care.)

Pain control and management

To use music therapy in pain control is common in terminal care, for people of all ages. The way music is selected and presented will be affected by several factors, such as individual preference for music style, associations with specific items, aphasia which inhibits verbal communication and so on. To involve the person in choice of music is the best approach since music one dislikes will not be helpful to relaxation. If the person is unable to express a preference because of aphasia, relatives can usually give us some idea of what will or will not be suitable.

Research on coping strategies in chronic pain revealed that these are not age-related. People who say they are able to cope with pain were shown to have lower levels of perceived pain and of depression, whereas those who tended to catastrophise problems had higher levels of psychological distress and of pain as well as higher levels of depression (Keefe and Williams 1990). The research also showed that self-talk about being able to cope was more helpful that mere distraction from pain.

This finding adds weight to the belief that the active use of music, to enhance feelings of control and self-esteem and to give opportunities for creativity and decision-making, is more effective in pain control than merely playing music to mask, for the time being, unpleasant thoughts.

The value of visual imagery combined with music as being of assistance to terminally ill patients has been described (Munro 1984; Porchet-Munro 1988). Both music and verbal input are used, and usually there is a spoken induction by the therapist which enhances the relaxing effect of the music.

Creating a peaceful atmosphere to enhance relaxation is a learned skill for the therapist, and since there may be visual imagery with associations that are far from relaxing, preliminary discussion is needed. As with choice of the music itself, family advice is helpful if the person is without speech.

Some people feel most relaxed when imagining themselves walking through a quiet forest, others when they envisage the seashore with gentle waves and seabirds hovering in the air. Others prefer to imagine themselves in a quiet garden with their favourite flowers in bloom, but some may feel happiest when remembering participation in an activity which is actually noisy and vigorous, and this remembered satisfaction brings its own peace.

The positive attitude towards ability to cope with pain is appropriately included in the verbal content of the relaxation work. Because the therapist cannot always be present when relaxation is needed, the preparation of music and verbal induction on tape is useful. Some people are in shared accommodation where total solitude is impossible, so that headphones achieve some separation from a noisy environment. The adverse feelings of some older people about 'equipment' can prevent the use of the headphones, and it may or may not be possible to use a tape player without headphones in the normal room. If necessary we must arrange opportunities for open listening if the patient can be moved to a room where others will not be disturbed.

Angry patients

Although the extremes of anger and self-isolative behaviour are uncommon in terminal care, some people are irritable and difficult, and people may also hide their angry feelings about untimely death and disappointment. We need to plan appropriate strategies. If there is an opportunity for individual work, it is helpful to find out, if possible, the reasons for hostility and withdrawal. When one learns the life story, the response is often better understood. It may, for example, be deflected from anger with life itself and its mode of ending. Encouraging people to talk about their reasons for anger and self-isolation may be all that is needed, or it may become clear that the patient needs in-depth counselling about a major emotional trauma, with permission to ventilate and perhaps gain some acceptance of whatever has caused the anger.

- One man's anger was focused upon the time at which food was served, but after he was given permission to ventilate his anger about death itself, anger with the kitchen staff evaporated.

- Another man was irritable because of changes of staff, but when he was allowed to talk of his disappointment in being so ill and thereby losing control of his life, and was also given a timetable of staff rosters so that he knew whom to expect on duty each morning, his anger disappeared.

- The anger of another man was found to have its origin in the statement that he had only three weeks to live, which was untrue and in any case an ill-advised statement. Having put his affairs in order and prepared himself for death, he became angry when life did not end.

Therapists find that people in a shared room seldom object to the sound of music therapy. They enjoy hearing music which is being played for someone else, and it may be possible to make contact with an angry person through the sharing of music in this way. But there are some who object strongly to what they see as disturbance. Some (but not all!) angry people are helped by an indirect approach and benefit from being asked for permission to play for the person in the next bed. This is often granted, and in many instances the isolative person first joins in the conversation, then asks for special pieces of music until ultimately he or she is ready to have individual music therapy.

If we are able to facilitate open discussion of the problems, the antagonism (whether generalised or specific) may well disappear. But if this is not effective, we can try another non-confrontational approach, such as 'I know you prefer not to have music, and it is fine to make your own decision, but I wonder whether you could give me an idea of what irritates you – it might help me to organise things better to know where you think that I am going wrong!'

The replies vary widely, and some may be unflattering: 'You don't play nearly as well as I used to and it makes me mad to listen'; 'My wife and I used to go to concerts together and now she is dead I don't want to hear any more music'; 'They tell me I am dying; I don't want to think about it, and the music makes me think'.

One angry lady was grieving over the loss of her piano-playing as a consequence of her illness, and wanted nothing to do with music because of her loss. After ventilation and counselling she came eventually to realise that she still had something to offer to others through her knowledge and, in helping me to plan music sessions for other people, came to an acceptance of her own mortality.

Some people need to maintain their anger or their denial of impending death to the very end. If we yearn to change this, it may be because we are trying to meet our own needs rather than theirs. For some therapists it is difficult to be non-judgmental, and I feel that the work of Kubler-Ross has been over-interpreted. It is seen as necessary for all terminally ill persons to go through all the stages of grief, in the same order, and following exactly the same timetable. If, however, we are to be true therapists, we allow people to make their own decisions, even if these do not fit the theoretical process of: denial, anger, bargaining and final acceptance.

The comatose patient

If we are asked to play to a previously unknown and comatose person, whose preference for music is unknown, the ethical position is complex. The capacity of the apparently unconscious person to hear what is going on makes it inadvisable to play songs which emphasise, for example, human love and the loss or gain of love, because these may have unhappy associations and there is no way in which resolution can be achieved.

If it is impossible to ask relatives about known preference, the therapist may decide that it is better not to play lest the music make the dying process harder. But if one does decide to play, the music should be, to the best of one's knowledge, emotionally neutral, instrumental (rather than vocal) items from music described as 'easy-listening' but also chosen with the ethnic and religious background of the individual in mind. It would, for example, be highly inappropriate to play Schubert's 'Ave Maria' to a person of Buddhist faith.

An elderly Polish man, expected to die within a few hours, was apparently unconscious, but I sat on the edge of the bed and sang softly to him the Polish religious song of his childhood which he had requested in the weeks beforehand. Each time this had been played for him he cried, yet each subsequent session he asked for it again. As I sang the song, he sobbed aloud, despite his apparently comatose state, and my thoughts were ambivalent: was it unkind to sing that song or was it evidence of my personal care for him? He had always asked for that song and had always cried when it was played, so perhaps my actions were correct.

Staff of the unit said they were glad for him that I had sung. All they could do was procedures such as two-hourly turns, pain-killing injections and the like, whereas that song was personal, a gift to him from me. They believed, and I came to share that belief, that death was made easier for him by hearing again his beloved childhood hymn.

Another elderly man, admitted for palliative care in terminal cancer, had asked for Bach's Organ Toccata and Fugue in D Minor because it was significant for him, but, in that conversation, had not explained its significance. On the day of his next session, I found that he had suffered a cardiac arrest and was dying. I took the tape and the tape player to the Intensive Care Unit and told him I had brought the promised music, asking whether he would like to hear it. He was barely conscious, unable to speak because of an oxygen mask, etc., but he was able to give a token nod. The music was turned on, and (only about 75 seconds into the piece) he died, with a smile on his face. It will never be known why that music was important to him, but I believe that hearing it gave him permission to let go of life.

As with so many other therapeutic decisions, each of us has to make the decision based upon the needs of the situation at any given time. The decision as to whether or not we try to intervene is a matter of enormous therapeutic empathy and skill, and we have to chart a middle course between the two extremes of too little or too much intervention.

Spiritual needs in terminal illness

It is sad that so many people who have had a life-long religious faith find that the frailty of old age deprives them of any communal expression of that faith. We know that spirituality is not to be equated with religious observance, but some older people do yearn for a formal expression of their faith by whatever means is available to them.

Whether the music therapist feels able to become involved in or contribute to the spiritual life and religious observance of patients may depend in part upon the therapist's own belief or absence of it, and also upon the atmosphere of the establishment in which the music therapy takes place, but a competent therapist will be able to play a number of appropriate vocal or instrumental items which bring comfort and peace.

In the Royal Victoria Hospital in Montreal, which can be regarded as the birthplace of music therapy in terminal care, there is a strong spiritual dimension to the whole of life in the palliative care service. No one who works there can fail to be aware of the importance of spiritual aspects of care for the dying, whether patients are Christian, Jewish, Buddhist, Muslim, of another faith or none.

Regular music therapy group occasions for patients, staff and families take place in the unit, and these include music, readings, etc. The sessions are called *partage*, the French word for sharing, and the programmes cover all aspects of life: musical, artistic, material and spiritual.

Patients from other wards who have recently been diagnosed as having a terminal illness, and who will therefore probably come into the palliative care unit at some time in the future, are also brought to the sessions. Their beds are wheeled in and placed in the large room where they can feel part of the session.

For many elderly people, the playing of favourite hymns or other pieces of religious music brings great comfort, and it is essential for all music therapists, whatever their belief or absence of belief, to include such items in their repertoire, just as one includes items of music from other countries in order to help clients of differing ethnic origins.

Summary

We shall all die one day. Most of us hope to live to a good age before that day arrives, and most of us have the unspoken proviso, 'But I hope I die peacefully in my sleep, in my own bed.' The patients with whom we work can be a frightening reminder that we do not all die peacefully in our sleep, nor do we necessarily die in our own beds.

We can learn courage and determination from our clients and, when we plan music sessions for elderly dying people, let us do so in answer to a private question: 'If I were in that bed or in that wheelchair, would I find this programme satisfying and helpful?'

CHAPTER 16

Summary

Captains of our Destiny
or Pawns of Circumstance?

As we look around at older people, and inwardly at ourselves, we realise that life is a mixture of unavoidable situations, avoidable circumstances and simple luck.

'Luck' is perhaps not quite the right word because it can have overtones of magic – 'I know I'm always lucky, it must be something about me!' – or of black magic and despair – 'Knowing my luck, it will go wrong, things always do!'

Yet 'luck' is the only way of describing some of the things which influence individual lives:

- the country we are born in, its affluence or poverty, its culture and its society
- the government of our country, its ethical standards, its attitudes to those who are poor, old or disadvantaged
- our genetic inheritance of intellect and our opportunities for education, whether these place us among the gifted, the retarded or somewhere in between
- the colour of our skin and whether we happen to be born into a social class at the top or find ourselves amongst the down-trodden
- the spiritual, emotional and moral attitudes of our families and friends
- our vulnerability or resilience to ill health and disability, which is often outside our control.

These factors all influence our lives for good or for ill and, if predominantly for ill, we may understandably become despairing victims. On the other hand if all these influences have been for good, placing us amongst the fortunate elite, we may fail to develop empathy for others and come to see ourselves as somehow deserving such good fortune.

The capacity for wholeness in old age depends, therefore, not simply on ourselves but also upon a host of circumstances, either of the present day or laid down in previous generations. What can we do to achieve wholeness or sufficient integrity to be able to cope with old age as a positive experience and not merely endure it to the end if possible?

Families which have long-term conflict, dysfunctional expression of emotion, coldness of affect, cannot nurture old age. Families with a positive and balanced atmosphere of acceptance, nurturing, support, affection and kindness can enhance old age, even when there are difficulties to cope with.

On the wider scene, we must not accept, and we must try to change, society's stereotypes about old age, disability, and frailty. The picture of older people as merely waiting for death, without purpose or function, distorts priorities in the mind of the taxpayer and thus in government funding.

Society must be reminded that each of us has some unique gift, whether it is the memory for a song of courtship which persists despite dementia, the smile of an aphasic person as a staff member comes on duty after a holiday, the scholarly writings of an elderly philosopher, the kindness of a welcoming grandparent, the family recipe for plum jam given to a newly married granddaughter.

We must not see ourselves, nor allow anyone else to see us, as the tenants of time, waiting impassively for our lease to expire. Neither are we puppets, dancing obediently to the strings pulled by our exploited fears. We are whole people!

References

Albert, M.L., Sparks, R.W., and Helm, N.A. (1973) 'Melodic intonation therapy for aphasia.' *Archives of Neurology 29*, 130–131.

Albert, S.A. and Catell, M.G. (1993) *Old Age in Global Perspective.* New York: Macmillan.

American Psychiatric Association (1987) *Diagnostic and Statistical Manual of Mental Disorders IIIR.* Washington DC: American Psychiatric Association.

American Psychiatric Association (1994) *Diagnostic and Statistical Manual of Mental Disorders IV.* Washington DC: American Psychiatric Association.

Ames, D. (1994) 'Depression in nursing and residential homes.' In E. Chiu and D. Ames (eds) *Functional Psychiatric Disorders in the Elderly.* Cambridge: Cambridge University Press.

Arie, T. (1994) 'Introduction.' In E. Chiu and D. Ames (eds) *Functional Psychiatric Disorders in the Elderly.* Cambridge: Cambridge University Press.

Armstrong, A. (1985) *Breath of Life.* London: British Broadcasting Corporation.

Ashman, A.F., Suttie, J. and Bramley, J. (1993) *Older Australians with an Intellectual Disability.* Brisbane: Fred and Eleanor Schonell Special Education Research Centre, University of Queensland.

Bailey, L. (1984) 'The use of songs in music therapy with cancer patients and their families.' *Music Therapy 4*, 1, 5–17.

Bancroft, J. (1994) 'Homosexual orientation. The search for a biological basis.' *British Journal of Psychiatry 164*, 4, 437–440.

Barker, R.G., Wright, B.A. and Gonick, M.H. (1946) *Adjustment to Physical Handicap and Disability.* New York: Social Science Research Bulletin 55.

Beaglehole, R. (1993) 'Changes in stroke incidence.' *Lancet 342*, 1470–1472.

Beale, B. (1996) 'Inside the mind of a killer [report of trial evidence].' *Sydney Morning Herald* 21 November.

Beats, B. (1989) 'Visual hallucinations as the presenting feature of dementia: a variant of Charles Bonnet syndrome.' *International Journal of Geriatric Psychiatry 4*, 197–201.

Beats, B. (1996) 'Biological origin of depression in later life.' *International Journal of Geriatric Psychiatry 11*, 349–354.

Beeson, P.B. and McDermott, W. (1975) *Textbook of Medicine.* Philadelphia: W.B. Saunders.

Berrios, G.E. and Quemala, J.I. (1990) 'Depressive illness in multiple sclerosis. Clinical and theoretical aspects of the association.' *British Journal of Psychiatry 156*, 10–16.

Berrios, G.E. (1990) 'Musical hallucinations. A historical and clinical study.' *British Journal of Psychiatry 156*, 188–194.

Bever, T.G. and Chiarello, R.J. (1974) 'Cerebral dominance in musicians and non-musicians.' *Science 185*, 537–539.

Bonita, R., Anderson, C.S., Broad, J.B., Jamrozik, K.D., Stewart-Wynne, E.G. and Anderson, N.E. (1994) 'Stroke incidence and fatality in Australasia. A comparison of the Auckland and Perth population-based stroke register.' *Stroke 25*, 2, 552–557.

Boxwell, A.O. (1988) 'Geriatric suicide: the preventable death.' *Nurse Practitioner 13*, 6, 10–19.

Braceland, F.J. (1973) 'Introduction: progression or regression?' In *Yearbook of Psychiatry and Applied Mental Health*. Chicago: Yearbook Medical Publishers.

Bright, R. (1972) *Music in Geriatric Care*. Sydney and London: Angus and Robertson; New York: St Martin's Press.

Bright, R. (1975) 'Amusia: the lateralisation of music function and its possible significance in rehabilitation.' *Proceedings, Australian Association of Gerontology 2*, 3, 145–149.

Bright, R. (1987) 'The use of music therapy with demented patients who are deemed "difficult to manage".' In T.L. Brink (ed) *The Elderly Uncooperative Patient*. New York: Haworth Press.

Bright, R. (1989) 'Music therapy and the brain-damaged alcoholic.' In J. Sheppard (ed) *Advances in Behavioural Medicine 6*, 301–314. Sydney: University of Sydney.

Bright, R. (1994) 'Music therapy.' In E. Chiu and D. Ames (eds) *Functional Psychiatric Disorders in the Elderly*. Cambridge: Cambridge University Press.

Bright, R. (1996) *Grief and Powerlessness: Helping People Regain Control of Their Lives*. London: Jessica Kingsley Publishers.

Bromet, E.J. (1996) 'The impact of trauma.' *Current Opinion in Psychiatry 9*, 2, 153–157.

Burch, E.A., Jnr (1994) 'Suicide attempt histories in alcohol-dependent men; differences in psychological profiles.' *International Journal of Addiction 29*, 11, 1477–1486.

Burston, G.R. (1975) 'Granny bashing.' *British Medical Journal 3*, 592.

Campbell, P.G. (1991) 'Graduates.' In R. Jacoby and C. Oppenheimer (eds) *Psychiatry in the Elderly*. Oxford: Oxford Medical.

Charlifue, S.W. (1993) 'Research into the aging process.' In G.G. Whiteneck, S.W. Charlifue, K.A. Gerhart, D.P. Lammertse, S. Manley and K.R. Seedroff (eds) *Aging with a Spinal Cord Injury*. New York: Demos.

Chiu, E. and Ames, D. (1994) 'Preface.' In E. Chiu and D. Ames (eds) *Functional Psychiatric Disorders of the Elderly.* Cambridge: Cambridge University Press.

Chochinov, H.M., Wilson, K.G., Enns, M. and Lander, S. (1994) 'Prevalence of depression in the terminally ill. Effects of diagnostic criteria and symptom threshold judgements.' *American Journal of Psychiatry 151,* 4, 537–540.

Cinesound (1942) *80,000 Women for the Workforce.* Item 16 on Cinesound review, *Homefront.* Sydney: News Corporation Limited.

Clarke, D.J., Littlejohns, C.S., Corbett, J.A. and Joseph, S. (1989) 'Pervasive developmental disorder and psychoses in adult life.' *British Journal of Psychiatry 155,* 692–699.

Cohen-Mansfield, J., Reisberg, B., Bonnema, J., Berg, B., Dastoor, D.P., Pfeffer, R.I. and Cohen, G.D. (1996) 'Staging methods for the assessment of dementia: perspectives.' *Journal of Clinical Psychiatry 57,* 5, 190–198.

Cooke, L.B. (1989) 'Hearing loss in aging mentally handicapped persons.' *Australia and New Zealand Journal of Developmental Disability 12,* 4, 321–327.

Corbet, B. (1993) 'What price independence?' In G.G. Whiteneck, S.W. Charlifue, K.A. Gerhart, D.P. Lammerste, S. Manley, R.R. Menter and K.R. Seedroff (eds) *Aging with a Spinal Cord Injury.* New York: Demos.

Cox, M. (1978) *Coding the Therapeutic Process.* Oxford: Pergamon. Reprinted (1988) London: Jessica Kingsley Publishers.

Crapper-McLachlan, D.R., Wen, G.Y. and Wis, H.M. (1985) 'Alzheimer's disease in clinicopathological studies.' *Neurology 35,* 957–961.

Crichton, J.U., Mackinnon, M. and White, C.P. (1995) 'Life expectation of persons with cerebral palsy.' *Developmental Medicine and Child Neurology 37,* 567–576.

Culebras, A. (1992) 'Update on disorders of sleep and sleep-wake cycle.' In J. Biller and R.G. Kathool (eds) *Psychiatric Clinics of North America. The Interface of Psychiatry and Neurology 15,* 2, 467–486.

Currie, D.M., Gerschkoff, A.M. and Cifu, D.X. (1993) 'Geriatric rehabilitation 3. Mid-and late-life effects of early-life disabilities.' *Archives of Physical Medicine and Rehabilitation 74,* S, 413–415.

Dalakas, M.C., Elder, G., Hallett, M., Ravits, J., Baker, M., Papadopoulos, N., Albrecht, P. and Sever, J. (1986) 'A long-term follow-up study of patients with post-poliomyelitis neuromuscular symptoms.' *New England Journal of Medicine 314,* 959–963.

Dawson, D.R. and Chipman, M. (1995) 'The disablement experienced by traumatically injured adults living in the community.' *Brain Injury 9,* 4, 339–353.

Desai, H.B., Donat, J., Shokeir, M.H.K. and Munz, D.G. (1990) 'Amyotrophic lateral sclerosis in a patient with Fragile X syndrome.' *Neurology 40,* 373–380.

Deveson, A. (1994) *Coming of Age*. Newham, Vic., Australia: Scribe Publications.

Diekstra, R.F.H. (1989) 'Suicide and the attempted suicide. An international perspective.' *Proceedings of Symposium on Suicide, Acta Psychiatrica Scandinavica, Supplement 354*, 80, 1–24.

Doka, K.J. (1989) *Disenfranchised Grief*. Lexington, MA: Lexington Books.

Draper, B. (1996) 'Editorial review article: attempted suicide in old age.' *International Journal of Geriatric Psychiatry 11*, 7, 577–587.

Einfeld, S.L. (1992) 'Clinical assessment of psychiatric symptoms in mentally retarded individuals.' *Australian and New Zealand Journal of Psychiatry 26*, 48–63.

Einfeld, S.L., Moloney, H. and Hall, W. (1989) 'Autism is not associated with Fragile X syndrome.' *American Journal of Medical Genetics 34*, 187–193.

Enoch, D. and Trethowan, W. (1991) *Uncommon Psychiatric Syndromes*. Oxford: Oxford University Press.

Erikson, E.H. (1973) *Childhood and Society*. Harmondsworth: Penguin.

Evans, L.K. and Strumpf, N.E. (1989) 'Tying down the elderly. A review of the literature on physical restraint.' *Journal of the American Geriatrics Society 37*, 65–74.

Faber, F.W. (1862) 'There's a wideness in God's mercy' (Hymn no. 666). In P. Dearmer, R. Vaughan Williams and M. Shaw (eds) *Songs of Praise*. London: Oxford University Press, 1931.

Foner, N. (1984) *Ages in Conflict. A Cross-cultural Perspective on Inequality Between Old and Young*. New York: Columbia University Press.

Friedan, B. (1993) *Fountain of Age*. London: Jonathan Cape.

Fuchs, T. and Lauter, H. (1992) 'Charles Bonnet syndrome and musical hallucinations in the elderly.' In C. Katona and R. Levy (eds) *Delusions and Hallucinations in Old Age*. London: Gaskell.

Gaincotti, G. (1993) 'The riddle of the right hemisphere's contribution to the recovery of languages. A review article.' *European Journal of Disorders of Communication 28*, 3, 227–246.

Galski, T., Bruno, L., Zorowitz, R. and Walker, J. (1993) 'Predicting length of stay, functional outcome and aftercare in the rehabilitation of stroke patients. The dominant role of higher-order cognition.' *Stroke 24*, 12, 1794–1800.

Gelder, M., Gath, D., Mayou, R. and Lowen, P. (1996) *Oxford Textbook of Psychiatry*, 3rd edition. Oxford: Oxford University Press.

Gerhart, G.G. (1993) 'Personal perspectives.' In G.G. Whiteneck, S.W. Charlifue, K.A. Gerhart, D.P. Lammertse, S. Manley and K.R. Seedroff (eds) *Aging with a Spinal Cord Injury*. New York: Demos.

Gilbert, W.S. and Sullivan, A. (1885) *The Mikado*. London: The Savoy Operas.

Glascock, A.P. (1990) 'By any other name, it is still killing; a comparison of the treatment of the elderly in America and other societies.' In J. Sokalovsky (ed) *The Cultural Context of Aging*. New York: Bergin and Garvey.

Gorbien, M.J., Bishop, J. and Beers, M.H. (1992) 'Iatrogenic illness in hospitalised elderly people.' *Journal of the American Geriatrics Society 40*, 1031–1047.

Gosling, P. (1985) 'Mourners without a death.' *British Journal of Psychiatry 137*, 397–398.

Graves, A.B., Mortimer, J.A., Larson, E.B., Wenzlow, A., Bowen, J.D. and McCormick, W.C. (1996) 'Head circumference as a measure of cognitive reserve. Association with severity of impairment in Alzheimer's disease.' *British Journal of Psychiatry 169*, 86–92.

Guttmann, D.J. (1980) 'Elderly self-transcendence.' In J.E. Birren and R.B. Sloane (eds) *Handbook of Mental Health and Ageing*. Englewood Cliffs, NJ: Prentice-Hall.

Hampshire, S. (1990) *Every Letter Counts*. London: Bantam.

Hanks, R.A. and Lichtenberg, P.A. (1996) 'Physical, psychological and social outcomes in geriatric rehabilitation patients.' *Archives of Physical Medicine and Rehabilitation 77*, 783–794.

Haugg, E. and Vaglum, P. (1995) 'Organised violence and the stress of exile: prediction of mental health in a community cohort of Vietnamese refugees three years after settlement.' *British Journal of Psychiatry 166*, 360–367.

Head, D.M., Portnoy, S. and Woods, R.T. (1990) 'The impact of reminiscence groups in two different setting.' *International Journal of Geriatric Psychiatry 5*, 295–302.

Heilman, K.M., Valenstein, E. and Watson, R.T. (1985) 'The neglect syndrome.' In J.A.M. Frederiks (ed) *Handbook of Clinical Neurology 45 (1 of new series)*. Amsterdam: Elsevier.

Hellman, R.E. (1996) 'Issues in the treatment of lesbian women and gay men with chronic mental illness.' *Seminars in Psychiatry 47*, 10, 1093–1098.

Hinton, J. (1967) *Dying*. Harmondsworth: Penguin.

Holmes, L.B., Moser, H.W., Halldorsen, S., Mack, C., Paul, S.S. and Matzilevich, B. (1972) *Mental Retardation: An Atlas of Diseases with Associated Physical Abnormalities*. London: Macmillan.

Holohan, C. and Sears, R. (1995) *The Gifted Group in Later Maturity*. Stanford, CA: Stanford University Press.

Hook, E.P. (1981) 'Down syndrome frequency in human populations and factors pertinent to variation in rates.' In F.F. de la Cruz and P.S. Gerald (eds) *Trisomy 21: Research Perspectives*. Baltimore: University Park Press.

Hsieh, R-L., Lein, I-N., Lee, W-C. and Lee, T-K. (1995) 'Disability among the elderly of Taiwan.' *American Journal of Physical Rehabilitation 74*, 5, 370–374.

Hurwitz, L. (1964) 'Improving mobility in severely disabled Parkinsonian patients.' In M. Swallow (ed) *Selected Papers of Leon Hurwitz.* Belfast: Brough Cox and Dunn.

Hurwitz, L. (1971) 'The word.' In M. Swallow (ed) *Selected Papers of Leon Hurwitz.* Belfast: Brough Cox and Dunn.

Ingham, J.G., Kreitman, N.B., Miller, P. McC., Sashidharan, S.P. and Surtees, P.G. (1986) 'Self-esteem, vulnerability and psychiatric disorder in the community.' *British Journal of Psychiatry 148,* 375–385.

Jacomb, P.A. and Jorm, A.F. (1996) 'Personality change in dementia of the Alzheimer type.' *International Journal of Geriatric Psychiatry 11,* 201–207.

Janicki, M.P. (1989) 'Aging, cerebral palsy and older persons with mental retardation.' *Australia and New Zealand Journal of Developmental Disability 15,* 3, 4, 311–320.

Jeste, D.V. (1996) 'Editorial: The growing disparity between need and reality. Research in geriatric psychiatry.' *Current Opinion in Psychiatry 9,* 1, 279–280.

Joffe, H.I., Joffe, C.F. and Brodaty, H. (1996) 'Ageing Jewish Holocaust survivors: anxieties in dealing with health professionals.' *Medical Journal of Australia 165,* 517–520.

Jorm, A.F. (1995) 'The epidemiology of depressive states in the elderly: implications for recognition, intervention and prevention.' *Social Psychiatry and Epidemiology 30,* 53–59.

Joukamaa, M., Saarijarvi, S., Muuriaisniemi, A-L. and Salokangas, R.K. (1996) 'Alexithymia in a normal elderly population.' *Comprehensive Psychiatry 37,* 2, 144–147.

Kane, R.L., Ouslander, J.G. and Abrass, I.B. (1994) *Essentials of Clinical Geriatrics.* New York: McGraw-Hill.

Keefe, F.J. and Williams, D.A. (1990) 'A comparison of coping stategies in chronic pain patients in different age-groups.' *Journal of Gerontology (Psychological Sciences Section) Special Issue 45,* 4, 161–165.

Kellett, J.M. (1989) 'Sex and the elderly.' *British Medical Journal 299,* 6705, 934.

Kertesz, A. (1985) 'Aphasia.' In J.A.M. Frederiks (ed) *Handbook of Clinical Neurology 45 (1* of new series). Amsterdam: Elsevier.

Kirmayer, L.J. and Robbins, J.M. (1993) 'Cognitive and social correlates of the Toronto Alexithymia Scale.' *Psychosomatics 34,* 41–52.

Klinger, R.L. and Cabaj, R.P. (1996) 'Characteristics of gay and lesbian relationships.' In J.M. Oldham, M.B. Riba and A. Tasman (eds) *Review of Psychiatry 12.* Washington DC: American Psychiatric Press.

Knoblauch, A. (1890) 'On disorder of the musical capacity from cerebral disease.' *Brain 13,* 317–340.

Krauss, T. and Galloway, H. (1982) 'Melodic Intonation Therapy with language delayed apraxic children.' *Journal of Music Therapy 19,* 2, 102–113.

Kreuler, M., Sullivan, M. and Siösteen, A. (1996) 'Sexual adjustment and quality of relationship in spinal paraplegia. A controlled study.' *Archives of Physical Medicine and Rehabilitation 70*, 541–548.

Kurrle, S.E., Sadler, P.M. and Cameron, I.D. (1992) 'Patterns of elder abuse.' *Medical Journal of Australia 157*, 673–676.

Ladame, F. (1992) 'Suicide prevention in adolescence. An overview of current trends.' *Journal of Adolescent Health 13*, 406–408.

Lawson, R. (1878) 'On the symptomatology of alcoholic brain disorder.' *Brain 1*, 182–194.

Lawton, F.G. and Hacker, N.F. (1989) 'Sex and the elderly [Letter].' *British Medical Journal 299*, 6710, 1279.

Levin, J.S., Markides, K.S. and Ray, L.A. (1996) 'Religious attendance and psychological well-being in Mexican Americans. A point analysis of three-generational data.' *The Gerontologist 36*, 4, 454–463.

Lichtenberg, P.A. and Strzepek, D.M. (1990) 'Assessment of institutionalised dementia patients' competence to participate in intimate relationships.' *The Gerontologist 30*, 1, 117–120.

Little, J.D. (1992) 'Staff responses to in-patient and out-patient suicide. What happened and what do we do?' *Australia and New Zealand Journal of Psychiatry 26*, 162–167.

Litz, B.T., Zeiss, A.M. and Davies, H.D. (1989) 'Sexual concerns of male partners of female Alzheimer disease patients.' *The Gerontologist 30*, 1, 113–116.

Mahler, M.E. (1992) 'Behavioural manifestations associated with multiple sclerosis.' In J. Biller and R.G. Kathool (eds) *Psychiatric Clinics of North America. The Interface of Psychiatry and Neurology 15*, 2, 427–438.

Maltsberger, J.T. (1988) 'Suicide danger: clinical estimation and decision.' *Suicide and Life-Threatening Behaviour 18*, 1, 47–54.

Marmar, C.R., Foy, D., Kagan, B. and Pynoos, R.S. (1993) 'An integrated approach to post-traumatic stress disorder.' In J.M. Oldham, M.B. Riba and A. Tasman (eds) *Review of Psychiatry 12*. Washington DC: American Psychiatric Association.

Marsden, C.D. (1977) 'Neurological disorders induced by alcohol.' In G. Edwards and M. Grant (eds) *Alcoholism: New Knowledge and New Responses*. London: Croom Helm.

Martin, J.B. and Gusella, J.F. (1986) 'Huntington's disease; pathogenesis and management.' *New England Journal of Medicine 315*, 1267–1276.

Mathur, S. (1996) *Aged Care Services in Australia's States and Territories. Aged Care Series 2*. Canberra: Australian Institute of Health and Welfare.

Mattick, R.P. and Heather, N. (1993) 'Development in cognitive and behavioural approaches to substance misuse.' *Current Opinion in Psychiatry 6*, 424–429.

McKenzie, D.M., Copp, P., Shaw, R.J. and Goodborn, G.M. (1996) 'Cognitive screening of the elderly.' *Psychological Medicine 26*, 2, 427–430.

McVicker, R.W., Shanks, O.E.P. and McClelland, R.J. (1994) 'Prevalence and associated features of epilepsy in adults with Down syndrome.' *British Journal of Psychiatry 164*, 528–532.

Menotti, A., Jacobs, D.R., Blackburn, H., Kromhout, D., Nissiven, A., Nedeljkovic, S., Buzina, R., Mohacek, I., Seccareccia, F., Gianipaoli, S., Dontas, A., Aravanis, C. and Toshima, H. (1996) '25-year prediction of stroke deaths in the 7-country study.' *Stroke 27*, 3, 381–387.

Menter, R.R. (1993) 'Issues in aging with spinal cord injury.' In G.G. Whiteneck, S.W. Charlifue, K.A. Gerhart, D.P. Lammertse, S. Manley and K.R. Seedroff (eds) *Aging with a Spinal Cord Injury.* New York: Demos.

Michelson, D., Strataker, C., Hill, L., Reynolds, J., Galliven, E., Chrousos, G. and Gold, P. (1996) 'Bone mineral density in women with depression.' *New England Journal of Medicine 335*, 1176–1181.

Miles, S. (1996) 'A case of death by physical restraint. New lessons from a photograph.' *Journal of the American Geriatrics Society 44*, 291–292.

Morgan, H.G. (1994) 'How feasible is suicide prevention?' *Current Opinion in Psychiatry 7*, 111–118.

Mori, E., Hirono, N., Yamashita, H. *et al.* (1997) Premorbid brain size as a determinant of reserve capacity against intellectual decline in Alzheimer's disease.' *American Journal of Psychiatry 154*, 18–24.

Morris, P.L.P., Robinson, R.G., Raphael, B. and Bishop, D. (1991) 'The relationship between the perception of social support and post-stroke depression in hospitalised patients.' *Psychiatry 54*, 306–316.

Mount, B. (1990) *Meaning in Dying [video].* Montreal: Palliative Care Service of the Royal Victoria Hospital.

Munro, S. (1984) *Music Therapy in Palliative and Hospice Care.* St Louis: MMB Music Inc.

Murray, T.J. (1995) 'The psychosocial aspects of multiple sclerosis.' In J.P. Antel (ed) *Neurologic Clinic (Volume One) Multiple Sclerosis.*

Nash, M.S. and Fletcher, M.A. (1993) 'The immune system.' In G.G. Whiteneck, S.W. Charlifue, K.A. Gerhart, D.P. Lammertse, S. Manley and K.R. Seedroff (eds) *Aging with a Spinal Cord Injury.* New York: Demos.

Nemiah, J.C. (1985) 'Chapter 20.5 on Somatiform disorders (comments on alexithymia).' In H.I. Kaplan and B.J. Sadock (eds) *Comprehensive Textbook of Psychiatry.* London: Williams and Wilkins.

Newton, E. (1979) *This Bed my Centre.* Melbourne: McPhee-Gribble.

Nydegger, C.N. (1983) 'Family ties of the aged in cross-cultural perspective.' *The Gerontologist 23*, 1, 26–32.

O'Brien, G. (1996) 'Case history: psychiatric management of adult autism.' *Advances in Psychiatric Treatment 2*, 173–177.

O'Callaghan, C. (1990) 'Music therapy skills used in songwriting within a palliative care setting.' *The Australian Journal of Music Therapy 1*, 15–22.

Oldfield, A. (1996) (Paper and Video) *Music Therapy with Mothers and Disabled Children*. Presented at the World Congress of the World Federation of Music Therapy, Hamburg (published as conference abstract).

Oppenheimer, C. (1991) 'Sexuality in old age.' In R. Jacoby and C. Oppenheimer (eds) *Psychiatry in the Elderly*. Oxford: Oxford University Press.

Penington, G.R. (1992) 'Benefits of rehabilitation in the presence of advanced age or severe disability.' *Medical Journal of Australia 157*, 665–666.

Phillips, J.B. (1986) *Your God is too Small*. New York: Phoenix Press/Walker and Company.

Philp, I. (1996) 'Measuring and promoting quality of life in health care of the elderly.' *Australian Journal on Ageing 15*, 3 Supplement, 17–20.

Pick, A. (1903) 'Clinical Studies III: On reduplicative paramnesia.' *Brain 26*, 260–267.

Plato (c. 380 BC) *The Republic*. Translated 1941 by F.M. Cornford. Oxford: Oxford University Press.

Porchet-Munro, S. (1988) 'Music therapy in support of cancer patients.' *Recent Results in Cancer Research 108*, 289–294.

Post, F. (1982) 'Sexuality.' In F. Post and R. Levy (eds) *The Psychiatry of Later Life*. Oxford: Blackwell.

Prasher, V.P. and Krishnan, V.H.R. (1993) 'Age of onset and duration of dementia in people with Down syndrome. Integration of 98 cases in the literature.' *International Journal of Geriatric Psychiatry 8*, 915–922.

Ragnarsson, K.T. (1993) 'The cardiovascular system.' In G.G. Whiteneck, S.W. Charlifue, K.A. Gerhart, D.P. Lammertse, S. Manley and K.R. Seedroff (eds) *Aging with a Spinal Cord Injury*. New York: Demos.

Rakien, A., Guilburd, J.N., Soustiel, J.F., Zaaroor, M. and Feinrod, M. (1995) 'Head injuries in the elderly.' *Brain Injury 9*, 2, 187–193.

Ralph, S. (1994) 'Existence without life: disability and genetics.' *Australian Disability Review 1-95*. Canberra, Commonwealth Department of Human Services and Health.

Raynes, N.V., Johnson, M., Sumpton, R.C. and Thorp, D. (1987) *Journal of Mental Deficiency Research 31*, 303–310.

Reeson, M. (1991) *No Fixed Address*. Sutherland, NSW, Australia: Albatross Books.

Reid, W.G.J., Hely, M.A., Morris, J.G.L., Broe, A.V., Adena, M., Sullivan, D.J.O. and Williamson, P.M. (1996) 'A longitudinal study of Parkinson's disease; clinical and neuropsychological correlates of dementia.' *Journal of Clinical Neuroscience 3*, 4, 327–333.

Restak, R.M. (1989) 'The brain, depression and the immune system.' *Journal of Clinical Psychiatry 50*, 5, Supplement, 23–26.

Ritchie, D. (1960) *Stroke. Diary of Recovery.* London: Faber.

Robinson, R.G., Starr, L.B., Kubos, K.L., Lipsey, J.R., Rao, K. and Price, T.R. (1985) 'A two-year longitudinal study of mood disorder following stroke: prevalence and duration at six-months follow-up.' *British Journal of Psychiatry 144*, 256–262.

Rosenberg, H.G. (1990) 'Complaint discourse, aging and care-giving.' In J. Sokolovsky (ed) *The Cultural Context of Aging: Worldwide Perspectives.* New York: Begin and Garvey.

Rosenman, S.J. and Tayler, H. (1986) 'Mania folowing bereavement. A case report.' *British Journal of Psychiatry 148*, 468–470.

Roth, M. and Cooper, A.F. (1992) 'A review of late paraphrenia and what is known of its aetiology.' In C. Katona and R. Levy (eds) *Delusions and Hallucination in Old Age.* London: Gaskell.

Rothschild, A. (1996) 'The diagnosis and treatment of later-life depression.' *Journal of Clinical Psychiatry 57* (supplement 5), 5–11.

Rovner, B.W., Zusselman, P.M. and Shmuely-Dulitski, Y. (1996) 'Depression and disability in older people with impaired vision.' *Journal of the American Geriatrics Society 44*, 2, 181–184

Rozzini, R., Bianchetti, A., Carabellene, C., Inzoli, M. and Trabucci, M. (1988) 'Depression, life events and somatic symptoms.' *The Gerontologist 28*, 2, 229–232.

Rutter, M. (1970) 'Autistic children: infancy to adulthood.' *Seminars in Psychiatry 2*, 4, 435–450.

Rutter, M. (1985) 'Resilience in the face of adversity.' *British Journal of Psychiatry 147*, 598–611.

Rybarczyk, B.D., Nyenhuis, D.L., Nicholas, J.J., Schultz, R., Slioto, R.J. and Blair, C. (1982) 'Social discomfort and depression in a sample of adults with leg amputations.' *Archives of Physical Medicine and Rehabilitation 73*, 12, 1169–1173.

Rybarczyk, B.D., Nyenhuis, D.L., Nicholas, J.J., Cash, S.M. and Kaiser, J. (1995) 'Body image, perceived social stigma and the prediction of psychosocial adjustment to leg amputation.' *Rehabilitation Psychology 40*, 2, 95–110.

Sack, W.H., Clarke, G.N., Kinney, R., Belestos, G., Him, C. and Seeley, J. (1995) 'The Khmer adolescent project II. Functional capacity in two generations of Cambodian refugees.' *Journal of Nervous and Mental Diseases 183*, 177–181.

Sacks, O. (1990) *Seeing Voices*. London: Picador.

Sacks, O. (1991) *A Leg to Stand On*. London: Picador.

Sacks, O. (1995) *An Anthropologist on Mars*. London: Picador.

Schmid, H., Manjee, K. and Shah, T. (1994) 'On the distinction of suicide ideation versus attempts in elderly psychiatric in-patients.' *The Gerontologist 34*, 3, 332–339.

Seidel, G. (1995) 'Suicide in the elderly in antiquity.' *International Journal of Geriatric Psychiatry 10*, 1077–1084.

Shah, A. (1994) 'Difficulties in the diagnosis of mental illness in elderly mentally handicapped patients.' *Australian Journal on Ageing 13*, 3, 115–118.

Shield, R.R. (1990) 'Liminality in a nursing home.' In J. Sokalovsky (ed) *The Cultural Context of Aging*. New York: Bergin and Garvey.

Sin, A.L., Beers, M.H. and Morgenstern, H. (1993) 'The geriatric "medical and public health" imperative re-visited.' *Journal of the American Geriatrics Society 41*, 78–84.

Snowdon, J. (1991) 'Our nursing homes.' *Medical Journal of Australia 155*, 120–121.

Sokalovsky, J. (ed) (1990) *The Cultural Context of Aging*. New York: Bergin and Garvey.

Solomon, J., Zimberg, S. and Shollar, E. (eds) (1993) *Dual Diagnosis*. New York: Plenum.

Somasundarem, D.J. and Sivayokan, S. (1994) 'War trauma in a civilian population.' *British Journal of Psychiatry 165*, 524–527.

Sparks, R.W., Helm, N. and Albert, M.L. (1974) 'Aphasia rehabilitation resulting from melodic intonation therapy.' *Cortex 10*, 303–316.

Stein, T.S. (1996) 'Changing perspectives on homosexuality.' In J.M. Oldham, M.B. Riba and A. Tasman (eds) *Review of Psychiatry 12*. Washington DC: American Psychiatric Press.

Swallow, M. (1996) *A Neurological Paradigm for the Healing Effects of Music*. Presented at the World Congress of the World Federation of Music Therapy, Hamburg (published as conference abstract).

Szollos, A.A. and McCabe, M.P. (1995) 'Sexuality of people with intellectual disability. Perceptions of clients and care-givers.' *Australia and New Zealand Journal of Developmental Disability 20*, 3, 205–222.

Szymanski, L.S. and Kaplan, L.C. (1991) 'Mental retardation.' In J. Wiener (ed) *Textbook of Child and Adolescent Psychiatry*. Washington DC: American Psychiatric Press.

Ticehurst, S. (1994) 'Substance use and abuse.' In E. Chiu and D. Ames (eds) *Functional Psychiatric Disorders of the Elderly.* Cambridge: Cambridge University Press.

Treischmann, R.B. (1987) *Aging With a Disability.* New York: Demos.

Tresch, D.D. and Aronow, W.S. (1996) 'Smoking and coronary heart disease.' In W.S. Aronow and D.D. Tresch (eds) *Clinics in Geriatric Medicine 12*, 1, 23–32

Vernon, M.J. (1996) 'Editorial: elder abuse.' *Geriatric Medicine 26*, 2, 16.

Vitiello, M.V. (1996) 'Sleep disorders and aging.' *Current Opinion in Psychiatry 9*, 1, 284–289.

Von Knorring, L., Perris, C., Eisemann, M., Eriksson, U. and Perris, H. (1983) 'Pain as a symptom in depressive disorders. II. Relationship to personaliy traits as assessed by means of KSP.' *Pain 17*, 377–384.

Wall, P.D. and Melzack, R. (eds) (1994) *Textbook of Pain*, 3rd edition. Edinburgh: Churchill-Livingstone.

Weibel-Orlando, J. (1990) 'Grandparenting styles: Native American perspectives.' In J. Sokalovsky (ed) *The Cultural Context of Aging.* New York: Bergin and Garvey.

Weinshenker, B.G. (1995) 'The natural history of multiple sclerosis.' In J.P. Antel (ed) *Neurologic Clinics (Volume One) Multiple Sclerosis.*

Wenger, N.K. (1996) 'Physical inactivity and coronary heart disease in elderly patients.' In W.S. Aronow and D.D. Tresch (eds) *Clinics in Geriatric Medicine 12*, 1, 79–88.

Whiteneck, G.G., Charlifue, S.W., Gerhart, K.A., Lammerste, D.P., Manley, S., Menter, R.R. and Seedroff, K.R. (eds) (1993) *Aging with a Spinal Cord Injury.* New York: Demos.

Whiteneck, G.G. and Menter, R.R. (1993) 'Where do we go from here?' In G.G. Whiteneck, S.W. Charlifue, K.A. Gerhart, D.P. Lammerste, S. Manley, R.R. Menter and K.R. Seedroff (eds) *Aging with a Spinal Cord Injury.* New York: Demos.

Wilkes, H.H. (1993) 'Aging with a disability. The spiritual component.' In G.G. Whiteneck, S.W. Charlifue, K.A. Gerhart, D.P. Lammerste, S. Manley, R.R. Menter and K.R. Seedroff (eds) *Aging with a Spinal Cord Injury.* New York: Demos.

Winchell, R.M. and Stanley, M. (1991) 'Self-injurious behavior: a review of the behavior / and biology of self-mutilation.' *American Journal of Psychiatry 148*, 306–317.

Wing, L. and Gould, J. (1979) 'Severe impairments of social interaction and associated abnormalities in children. Epidemiology and classification.' *Journal of Autism and Developmental Disabilities 9*, 1, 11–29.

Wing, L. (1981) 'Asperger's syndrome; a clinical account.' *Psychological Medicine 11*, 115–129.

World Health Organisation (1980) *International Classification of Impairment, Disability and Handicap. A Manual of Classification Relating to the Consequences of Disease.* Geneva: United Nations World Health Organisation.

World Health Organisation (1992, reprinted 1993, 1994) *ICD 10; A Classification of Mental and Behavioural Disorders.* Geneva: United Nations World Health Organisation.

Wright, B. (1960) *Physical Disability: A Psychological Approach.* New York: Harper.

Yancey, P. (1977) *Where is God When it Hurts?* Grand Rapids, MI: Zondervan.

Yancey, P. (1988) *Disappointment with God. Three Questions No One Asks Aloud.* New York: Harper-Collins.

Subject Index

Author Index